VEDANTIC THOU
MĀYĀ, MITH
BRAH

Prof. (Dr.) Jai Paul Dudeja

Made with ♥ on the Notion Press Platform

www.notionpress.com

This book is humbly dedicated to Maharshi Bādarāyaṇa,
The Author of 'Brahma Sutras', A Component of Vedanta

CONTENTS

PREFACE 1

ACKNOWLEDGEMENTS 3

ABOUT THE AUTHOR 4

CHAPTER 1 THREE SOURCES OF VEDANTA: PRASTHANATRAYI 6

1.1 PRASTHANATRAYI (UPANISHADS, BRAHMA SŪTRAS, BHAGAVAD GITA) 6
1.2 THE VEDAS 9
1.3 THE UPANISHADS 10
1.4 THE BRAHMA SŪTRAS 15
1.5 THE BHAGAVAD GĪTĀ 17
1.6 TRADITIONS OF VEDANTA PHILOSOPHY 20
1.7 MORE ON THE ADVAITA VEDANTA PHILOSOPHY OF SRI SANKARA 30

CHAPTER 2 MĀYĀ, MITHYĀ, AND THE BRAHMAN IN VEDANTA: OVERVIEW 32

2.1 DARSHANA (PHILOSOPHY IN HINDUISM) 32
2.2 POST SHANKARA ADVAITA 44

CHAPTER 3 INTRODUCTION OF MĀYĀ 47

3.1 WHAT IS MĀYĀ? 47
3.2 MĀYĀ – NATURE, MEANING AND CONNOTATION 48
3.3 PRAKRITI VERSUS MĀYĀ 54
3.4 MĀYĀ IS OF THE NATURE OF ADHYASA 64
3.5 MĀYĀ IS THE BEDROCK AND OBJECT OF BRAHMAN 65
3.6 CONCEPT OF MĀYĀ IN VEDAS 66

CHAPTER 4 MĀYĀ IN UPANISHADS 73

4.1 MĀYĀ IN UPANISHADS 73
4.2 MĀYĀ IN AITAREYA UPANISHAD 75
4.4 MĀYĀ IN TAITTIRIYOPANISHAD 81
4.5 MĀYĀ IN SHVETASHVATARA UPANISHAD 83
4.6 MĀYĀ IN MANDUKYA KARIKA 87
4.7 MĀYĀ IN MANTRIKA UPANISHAD 89
4.8 MĀYĀ IN SARVA SARA UPANISHAD 91
4.9 MĀYĀ IN BRIHADARANYAKA UPANISHAD 97

4.10 MĀYĀ IN KAIVALYA UPANISHAD 98
4.11 MĀYĀ IN MAITRAYANIYA UPANISHAD 99
4.12 MĀYĀ IN NRISIMHA POORVA TAPANIYA UPANISHAD 101
4.13 MĀYĀ IN TEJO-BINDU UPANISHAD 103
4.14 MĀYĀ IN YOGA TATTVA UPANISHAD 104
4.15 MĀYĀ IN ANNAPURNA UPANISHAD 105

CHAPTER 5 MĀYĀ IN BRAHMA SUTRAS 107

5.1 MAHARSHI BĀDARĀYAṆA: THE AUTHOR OF 'BRAHMA SUTRAS' 107
5.2 MĀYĀ IN BRAHMA SUTRAS 108

CHAPTER 6 MĀYĀ IN SRIMAD BHAGAVAD GITA AND THE MOKSHA GITA 114

6.1 MĀYĀ IN SRIMAD BHAGAVAD GITA 114
6.2 MĀYĀ IS NOT JUST ILLUSION – IT IS ALSO THE AGENCY THAT BRINGS ABOUT ILLUSION 115
6.3 CONCEPT OF MĀYĀ IN THE MOKSHA GITA (CHAPTER 3) 123

CHAPTER 7 THE CONCEPT OF MITHYĀ 136

7.1 INTRODUCTION TO MITHYĀ IN ANCIENT HINDU TEXTS 138
7.2 MITHYĀ IN ADVAITA VEDANTA 140
7.3 JAGAT MITHYĀ 147
7.4 MORE ON MITHYĀ 151
7.5 STORY OF RAMAKRISHNA AND ADVAITA VEDANTA OF TOTAPURI.... 154

CHAPTER 8 THE BRAHMAN: AN INTRODUCTION 158

8.1 INTRODUCTION TO BRAHMAN 158
8.2 BRAHMAN AS THE ULTIMATE REALITY 161
8.3 BRAHMAN AS EXISTENCE OR BEING 166
8.4 PANCHA KOSHAS AND THE BRAHMAN 171

CHAPTER 9 THE BRAHMAN IN UPANISHADS 181

9.1 BRAHMAN IN UPANISHADS 181
9.2 BRAHMAN IN TAITTIRĪYA UPANISHAD 181
9.3 BRAHMAN IN KATHA UPANISHAD 182
9.4 BRAHMAN IN KENA UPANISHAD 186

CHAPTER 10 THE BRAHMAN IN BRAHMA SUTRAS 192

10.1 THE ENQUIRY INTO BRAHMAN AND ITS PRE-REQUISITES (BS 1.1.1) 192
10.2 DEFINITION OF BRAHMAN (BS 1.1.2) 192
10.3 BS 1.1.10: 192

10.4 BS 1.1.11: 193
10.5 Anandamaya is Para Brahman (BS 1.1.12) 193
10.6 BS 1.1.15: 193
10.7 The being or person in the Sun and the eye is Brahman (BS 1.1.20) 193
10.8 The word Akasa must be understood as Brahman (BS 1.1.22) 194
10.9 The word 'Prana' must be understood as Brahman (BS 1.1.23) 194
10.10 The light is Brahman (BS 1.1.24) 194
10.11 BS 1.1.28: 195
10.12 BS 1.1.30: 195
10.13 The Manomaya is Brahman (BS 1.2.1) 195
10.14 BS 1.2.2: 196
10.15 BS 1.2.7: 196
10.16 The Eater is Brahman (BS 1.2.9) 196
10.17 BS 1.2.10: 197
10.18 The dwellers in the cave of the heart are the individual soul and Brahman(1.2.11) 197
10.19 The person within the eye is Brahman (1.2.13) 197
10.20 The internal ruler is Brahman (BS 1.2.18) 198
10.21 That which cannot be seen is Brahman (BS 1.2.21) 198
10.22 Vaisvanara is Brahman (BS 1.2.24) 198
10.23 BS 1.2.28: 199
10.24 The abode of heaven, earth etc. is Brahman (BS 1.3.1) ... 199
10.25 Bhuma is Brahman (BS 1.3.8) 199
10.26 Akshara is Brahman (BS 1.3.10) 199
10.27 The Highest person to be meditated upon is the Highest Brahman 200
(BS 1.3.13) 200
10.28 BS 2.3.5: 200
10.29 When meditating on a symbol, the symbol should be considered as Brahman and not Brahman as the symbol (BS 4.1.5) .. 200

CHAPTER 11 THE BRAHMAN IN SRIMAD BHAGAVAD GITA 202

11.1 The Brahman in Srimad Bhagavad Gita 202

CHAPTER 12 QUANTUM SCIENCE INTERPRETATION OF MĀYĀ AND THE BRAHMAN 220

12.1 Classical Physics vs. Quantum Physics 220

PREFACE

Dear Readers,

I am extremely happy to see this book titled, **"Vedantic Thoughts on Māyā, Mithyā, and the Brahman",** in your hands. It is my firm belief that you have chosen to read this book with a specific aim in mind, and I assure you that you will not be disappointed with it.

The Upanishads, the Brahma Sūtras and the Bhagavad Gita constitute the three component sources of Vedanta. Māyā, literally means "illusion". It is unstable, ever-changing, impermanent, unreliable and never the same. According to Advaita Vedanta, this world is Māyā. Mithyā means "false belief". One example of Mithyā is perceiving a rope as a snake in the in insufficient light or in dark. There is a famous Sanskrit verse: *"Brahma Satyam, Jagat Mithyā"*; that means: Brahman is the truth. The world is a false belief.

These concepts of Māyā, Mithyā, and the Brahman, as viewed by the Vedanta, are explained in details, in this book consisting of twelve chapters.

After the first introductory chapter on the Upanishads, Brahma Sūtras and the Bhagavad Gita, the second chapter gives an overview of Māyā, Mithyā, and the Brahman in Vedanta. The next four chapters (3-6) are devoted to the topic of Māyā; out of which three chapters (4-6) describe Māyā as it appears in the Upanishads, Brahma Sūtras and the Bhagavad Gita, respectively. Chapter 7 is dedicated to the concept of Mithyā in Vedanta. The next four chapters (8-11) are devoted to the topic of Brahman; out of which three chapters (9-11) describe Brahman as it appears in the

Upanishads, Brahma Sūtras and the Bhagavad Gita, respectively. The last chapter (Chapter 12) titled "Quantum Physics Interpretation of Māyā and The Brahman" should be an intellectual treat to those scientists interested in the interpretation of Māyā and the Brahman by the Quantum Physics.

The book is strongly supported by **over 150 verses in Sanskrit** (shlokas) along with their Roman script, translation and explanation in English language.

This book is humbly dedicated to Maharshi Bādarāyaṇa, the Author of 'Brahma Sutras', a component of Vedanta.

The author sincerely believes that a book of this nature will be appreciated by all the readers across the globe who wish to get a deep insight into various aspects of Vedantic thoughts on Māyā, Mithyā and the Brahman, and their significance in their own spiritual growth.

The author would open heartedly love to receive any encouraging/critical comments as well as feedback from the dear readers at his Email ID: drjpdudeja@gmail.com

Sincerely

2023
Prof. (Dr.) Jai Paul Dudeja

ACKNOWLEDGEMENTS

The seeds of my interest in spirituality were lovingly sown by my revered parents: **Late (Dr.) Shanti Sawrup Dudeja and (Late) Mrs. Jai Devi Dudeja.** I am sure that they are watching me every moment from wherever they are in the other world and continuously sending their blessings to me.

I have greatly benefitted in going through the books and articles referred in the 'Bibliography' in this Book. I gratefully acknowledge these authors for enhancing my understanding on the subject matter of this book.

My greatest admiration is reserved for **Mrs. Rita Dudeja**, **my wife** and my best friend. She is a continual source of inspiration for me and is a co-traveller on this path of trust and truth.

2023
Prof. (Dr.) Jai Paul Dudeja

ABOUT THE AUTHOR

Born in June 1948, Prof. (Dr.) Jai Paul Dudeja holds a brilliant academic record. He did his Master's degree from Birla Institute of Technology and Science (BITS), Pilani (India), and Ph.D. degree from the Indian Institute of Technology (IIT), Delhi. He has been in regular employment as a Scientist, Professor, Dean, Director, Principal and a Senior Administrator in various educational institutions, universities, laboratories, public and private organizations. He superannuated as a Senior Scientist and Additional Director in May 2008 from the Defence Research and Development Organisation (DRDO), Government of India. After DRDO, he served for over 11 years, till his last posting as a Director at Amity University Gurgaon, from where he retired in Nov 2019.

Till date, Dr. Dudeja has published/presented about 90 research papers in various national and international journals/conferences. Out of these, over 20 research papers are on spirituality and consciousness etc. Besides this, he has authored the following **twenty books** on spirituality and consciousness and 'science of spirituality':

1. Gayatri Mantra: A GPS to Enlightenment,
2. Maha Mrityunjaya Mantra: An Invincible Armour for Conquering Death
3. Ajapa-Japa Sohum-Humsa Mantra: An Eternal Mantra for Inner Consciousness
4. The Third Eye: A Spiritual Laser for Stimulating Inner Awakening

5. Quantum Physics of Consciousness and Non-Duality in Eastern Philosophy
6. Quantum Science of Love, Healing, Happiness, and Bliss in Ancient Wisdom
7. Chakras Healing and Kundalini Awakening by Yogic Techniques,
8. Meditation Practices across the Globe and their Beneficial Effects.
9. Comparative Analysis of Hindu, Buddhist, and Jain Philosophies
10. Mantras for Happiness
11. Om Namah Shivaya: A Powerful Mantra for Mastering Five Elements
12. Trataka: A Concentrated Gazing Technique for Mystical Powers
13. Walking Meditation: Techniques and Benefits
14. Quantum Science of Ganesha Consciousness
15. Tantra Science
16. Quantum Brain, Mind, and Thinking
17. Profound Meditation Techniques in Tibetan Buddhism
18. REIKI: A Holistic Energy Healing Technique
19. SHAKTIPĀT : Instant Transmission of Spiritual Energy from a Siddha Guru to the Disciple.
20. Vāstu Shāstra: Ancient Indian Science of Architecture

Dr. Dudeja has delivered many invited lectures in international conferences on Spirituality and Consciousness in India and abroad.

He has been initiated to more than half-a-dozen meditation techniques.

Dr. Dudeja has been recognized as the "World's Who's Who in Science & Engineering".

CHAPTER 1

THREE SOURCES OF VEDANTA: PRASTHANATRAYI

1.1 Prasthanatrayi (Upanishads, Brahma Sūtras, Bhagavad Gita)

The Upanishads, the Brahma Sūtras and the Bhagavad Gita constitute the three component sources of Vedanta. All schools of Vedanta propound their philosophy by interpreting these texts, collectively called the Prasthanatrayi, literally, the three sources:

(i) **The *Upanishads***, or *Śruti prasthana*; considered as the *Śruti*, the "heard" (and repeated) foundation of Vedanta.

(ii) **The *Brahma Sūtras***, or *Nyaya prasthana/Yukti prasthana*; considered as the reason-based foundation of Vedanta; and

(iii) **The *Bhagavad Gita***, or *Smriti prasthana*; considered the *Smriti* (remembered tradition) foundation of Vedanta.

Vedantic Granthas are of **two kinds**:
the Pramana-granthas, and
the Prameya-granthas.

Granthas like the Advaitasiddhi, Chitasukhi, Khandanakhandakhadya, **Brahmasūtras, etc., are Pramana-granthas**, because they refute other theories and establish the Advaita-Tattva through logic and argumentation. Texts like the **Upanishads, the Bhagavad-**

Gita and the Yogavasishtha are **Prameya-granthas**, for they merely state the Absolute Truth with authority and do not indulge in reasoning for refuting or establishing anything. They are intuitional works, whereas the formers are intellectual.

The Brahma Sūtras attempted to synthesize the teachings of the Upanishads. The diversity in the teaching of the Upanishads necessitated the systematization of these teachings. This was likely done in many ways in ancient India, but the only surviving version of this synthesis is the Brahma Sūtras of Maharshi Bādarāyaṇa. *(This book is humbly dedicated to Maharshi Bādarāyaṇa).*

Vedanta philosophies discuss three fundamental metaphysical categories and the relations between them:

(i) Brahman or *Ishvara*: the ultimate reality;

(ii) Atman or *Jivatman*: the individual soul, self: and

(iii) Prakriti/Jagat (the world): the empirical world, ever-changing physical universe, body and matter.

1.1.1 Brahman/Ishvara – Conceptions of the Supreme Reality

Shankara, in formulating Advaita, talks of two conceptions of *Brahman*: The higher *Brahman* as undifferentiated Being, and a lower *Brahman* endowed with qualities as the creator of the Universe.

(i) Higher Brahma (Para Brahma):

Para Brahma is unconditioned, indeterminate and beyond attributes (Nirguna). It is trans-empirical, non-phenomenal and transcendental. Existence (Sat), consciousness (Chitta) and bliss (Ananda) constitute its essence. It is indefinable and inexpressible. It is incomprehensible by mind and imperceptible by sense organs. It is known by right intuition.

(ii) The lower Brahma (Apara Brahma):

Apara Brahma is conditioned, determinate and qualified attributes (Saguna). It is empirical and phenomenal. It is immanent. Brahman associated its potency (shakti) may appear as the qualified Brahman or Saguna or Apara Brahman or Ishvara who is the creator, preserver and destroyer of this world which is his appearance. In other words Brahma appears to be the Lord of the empirical selves and the empirical world of phenomena.

The schools of Vedanta differ in their conception of the relation they see between *Atman/jivatman* and *Brahman/Ishvara*:

(i) According to Advaita Vedanta, *Atman* is identical with *Brahman* and there is no difference.

(ii) According to Vishishtadvaita, *Jivatman* is different from *Ishvara*, though eternally connected with Him as His mode. The oneness of the Supreme Reality is understood in the sense of an organic unity (*vishistaikya*). *Brahman/Ishvara* alone, as organically related to all *Jivatman* and the material universe is the one Ultimate Reality.

(iii) According to Dvaita, the *Jivatman* is totally and always different from *Brahman/Ishvara*.

(iv) According to Shuddhadvaita (pure monism), the *Jivatman* and *Brahman* are identical; both, along with the changing empirically-observed universe being Lord Krishna.

1.2 The Vedas

Veda means the supreme knowledge. The Vedas are a large body of Hindu texts originating in ancient India, with its Samhita and Brahmanas complete before about 800 BCE. Composed in Vedic Sanskrit, the texts constitute the oldest layer of Sanskrit literature and the oldest scriptures of Hinduism. Hindus consider the Vedas to be *apauruṣheya*, which means "not of a human origin, superhuman" and "impersonal, authorless". They were not written by any individual. They came out from the breath of Hiranyagarbha (Lord Brahma).The knowledge in the Vedas is believed in Hinduism to be eternal, uncreated, neither authored by human nor by divine source, but seen, heard and transmitted by sages.

There are four Vedas: the Rig Veda, the Yajur Veda, the Sam Veda and the Atharv Veda.

(i) **Rig Veda:** Some of the topics covered in this Veda are: Spiritual well-being and fulfilment, self-realization, peace of mind, Nirvana (Salvation), dutifulness, love, *Tapa,* compassion, human service etc. fall under the Rig Veda.

(ii) **Yajur Veda:** Some of the topics covered in this Veda are: Generosity, valour, courage, gallantry, self-defence, leadership, fame, victory, power, dignity etc. fall under Yajur Veda.

(iii) **Sam Veda:** Sam Veda deals with games, sports, amusement, recreation, music, arts, literature, sensual enjoyment, beauty, harmony, poetic imagery, dynamism, refined taste, gratification etc.

(iv) **Atharv Veda:** Some of the topics covered in this Veda are: Wealth, prosperity, accumulation of money and resources, animals, medicines, food grains, materials, metals, buildings, vehicles and similar other materials of worldly being fall within the purview of Atharv Veda.

Rik is also known as righteousness (*Dharma*), Yajur as liberation (*Moksha*), Sam as sensual pleasure (*Kama*) and Atharva as prosperity (*Arth*). **These are the four faces of Brahma**.

Each Veda has been sub classified into four major text types – the Samhitas (mantras and benedictions), the Aranyakas (text on rituals, ceremonies, sacrifices and symbolic-sacrifices), the Brahmanas (commentaries on rituals, ceremonies and sacrifices), and the **Upanishads** (text discussing meditation, philosophy and spiritual knowledge).

1.3 The Upanishads

Upanishads are one of four genres of texts that together constitute each of the Vedas, the sacred scriptures of most Hindu traditions. Each of the four Vedas—the Rigveda, Yajurveda, Samaveda, and Atharvaveda—consists of a Samhita (a "collection" of hymns or sacred formulas); a liturgical prose exposition called a Brahmana; and two appendices to the Brahmana—an Aranyaka ("Book of the Wilderness"), which contains esoteric doctrines meant to be studied by the initiated in the forest or some other remote place, and an Upanishad, which speculates about the ontological connection between humanity and the cosmos.

Because the Upanishads constitute the concluding portions of the Vedas, they are called Vedanta ("the conclusion of the Vedas"), and they serve as the foundational texts in the theological discourses of many Hindu traditions that are also known as Vedanta.

The word Upanishad literally means "sitting down near" and implies studying with a spiritual teacher. The six Upanishads presented are drawn from the principal Upanishads. These Upanishads are not to be seen as uniform books – each text is connected to the Veda in which it occurs. The Upanishadic teaching is often presented in the context of a particular Vedic hymn or ritual. In the Vedanta traditions, the Upanishads are referred to as the Shruti prasthana, i.e., revealed scripture, from which knowledge of Brahman is obtained. The triad in Mundaka refers to the first three Vedas, while the triad in Svetasvatara 1 seems to refer to three aspects of God. The present block consists of five units.

The exact number of the Upanishads is not clearly known. The original Upanishads are the end portions of the four Vedas, and thereby came to be identified with "Vedanta", which literally means the end of the Vedas. They dealt with the philosophical aspects of the Vedas and were taught in ancient India to highly qualified and selected individuals. Today there are estimated to be about 350 Upanishads, some well-known and some least known. The Bhagavad-Gita of Lord Krishna is also considered an Upanishad because it contains the essence of many of the Upanishads. The *mukhya* Upanishads are found mostly in the concluding part of the *Brahmanas* and *Aranyakas* and were, for centuries, memorized by each generation and passed down verbally. The early Upanishads all predate the Common Era, some in all likelihood pre-Buddhist (6th century BCE), down to the Maurya period. Of the remainder, some 95 Upanishads are part of the Muktika canon, composed from about the start of common era through medieval Hinduism. New Upanishads, beyond the 108 in the Muktika canon, continued to being composed through the early modern and modern era, though often dealing with subjects unconnected to Hinduism.

The Upanishadic texts are part of the Shruti literature and are considered to be divine in origin. They are associated with the names of several ancient seers. Some of these lived at least twenty generations before Lord Krishna and the probable date of the Mahabharata war. Prominent among these sages were Yagnavalkya, Uddalaka Aruni, Shandilya, Aitareya, Pipplapada and Sanatkumara.

As per the list contained in the Muktikopanishad, **108 Upanishads** are given below. These are arranged in four categories according to the particular Veda to which each of them belong.

1.3.1 Vedas and Associated Upanishads

Vedas (No. of Associated Upanishads)	**Associated Upanishads**
Rigveda (10)	Aitareya, Atmabodha, Kaushitaki, Mudgala, Nirvana, Nadabindu, Akshamaya, Tripura, Bahvruka, Saubhagyalakshmi.
Yajurveda (50)	Katha, Taittiriya, Isavasya, Brihadaranyaka, Akshi, Ekakshara, Garbha, Prnagnihotra, Svetasvatara, Sariraka, Sukarahasya, Skanda, Sarvasara, Adhyatma, Niralamba, Paingala, Mantrika, Muktika,

	Subala, Avadhuta, Katharudra, Brahma, Jabala, Turiyatita, Paramahamsa, Bhikshuka, Yajnavalkya, Satyayani, Amrtanada, Amrtabindu, Kshurika, Tejobindu, Dhyanabindu, Brahmavidya, Yogakundalini, Yogatattva, Yogasikha, Varaha, Advayataraka, Trisikhibrahmana, mandalabrahmana, Hamsa, Kalisantaraaa, Narayana, Tarasara, Kalagnirudra, Dakshinamurti, Pancabrahma, Rudrahrdaya, SarasvatIrahasya.
Samaveda (16)	Kena, Chandogya, Mahat, Maitrayani, Vajrasuci, Savitri, Aruneya, Kundika, Maitreyi, Samnyasa, Jabaladarsana, Yogachudamani, Avyakta, Vasudeva, Jabali, Rudrakshajabala.
Atharvaveda (32)	Prashna, Mandukya, Mundaka, Atman, Surya, Narada-Parivrajakas, Parabrahma, Paramahamsa-Parivrajakas, Pasupatha-Brahma, Mahavakya, Sandilya, Krishna, Garuda, Gopalatapani, Tripadavibhuti-mahnarayana, Dattatreya, Kaivalya, Nrsimhatapani, Ramatapani, Ramarahasya, HayagrIva, Atharvasikha, Atharvasira, Ganapati, Brhajjabala, Bhasmajabala, Sarabha, Annapurna, Tripuratapani, Devi, Bhavana, SIta.

The Upanishads' impact on later theological and religious expression and the abiding interest they have attracted are greater than that of any of the other Vedic texts. The Upanishads became the subject of many commentaries and sub-commentaries, and texts modelled after them and bearing the name "Upanishad" were composed through the centuries up to about 1400 C.E. to support a variety of theological positions. The earliest extant Upanishads date roughly from the middle of the 1st millennium BCE. Western scholars have called them the first "philosophical treatises" of India, though they neither contain any systematic philosophical reflections nor present a unified doctrine. Indeed, the material they contain would not be considered philosophical in the modern, academic sense. For example, some Upanishads describe rites or performances designed to grant power or to obtain a particular kind of son or daughter.

Contrary to the assertion of early Western scholars, the Sanskrit term Upanishad did not originally mean "sitting around" or a "session" of students assembled around a teacher. Rather, it meant "connection" or "equivalence" and was used in reference to the homology between aspects of the human individual and celestial entities or forces that increasingly became primary features of Indian cosmology. Because this homology was considered at the time to be an esoteric doctrine, the title "Upanishad" also became associated during the middle of the 1st millennium BCE with a genre of textual works claiming to reveal hidden teachings. The Upanishads present a vision of an inter-connected universe with a single, unifying principle behind the apparent diversity in the cosmos, any articulation of which is called **Brahman**. Within this context, the Upanishads teach that Brahman resides in the Atman, the unchanging core of the human individual. Many later Indian theologies viewed the **equation of Brahman with Atman as the Upanishads' core teaching**.

1.4 The Brahma Sūtras

The Brahma Sūtras is one of three most important texts in Vedanta along with the Principal Upanishads and the Bhagavad Gita. Brahma Sutras is the Science of the Soul. It has been influential to various schools of Indian philosophies, but interpreted differently by the non-dualistic Advaita Vedanta sub-school, the theistic Vishishtadvaita and Dvaita Vedanta sub-schools, as well as others.

The Brahma Sūtras, also known as the Vedanta Sūtras, Sariraka Sūtras, or Bhikshu Sūtras, are a Sanskrit text which synthesizes and harmonizes Upanishadic ideas and practices. The Brahma Sūtras are attributed to Maharshi Bādarāyaṇa. In some texts, Bādarāyaṇa is also called Vyasa, which literally means "one who arranges". The book was completed in its surviving form in approx. 400–450 CE. The oldest version may be composed between 500 BCE and 200 BCE, with 200 BCE being the most likely date.

The Brahma Sūtras consist of 555 aphorisms or sūtras, dealing with attaining the knowledge of Brahman. in four chapters (adhyāya), with each chapter divided into four parts (pāda). Each part is further subdivided into sections called Adhikaraṇas with Sūtras. The Brahma Sūtras text has 189 Adhikaranas. Each section in the text opens with the Mukhya (chief, main) Sūtra that states the purpose of that section, and the various sections of the Brahma Sūtras include Vishaya-Vakyas (cite the text sources and evidence they use).

The total number of 555 Sūtras in the Brahma Sūtras are distributed as follows:

Adhyaya-1 (1st Pada: 31 Sūtras, 2nd Pada: 32 Sūtras, 3rd Pada: 43 Sūtras, 4th Pada: 28 Sūtras, Total 134 Sūtras).

Adhyaya-2 (1st Pada: 37 Sūtras, 2nd Pada: 45 Sūtras, 3rd Pada: 53 Sūtras, 4th Pada: 22 Sūtras, Total 157 Sūtras).

Adhyaya-3 (1st Pada: 27 Sūtras, 2nd Pada: 41 Sūtras, 3rd Pada: 66 Sūtras, 4th Pada: 52 Sūtras, Total 186 Sūtras).

Adhyaya-4 (1st Pada: 19 Sūtras, 2nd Pada: 21 Sūtras, 3rd Pada: 16 Sūtras, 4th Pada: 22 Sūtras, Total 78 Sūtras). **Total: 555 Sūtras.**

The different Acharyas (founders of different schools of thought) have given their own interpretations of the Sūtras to establish their own doctrines. The Bhashya (lucid commentary) of Sri Sankara on Brahma Sūtras is known as Sariraka Bhashya. His school of thought is Kevala Advaita. The Bhashya of Sri Ramanuja who founded the Visishtadvaita School is called Sri Bhashya. The commentary of Sri Nimbarkacharya is known as Vedanta-parijata-saurabha. Sri Vallabhacharya expounded his system of philosophy of Shuddhadvaita (pure monism) and his commentary on the Brahma Sutras is known as Anu Bhashya.

The erroneous identification of the body with the pure Atman is the root cause for human sufferings and miseries and for births and deaths. You identify yourself with the body and say, 'I am fair, dark, stout or thin. I am a Brahmin, I am a Kshatriya, I am a doctor'. You identify yourself with the senses and say, 'I am blind, I am dumb'. You identify yourself with the mind and say, 'I know nothing. I know everything. I became angry. I enjoyed a good meal. I am suffering from this disease'. The entire object of the Brahma Sūtras is to remove this erroneous identification of the Soul with the body which is the root cause of your sufferings and miseries, which is the product of Avidya (ignorance) and help you in the attainment of the final emancipation through knowledge of Brahman.

1.5 The Bhagavad Gītā

The Bhagavad Gita (romanized: śrīmad bhagavad gītā, lit. 'The Song by God' often referred to as the Gita (IAST: gītā), is a **700-verses** Hindu scripture, which is part of the epic Mahabharata. It forms **18 chapters (**chapters 23–40 of the book 6 of the Mahabharata called the Bhishma Parva. The work is dated to the second half of the first millennium BCE. Typical of the Hindu synthesis, it is considered to be one of the holy scriptures of Hinduism and one of three texts in Vedanta, Prasthanatrayi: along with Upanishads, and Brahma Sūtras.

The Bhagavad Gita is set in a narrative framework of dialogue between Pandava prince Arjuna and his guide and charioteer (sarathi), Krishna. At the start of the dharma yuddha (or the "righteous war") between the Pandavas and their cousins, the Kauravas, Arjuna is preoccupied by a moral and emotional dilemma and despairs about the violence and death the war will cause in the battle against his kin. Wondering if he should renounce the war, he seeks Krishna's counsel, whose answers and discourse constitute the Gita. Krishna counsels Arjuna to "fulfil his Kshatriya (warrior) duty to uphold the dharma" through Karma ("action"). The Krishna–Arjuna dialogues cover a broad range of spiritual topics, touching upon ethical dilemmas and philosophical issues that go far beyond the war that Arjuna faces.

The Bhagavata Gita is attributed to the sage Vyasa. The Bhagavad Gita presents a synthesis of Hindu ideas about dharma, theistic bhakti, and the yogic ideal of moksha. The text covers Jñāna, Bhakti, Karma, and Rāja yogas (spoken of in the 6th chapter), while incorporating ideas from the Samkhya-Yoga philosophy. The Bhagavad Gita is one of the most revered Hindu texts.

The text of Gita has occasional pre-classical elements of the Sanskrit language, such as the prohibitive mā instead of the expected na (not) of classical Sanskrit. This suggests that the text was composed after the Pāṇini era, but before the long compounds of classical Sanskrit became the norm. This would date the text as transmitted by the oral tradition to the later centuries of the 1st-millennium BCE, and the first written version probably to the 2nd or 3rd century CE.

The synthesis in Bhagavad Gita addresses the question of what constitutes the virtuous path that is necessary for spiritual liberation or release from the cycles of rebirth (moksha). It discusses whether one should renounce a householder lifestyle for a life as an ascetic, or lead a householder life dedicated to one's duty and profession, or pursue a householder life devoted to a personalized God in the revealed form of Krishna. Thus, Gita discusses and synthesizes the three dominant trends in Hinduism: enlightenment-based renunciation, dharma-based householder life, and devotion-based theism. The Bhagavad Gita attempts "to forge a harmony" between these three paths.

The Bhagavad Gita's synthetic answer recommends that one must resist the "either-or" view, and consider a "both-and" view. It states that the dharmic householder can achieve the same goals as the renouncing monk through "inner renunciation" or "motiveless action". One must do the right thing because one has determined that it is right, states Gita, without craving for its fruits, without worrying about the results, loss or gain. Desires, selfishness, and the craving for fruits can distort one from spiritual living. The Gita synthesis goes further, according to its interpreters such as Swami Vivekananda, and the text states that there is Living God in every human being and the devoted service to this Living God in everyone – without craving for personal rewards – is a means to spiritual development and liberation. The teachings in the Gita differ from other Indian religions that encouraged extreme austerity and self-torture of various forms. The Gita disapproves of these, stating that not only is it against tradition but against Krishna himself, because "Krishna dwells within all beings, in torturing the body the ascetic would be torturing him". Even a monk should strive for "inner renunciation" rather than external pretensions.

The Gita synthesizes several paths to spiritual realization based on the premise that people are born with different temperaments and tendencies (guna). The text acknowledges that some individuals are more reflective and intellectual, some affective and engaged by their emotions, some are action driven, yet others favour experimentation and exploring what works. It then presents different spiritual paths for each personality type respectively: the path of knowledge (jnana yoga), the path of devotion (bhakti yoga), the path of action (karma yoga), and the path of meditation (raja yoga). The guna premise is a synthesis of the ideas from the Samkhya school of Hinduism. The Gita states that none of these paths to spiritual realization is "intrinsically superior or inferior", rather they "converge in one and lead to the same goal".

The Bhagavad Gita is a poem written in the Sanskrit language. Its 700 verses are structured into several ancient Indian poetic meters, with the principal being the shloka (Anushtubh chanda). It has 18 chapters in total. Each shloka consists of a couplet; thus, the entire text consists of 1,400 lines. Each shloka has two quarter verses with exactly eight syllables. Each of these quarters is further arranged into two metrical feet of four syllables each. The metered verse does not rhyme. While the shloka is the principal meter in the Gita, it does deploy other elements of Sanskrit tradition. At moments, it uses the tristubh meter found in the Vedas, where each line of the couplet has two quarter verses with exactly eleven syllables.

There are total 18 chapters and 700 verses in Gita. These are:

Chapter No.	Name of Chapter	Total Verses
1	Arjuna Vishada Yoga	47
2	Sankhya Yoga	72
3	Karma Yoga	43
4	Jnana-Karma-Sanyasa Yoga	42
5	Karma-Sanyasa Yoga	29
6	Atma-Samyama Yoga	47
7	Jnana-Vignana Yoga	30
8	Aksara-ParaBrahma Yoga	28
9	Raja-Vidya-Raja-Guhya Yoga	34
10	Vibhuti Yoga	42
11	Vishwarupa-Darsana Yoga	55
12	Bhakti Yoga	20
13	Ksetra-Ksetrajna-Vibhaga Yoga	34
14	Gunatraya-Vibhaga Yoga	27
15	Purushottama Yoga	20
16	Daivasura-Sampad-Vibhaga Yoga	24
17	Shraddhatraya-Vibhaga Yoga	28
18	Moksha-Sanyasa Yoga	78
Total		**700**

1.6 Traditions of Vedanta Philosophy

There are six traditions of Vedanta philosophy:

(i) Bhedabheda,
(ii) Advaita (monistic),
(iii) Vishishtadvaita (qualified monism),
(iv) Dvaita (dualism),
(v) Suddhadvaita (purely non-dual), and
(vi) Achintya-Bheda-Abheda (inconceivable difference and non-difference)

1.6.1 Bhedabheda (difference and non-difference), was proposed as early as the 7th century CE, or even the 4th century CE.

The characteristic position of all the different Bhedābheda Vedānta traditions is that the individual self (jīvātman) is both different and not different from the ultimate reality known as Brahman. Each thinker within the Bhedābheda Vedānta tradition has his/her own particular understanding of the precise meanings of the philosophical terms "difference" and "non-difference". Bhedābheda Vedāntic ideas can be traced to some of the oldest Vedāntic texts, including quite possibly **Bādarāyaṇa Brahma Sūtra** (c. 4th century CE).

Bhedābheda is distinguished from the positions of two other major schools of Vedānta. The Advaita (Non-dual) Vedānta that claims that the individual self is completely identical to Brahman, and the Dvaita (Dualist) Vedānta (13th century) that teaches complete difference between the individual self and Brahman.

Bhedābheda ideas had an enormous influence on the devotional (bhakti) schools of India's medieval period. Among the medieval Bhedābheda thinkers are:

(i) **Niambra** (dates proposed by scholars range from 7th century – 15th century), who founded the Svābhābika Dvaitādvaita school.

(ii) **Bhāskara** (8th and 9th centuries), who founded the Aupādhika Bhedābheda school.

(iii) **Chaitanya** (1485–1533), the founder of Gaudiya Vaishnavism based in the eastern Indian State of West Bengal , and the theological founder of Achintya Bheda Abhedavedanta

Other major names are **Rāmānuja's teacher Yādavaprakāśa,** and **Vijñānabhikshu** (16th century).

1.6.2 Advaita (monistic), associated with the most prominent Gaudapada (~500 CE) and **Adi Shankaracharya** (8th century CE).

Advaita Vedanta (Advaita Vedānta) is a school of Hindu philosophy and a Hindu sadhana, a path of spiritual discipline and experience. In a narrow sense it refers to the oldest extant scholarly tradition of the orthodox Hindu school Vedānta.

The term Advaita (literally "non-secondness", but usually rendered as "nondualism", and often equated with monism) refers to the idea that **Brahman alone is ultimately real,** while the transient phenomenal world is an illusory appearance **(Māyā**) of Brahman. In this view, jivatman, the experiencing self, is ultimately non-different from Ātman-Brahman, the highest Self or Reality. The jivatman or individual self is a mere reflection or limitation of singular Ātman in a multitude of apparent individual bodies.

In the Advaita tradition, moksha (liberation from suffering and rebirth) is attained through recognizing this illusoriness of the phenomenal world and disidentification from the body-mind complex and the notion of 'doership', and acquiring Vidyā (knowledge) of one's true identity as Atman-Brahman, self-luminous (svayaṃ prakāsha) awareness or Witness-consciousness. While the prominent 8th century Vedic scholar and teacher (acharya) **Adi Shankara** emphasized that, since Brahman is ever-present, Brahman-knowledge is immediate and requires no 'action' or 'doership', that is, striving (to attain) and effort.

Shankara and his followers regard Atman/Brahman to be the ultimate Real, and jivanatman "ultimately [to be] of the nature of Atman/Brahman.

The swan is an important motif in Advaita. The swan symbolises the ability to discern Satya (Real, Eternal) from Mithyā (Unreal, Changing), just like the mythical swan Paramahamsa discerns milk from water.

Classical Advaita Vedānta states that all reality and everything in the experienced world has its root in Brahman, which is unchanging Consciousness. To Advaitins, there is no duality between a Creator and the created universe. All objects, all experiences, all matter, all consciousness, all awareness are somehow also this one fundamental reality Brahman. Yet, the knowing self has various experiences of reality during the waking, dream and dreamless states, and Advaita Vedānta acknowledges and admits that from the empirical perspective there are numerous distinctions.

The jivatman or individual self is a mere reflection of singular Atman in a multitude of apparent individual bodies. It is "not an individual subject of consciousness," but the same in each person and identical to the universal eternal Brahman, a term used interchangeably with Atman.

1.6.3 Vishishtadvaita (qualified monism), prominent scholars are Nathamuni, Yamuna and Ramanuja (1017–1137 CE)

Vishishtadvaita is a highly regarded school of Hindu philosophy belonging to the Vedanta tradition. Vedanta refers to the profound interpretation of the Vedas based on Prasthanatrayi (Upanishads, Brahma Sutras, and Bhagavad Gita). Vishishta Advaita, meaning "non-duality with distinctions", is a non-dualistic philosophy that recognizes Brahman as the supreme reality while also acknowledging its multiplicity. This philosophy can be characterized as a form of qualified monism, attributive monism, or qualified non-dualism. It upholds the belief that all diversity ultimately stems from a fundamental underlying unity.

Ramanuja, the 11–12th century philosopher and the main proponent of Vishishtadvaita philosophy contends that the Prasthanatrayi, namely the Upanishads, the Bhagavad Gita, and the Brahma Sutras, are to be interpreted in a way that shows this unity in diversity, for any other way would violate their consistency.

Ramanuja continues along the line of thought of his predecessors while expounding the knowledge expressed in the Upanishads, Brahma Sutras and Bhagavad Gita. **Vedanta Desika and Pillai Lokacharya,** disciples in the tradition of Ramanuja, had minor disagreements not on the philosophy, but on some aspects of the theology, giving rise to the Vadakalai and Tenkalai schools of thought.

The Vishishtadvaitic philosophy is believed to have a long history, with its earliest works no longer available. The names of these earliest philosophers are only mentioned in Ramanuja's Vedartha samgraha. Bodhayana, Dramida, Tanka, Guhadeva, Kapardi, and Bharuci are some of the well-known philosophers in the line of those who are thought to have developed the Vishishtadvaitic system.

Bodhayana is considered to have written an extensive vritti (commentary) on the Purva and Uttara Mimamsas. **Tanka** is attributed with having written commentaries on Chandogya Upanishad and Brahma Sutras. **Nathamuni** of the ninth century AD, the foremost Acharya of the Vaishnavas, collected the Tamil prabandhas, classified them, made the redaction, set the hymns to music and spread them everywhere. He is said to have received the divine hymns straight from **Nammalva**r, the foremost of the twelve Alvars, by yogic insight in the temple at Alwar Thirunagari, which is located near Tirunelveli in South India. **Yamunacharya** renounced kingship and spent his last days in the service of the deity at Srirangam and in laying the fundamentals of the Vishishtadvaita philosophy by writing four basic works on the subject.

Swaminarayan, the founder of Swaminarayan Sampraday, propagated a related philosophy, and based the Swaminarayan Sampraday (original name is Uddhava Sampraday) partly on these ideals.

1.6.4 Dvaita (dualism), founded by Madhvacharya (1199–1278 CE)

Dvaita Vedanta ((originally known as Tattvavada), is a sub-school in the Vedanta tradition of Hindu philosophy. The term Tattvavada literally means "arguments from a realist viewpoint". The Tattvavada (Dvaita) Vedanta sub-school was founded by the 13th-century Indian philosopher-saint **Madhvacharya**. Madhvacharya believed in three entities:

God, Jiva (soul), and Jada (Māyā, matter). The Dvaita Vedanta school believes that God and the individual souls (jīvātman) exist as independent realities, and these are distinct, being said that Vishnu (Narayana) is independent (Swatantra), and souls are dependent (paratantra) on him.

The Dvaita school contrasts with the other two major sub-schools of Vedanta, the Advaita Vedanta of Adi Shankara which posits nondualism—that ultimate reality (Brahman) and human soul (Ātman) are identical and all reality is interconnected oneness, and Vishishtadvaita of Ramanuja which posits qualified nondualism—that ultimate reality (Brahman) and human soul are different but with the potential to be identical.

Dvaita means "duality, dualism". The term refers to any premise, particularly in theology on the material and the divine, where two principles (truths) or realities are posited to exist simultaneously and independently.

The term Advitīyatva has been interpreted by Madhva, in the Chandogya Bhashya, in terms of "absence of peer and superior" to Brahman, conceding by implication, the existence, the reality of "lesser reals" like matter and souls under the aegis of God. The first part of the text has been taken to emphasize the unity of God-head by excluding internal distinctions of substance and attributes in Brahman in conformity with text like नेह नानास्ति किंचना (Neha nanasti kinchana), which are understood as nagating some internal distinctions (nānātva) alone in Brahman. The only internal distinctions that are logically conceivable in Brahman, are those of attributes. This is negated by the way of significant negation. The adjunct Swatantra would thus serve to emphasize the transcendence of the supreme over the other reals and its immanence in them and show how the conception of Brahman, here, differs from the Nirviśeṣādvaita of Adi Shankara.

1.6.5 Shuddhadvaita (pure non-dualism)

Shuddadvaita (pure non-dualism) is the "purely non-dual" philosophy propounded by **Vallabhacharya** (1479-1531 CE), the founding philosopher and guru of the Vallabhā sampradāya ("tradition of Vallabh"), a Hindu Vaishnava tradition focused on the worship of Krishna. Vallabhacharya's pure form (nondualist) philosophy is different from Advaita. The Shrinathji temple at Nathdwara, and compositions of eight poets (ashṭachap), including Surdas, are central to the worship by the followers of the sect.

The school of in-essence monism or purified non-dualism of Vallabha sees equality in "essence" of the individual self with God. There is no real difference between the two (like the analogy of sparks to fire). However, unlike Shankara's Advaita, Vallabha does not deny God as the whole and the individual as the part. The individual soul is not the Supreme (Satcitananda) clouded by the force of avidya, but is itself Brahman, with one attribute (Ananda) rendered imperceptible. The soul is both a doer and enjoyer. It is atomic in size, but pervades the whole body through its essence of intelligence (like sandalwood makes its presence felt through its scent even if sandalwood can't be seen).

Unlike Advaita, the world of **Māyā)** is not regarded as unreal, since Māyā) is nothing else than a power of Ishvara. He is not only the creator of the universe but is the universe itself. Vallabha cites the Brihadaranyaka Upanishad account, that Brahman desired to become many, and he became the multitude of individual souls and the world.

Although Brahman is not known, He is known when He manifests Himself through the world.

Bhakti is the means of salvation, though Jnana is also useful. Karmas precede knowledge of the Supreme, and are present even when this knowledge is gained. The liberated perform all karmas. The highest goal is not Mukti or liberation, but rather eternal service of Krishna and participation along with His activities in His Divine abode of Vrindavana. Vallabha distinguishes the transcendent consciousness of Brahman as Purushottama. Vallabha lays a great stress on a life of unqualified love and devotion towards God.

1.6.6 Achintya-Bheda-Abheda (inconceivable difference and non-difference)

Achintya-Bheda-Abheda is a school of Vedanta representing the philosophy of inconceivable one-ness and difference. In Sanskrit Achintya means 'inconceivable', bheda translates as 'difference', and Abheda translates as 'non-difference'.

Chaitanya Mahaprabhu (1486–1534 CE), the founder of Achintya Bheda Abheda school and Gaudiya Vaishnavism.

The Gaudiya Vaishnava religious tradition employs the term in relation to the relationship of creation and creator (Krishna, Svayam Bhagavan), between God and his energies. It is believed that this philosophy was taught by the movement's theological founder Chaitanya Mahaprabhu (1486–1534) and differentiates the Gaudiya tradition from the other Vaishnava Sampradayas. It can be understood as an integration of the strict dualist (Dvaita) theology of Madhvacharya and the qualified monism (Vishishtadvaita) of Ramanuja.

The theological tenet of Achintya-bheda-Abheda tattva reconciles the mystery that God is simultaneously "one with and different from His creation". In this sense Vaishnava theology is panentheistic as in no way does it deny the separate existence of God (Vishnu) in His own personal form. However, at the same time, creation (or what is termed in Vaishnava theology as the 'cosmic manifestation') is never separated from God. He always exercises supreme control over his creation. Sometimes directly, but most of the time indirectly through his different potencies or energies (Prakrti). Examples are given of a spider and its web; earth and plants that come forth and hair on the body of human being.

One who knows God knows that the impersonal conception and personal conception are simultaneously present in everything and that there is no contradiction. Therefore, Lord Chaitanya established His sublime doctrine: Achintya bheda-and-Abheda-tattva -- simultaneous oneness and difference. The analogy often used as an explanation in this context in the relationship between the Sun and the Sunshine. For example, both the sun and sunshine are part of the same reality, but there is a great difference between having a beam of sunshine in your room, and being in close proximity to the sun itself. Qualitatively the Sun and the Sunshine are not different, but as quantities they are very different. This analogy is applied to the living beings and God - the Jiva being of a similar quality to the Supreme being, but not sharing the qualities to an infinite extent, as would the Personality of Godhead himself. Thus, there is a difference between the souls and the Supreme Lord.

1.6.7 Some Common Features of Vedanta Traditions

Despite their differences, all schools of Vedanta share:

(i) Vedanta is the pursuit of knowledge into the **Brahman and the Atman**.

(ii) The Upanishads, the Bhagavad Gita and the Brahma Sutras constitute the basis of Vedanta, providing reliable sources of knowledge.

(iii) Brahman/Ishvara (God, Vishnu), exists as the unchanging material cause and instrumental cause of the world. The only exception here is that Dvaita Vedanta does not hold Brahman to be the material cause, but only the efficient cause.

(iv) The self (Atman/Jiva) is the agent of its own acts (karma) and the recipient of the consequences of these actions.

(v) Belief in rebirth and the desirability of release from the cycle of rebirths, (moksha).

(vi) Rejection of Buddhism and Jainism and conclusions of the other Vedic schools (Nyaya, Vaisheshika, Samkhya, Yoga, and, to some extent, the Purva Mimamsa.)

1.7 More on the Advaita Vedanta Philosophy of Sri Sankara

According to Sri Sankara, there is one Absolute Brahman who is ***Sat-Chit-Ananda***, who is of an absolutely homogeneous nature. The appearance of this world is due to ***Māyā*** -the illusory power of Brahman which is neither Sat nor Asat. This world is unreal. This world is a Vivarta or apparent modification through Māyā. Brahman appears as this universe through Māyā. ***Brahman is the only reality***.

The individual soul has limited himself through Avidya and identification with the body and other vehicles. Through his selfish actions he enjoys the fruits of his actions. He becomes the actor and enjoyer. He regards himself as atomic and as an agent on account of Avidya or the limiting Antahkarana. The individual soul becomes identical with Brahman when his Avidya is destroyed. In reality Jiva is all-pervading and identical with Brahman. Isvara or Saguna Brahman is a product of Māyā. Worship of Isvara leads to Krama Mukti. The pious devotees (the knowers of Saguna Brahman) go to Brahmaloka and attain final release through highest knowledge. They do not return to this world. They attain the Nirguna Brahman at the end of the cycle. Knowledge of Nirguna Brahman is the only means of liberation. The knowers of Nirguna Brahman attain immediate final release or Sadyomukti. They need not go by the path of gods or the path of Devayana. They merge themselves in Para Brahman. They do not go to any Loka or world. Sri Sankara's Brahman is Nirvisesha Brahman (Impersonal Absolute) without attributes.

Following is the summary of the concept of Brahman and Māyā, according to Sankara:

1. That the only true existence is that of Brahman.

2. That Brahman is identical with the Atman. Shakara holds that the two are identical (Advaita).

3. That the universe is Māyā, having only a phenomenal or relative existence.

CHAPTER 2

MĀYĀ, MITHYĀ, AND THE BRAHMAN IN VEDANTA: OVERVIEW

2.1 Darshana (Philosophy in Hinduism)

Man is often described as a rational animal. Once, as the animal in him is reasonably satisfied by the provision of basic biological, material and some psychological needs, the rational part gets an opportunity to evolve to higher levels. Philosophy, including metaphysics, is one of the highest aspects of this evolution.

The Indian philosophical systems have developed not only as a result of intellectual speculation but also of mystical intuition. Hence the name 'Darshana' (lit., 'seeing'), is usually applied to them.

The topics most commonly discussed by these darshanas are generally four:

(a) nature of the physical world, its origin and evolution;
(b) nature of man and other living beings;
(c) existence of God, his nature and attributes; and
(d) the goal of human life and the way of attaining it.

Different standpoints and differing views of these topics of discussion have naturally led to a variety of schools. These schools are broadly divided into two classes: the āstika and the nāstika.

The former accept the authority of the Vedas whereas the latter do not.

ब्रह्म सत्यं जगन्मिथ्या जीवो ब्रह्मैव नापरः

Brahma Satyam, Jagat Mithyā, Jivo Brahmaiva naparah

(While this verse is frequently attributed to the Vivekachudamani, in fact it comes from Verse 20 of the Brahma Jnana Vali Mala).

Translation: "Brahman is the truth. The world is illusory. There is ultimately no difference between a living being and Brahman.

In the beginning (before creation) 'Reality (or Brahman) alone existed, the one without a second' (Chāndogya Upanishad 6.2.1). However, the world of multiplicity is a matter of our day-to-day experience. Hence it becomes necessary to offer an explanation as to how Brahman, the One without a second, appears as this world of multiple names and forms. The explanation offered by Advaita is anirvacanīya-khyāti , its theory of erroneous cognition, which defies logic. Perceiving silver in the sea-shell in moonlight or snake in the rope in insufficient light: are the stock examples given by the Advaitins. In both cases there is an erroneous perception brought about by the impression of silver and snake from an earlier idea of the same, now superimposed upon shell and rope under conditions favorable to the error. This superimposition, called 'adhyāsa' or 'adhyāropa,' is responsible for the mithyā-jñāna (false knowledge) that the object perceived is silver or snake. The silver or the snake perceived is neither 'sat' (real) nor 'asat' (unreal). It is not 'asat' or unreal like 'the son of a barren woman' since it is actually perceived. Neither is it 'sat' or real since it disappears as soon as the substratum (the sea-shell or the rope) is perceived as it is. To explain such a peculiar phenomenon Shankara creates, out of logical necessity, a third type of perceived objects which is 'sadasad-vilasaṇa' (different from both the real and the unreal). The 'khyāti' or the cognition itself is described as 'anirvacaniya,' incapable of any precise definition or description.

2.1.1 Jagat Mithyā

The word Jagat embraces in itself this entire world, this cosmos. All that which is or can be an 'object' of our knowledge. It includes not only the gross but also the subtle 'objects'. The thoughts, emotions, the energy all come under this word 'Jagat'. That which is near or far, inside or outside, now or later, good or bad everything is part of this Jagat. This word has been described as referring to that which is ***'Jayate gachati iti jagat'***, i.e., that which is born & dies is jagat. Birth & death are movements in time. That which is in time constantly changes, there is a constant flux. Something starts this process of activation & manifestation of time and thus we see this dynamic flux. It is comparable to being in a dream world. Mithyā is that which is not there in all three periods of time. That which had a birth at a particular time and that which will certainly die at some point of time. It is there in this present moment, because of some reason - known or unknown. The above aphorism of 'Jagat Mithyā thus implies that all what is available for experience is transient (Kshanika).

Mithyā also implies that it is certainly beautiful, in fact very beautiful, it is also true that 'objects' of the world alone are useful for our worldly needs & purposes, but at the same time this is also a fact that we basically remain where we were. It is like eating a dream food, with which we never satiate our hunger. However much we eat the dream food, we will still remain basically hungry. Whatever we have sought in this world may have helped our life to get comfortable & organized, but has certainly not helped us in eliminating the fundamental desire 'to seek' something more. Like hunger the seeking still remains as it is.

2.1.2 Jivo Brahmaiva Naparah

This sutra means that 'every Jiva - the apparent limited & finite entity is basically the infinite & limitless Brahman, and nothing else. The truth & essence of an individual is the truth & essence of this whole world or rather God. Every Jiva is basically God himself wearing a cloak of limited equipment, and moreover, identified with the one's equipment he lives a limited & transient life. It is basically a case of non-apprehension followed by misapprehension of the truth of oneself. We take ourselves to be limited and therefore we are & remain limited. Body & all our equipment are certainly limited in time & space but 'I' who knows and objectifies all these is not. A seer is always different from seen. We are conscious of the body & mind complex so we have to be different from them. We are that which knows, that which illumines, that eternal life principle - Brahman. The Upanishads reveal that whoever knows his or her true reality is a healthy person, rest are diseased. They are certainly not at ease, there seems to be some bug in them. It is the bug of misapprehension of one's true self as a limited guy. If we were really limited then someone 'could' have helped us, but when we just erroneously take ourselves to be limited then it is something which God also cannot do anything about, except come and provide right knowledge. It is we who have to pause, think, deliberate, meditate & realize.

Everything of this individual gets changed, except the 'I' - the self-effulgent, blissful essence. One who knows that alone lives a true life, which every human deserves to live.

That alone was the secret of all saints, sages & even the avatar purushas. This alone is the real teaching of all our scriptures.

The awakening of limited Jiva to the realm of limitless Brahman is not a journey in the realm of time, but it is by transcending the very time, by right knowledge. Karma is a means to attain something in the realm of time, so it is not really relevant here. With karma we attain that which is unattained. In karma we turn our attention to that which should be rather than that which is. So in order to awake to our true self, one has to keep aside all cravings to 'do or achieve something'. One has to relax and be highly observant and see some fundamental facts of life & our true self. That which is limitless & infinite is not something to be attained but that which is to be known. It is already attained, one should realize that 'I am already that', We just have to directly know it. All sadhanas are directed only for this ultimate goal of life. This is the objective of Sanyas & Moksha. Drop the hankering for everything, relax, and see that which alone is.

2.1.3 Ajñāna or Avidyā

The basic cause of this erroneous perception is termed as ajñāna or avidyā (ignorance) which is said to be bhāvarūpa (existent) and is endowed with two shaktis or powers viz., 'āvaraṇashakti' (veiling power) and vikshepashakti' (transforming power). It veils the true nature of sea-shell and rope, and shows up silver and snake in their place by apparently transforming them. Such an apparently transformed object is called a 'vivarta' of the original and the theory that propounds this is known as Vivartavāda . Since this avidyā does not make the sea-shell and the rope completely disappear from view, but only makes them appear as something else, it is described as 'bhāvarūpa' or existent.

2.1.4 Māyā

An attempt may now be made to explain how this world of duality has evolved out of the nondual Reality called Brahman in the Upanishads. The world of duality can be broadly divided into 'dṛk' (the seer) and 'drishya' (the seen). Both these, again, are divided into the innumerable living beings (jīvas) and countless objects of creation. How does Brahman the Absolute, the One without a second, the indivisible Reality, appear divided into innumerable beings on the one side and countless objects on the other? It is avidyā that causes the one.

The world governs with Māyā. The mundane world, the entire cosmos rotates around the God's Māyā. Māyā, the word refers to concepts of "illusion". Māyā, is the principal concept which manifests, perpetuates and governs the illusion and dream of duality in the phenomenal universe. Literally speaking, Māyā, a Sanskrit word, ***Mā- not and yā – that is i.e "that is not" is Māyā,*** which really supplements the word Virtual reality is a reality is just miles away from truth. Māyā on Hindu mythology consist of Jeeva, Jagat and Brahma. All the three are vital for the existence of the world existence. One is Creature (Jeeva). It is being created by Creator (Brahma) and it sustains on the world (Jagat).

Māyā allures us attain those things which are not real. The example of "*Mrigtrishna" (Mirage)* is quite popular. The poor deer smells the Kasturi (highly smelling element) and tries to find it in all possible places except inside. The "Mirage" of the desert is best example of Virtual reality. The far desert sand just resembles like water and the person looking for water is not able to find a single drop over there.

Human behaviour is also as such; we had been born and brought up to look the virtues and qualities outside. We newer try to look inside the physical sheath. The reality is that reality which we are looking for doesn't exist outside. It is just within us and in the form of panchtatva (5 basic elements of existence: Prithvi, Jal, Vayu, Agni, Akasha).

Sakti adher jevarhee bhram chookaa nihchal siv ghari vaasaa. (Sri Guru Granth Sahib, 332)

In the darkness of māyā, I mistook the rope for the snake, but that is over, and now I dwell in the eternal home of the Lord.

2.1.5 Difference between Māyā and Mithyā

The concept of Māyā and Mithyā are central to Advaita Vedanta, yet they are misunderstood by many.

The statements like "Māyā means illusion" or "the world doesn't exist". These types of statements are true from certain points of reference, and false from other frames of reference. As an example, consider a flying airplane. If you are in it, the airplane is not moving; if you are on the ground, the airplane is moving; if you are in space, both the ground and airplane are moving. So it is important to mention your frame of reference when you make such statements.

The classic example of a Mithyā caused by avidya is a rope on the ground mistaken for a snake. The "Avarana" or covering power of avidya conceals the reality of the rope; the "vikshepa" or projection power of avidya makes one believe it is a snake. This type of error is of "adhyāsa" or superposition.

Another example of Mithyā is the ocean and waves. Both are Mithyā. Why? Both ocean are waves are just water, with different forms. They are dependent on water for existence. Oceans and waves exist; they are not illusory in nature.

We can take this one step further and examine matter and consciousness. The existence of any object is proved only when it is observed. Let us say there is an object that has never been observed. No one would acknowledge that object as valid! Therefore, some Consciousness must observe this object to prove its existence. So, any object is dependent on Consciousness to be validated. So it is Mithyā.

Whereas, Consciousness is itself proof of its existence. Even if I am suspended in deep space with nothing around me, I know I am, and therefore I myself am the proof of my existence. Therefore, Vedanta says Consciousness has Independent Existence (Satyam) and any object or matter has Dependent Existence (Mithyā). Vedanta tells us that Consciousness (Brahman) alone is Satyam.

Avidya is the ignorance of the Jiva regarding his/her true nature. In the Absolute Paramarthika Reality, Jiva is the same as Brahman. Ignorance of this truth is Avidya. We can also say that due to Avidya, Jiva perceives himself as different than Brahman.

IGNORANCE means Avidya, the separative consciousness and the egoistic mind and life that flow from it and all that is natural to the separative consciousness and the egoistic mind and life. This Ignorance is the result of a movement by which the cosmic intelligence separated itself from the light of the Super mind and lost the Truth. It is this that some of the ancient thinkers like Shankara, not perceiving the greater Truth-Force behind, stigmatized as Māyā and thought to be the highest creative power of the Divine. Māyā is Cosmic

Avidya at the macro level. Māyā makes the world appear as different than Brahman. In other words, Māyā is Matter, Brahman is Consciousness.

Sarvasara Upanishad refers to two concepts: Mithyā and Māyā. It defines Mithyā as illusion and calls it one of three kinds of substances, along with Sat (Be-ness, True) and Asat (not-Be-ness, False). Māyā, Sarvasara Upanishad defines as all what is not Atman. Māyā has no beginning, but has an end. Māyā, declares Sarvasara, is anything that can be studied and subjected to proof and disproof, anything with Gunas. In the human search for Self-knowledge, Māyā is that which obscures, confuses and distracts an individual.

2.1.6 Ātman (the Self)

Incidentally, the Upanishads use both words, Ātman and Brahman, to indicate the same Reality--appear as many jīvas and it is māyā that causes the world of phenomena. Māyā is avidyā at the cosmic level.

2.1.7 Three Degrees of Reality

Shankara accepts three degrees of reality.

The first, known as 'prātibhāsika-satya' (apparent truth, illusory appearance) is illustrated in the wrong perception of silver in sea-shell or snake in rope.

The second, called 'vyāvahārika-satya' is illustrated by this world of our day-to-day experience. This world appearance has a much higher degree of reality and lasts till one gets ātma-jñāna or brahma-jñāna, realization of Truth. It is satya or true for all purposes of vyavahāra i.e., day-to-day existence or practical life.

The third, designated as 'pāramārthika-satya', is the highest Truth and the only truth that really exists. It is Brahman or Ātman, which is nirguṇa (without attributes) and nirākāra (without forms), hence incapable of being described except in a negative way ('neti, neti'—'not this, not this').

2.1.8 Creation (The World etc.)

Brahman associated with **māyā** is Saguṇa Brahman (Brahman with attributes) or Ishvara (Lord of creation, God). It is this aspect of Brahman that is responsible for creation, preservation and destruction of the world. As for the actual order of evolution of the created world, the descriptions given in the Upanishads are accepted. For Shankara, who holds that the world process is only a vivarta (illusory appearance) due to adhyāsa (superimposition on Brahman), the very attempt to describe the various steps of evolution is a futile exercise. However, since the shruti (revealed scripture, the Upanishads) has done so, a place of honor must somehow be accorded to it. So, he characterizes such descriptions as giving 'tatastha-lakshana' (accidental or casual characteristics) of Brahman helping us to be directed towards it, even as the branch of a tree helps us to locate the crescent in the sky. On the other hand, Brahman, as it is, can be comprehended only through its 'swarūpa-lakshaṇa' (integral or essential characteristics), which is 'sat-chit-ānanda.' 'Sat' (eternal reality), 'chit' (pure consciousness), and 'ānanda' (unalloyed bliss) are not really its characteristics but its very essence.

2.1.9 Jiva

This Brahman or Ātman which is sat-chit-ānanda, has inexplicably got itself involved in the body-mind complex, the involvement being due to avidyā. Since the origin of this involvement can never be logically or satisfactorily explained, avidyā is stated to be anādi or beginningless. The involved Ātman is designated as 'jīva.' This jīva, the Ātman in bondage, has five koshas or sheaths, three sharīras or bodies, performs actions motivated by desires, experiences pleasure and pain due to karma and undergoes transmigration until liberation. Shankara declares that this jīva, when shorn of its upadhis or the limiting adjuncts like the body and the mind, is identical with Brahman, since its essential nature also is sat-chit-ānanda.

2.1.10 Sadhanas and Mukti

The main trouble with the Ātman becoming jīva is the tādātmya or the false identification with the mind and the body, brought about by adhyāropa or adhyāsa (superimposition). Hence the only way of remedying it is by apavāda or de-superimposition, by denying this identification. For this, one has first to prepare oneself by the preliminary four-fold discipline or sadhana-chatushtaya, viz., (i) viveka (discrimination between the eternal and the non-eternal), (ii) vairagya (dispassion), (iii) shamādishatka (cultivation of the six virtues like self-control) and (iv) Mumukshutva (desire for liberation). Then one has to approach a competent guru (spiritual preceptor) and learn the truth from him by shravaṇa (hearing), manana (reflection) and nidi-dhyāsana (contemplation). The most important part of the guru's teaching will be in the form of 'Mahavakyas' (great sentences) like ***'tat tvam asi*** ('That thou art') or ***'aham brahmāsmi'*** ('I am Brahman'). Shravaṇa and manana produce the deep-rooted conviction that one is the spirit. Hence in nidi-dhyāsana, de-superimpostion in the form of 'I am not the body, nor the sense-organs, nor the mind, nor even the ego' and so on, can be practiced leading ultimately to the realization that one is the Ātman. This realization, resulting in mukti or liberation, can be had even while one is living in this body. It is known as 'jīvanmukti.' He will attain 'videhamukti' (liberation from future bodies) after the body falls off, the continuance of the body between the two states being due to prārabdha-karma (actions that have caused this body). Mukti or liberation from transmigration is not the gaining of a new state but recognizing the already existing original state.

2.1.11 Jīvanmukti and Videhamukti

Two kinds of mukti: jīvanmukti and videhamukti, are envisaged in the Advaitic works. The Vivaraṇa school upholds the theory that mukti is simultaneous with jñāna. Hence Jīvanmukti is not only possible, but the only mukti that can be recognized. Continuance of the body for some more time, due to prārabdha-karma, has no effect upon jñāna. On the other hand, the Bhāmatī school holds that even after jñāna, if the body continues due to prārabdha-karma, this imposes a limitation, thereby implying the existence of a trace of avidyā. The death of the body puts an end even to this trace of avidyā and real mukti is obtained then. Since this comes after the death of the body, it is called 'videhamukti.'

2.1.12 Locus of Avidyā

A favorite topic of discussion that frequently crops up in Advaita metaphysical works is the locus of avidyā. Since Brahman is the only reality that exists, it alone is the āśraya (locus) as also the vishaya (object) of avidyā. This is one school. Sureshvara and Padmapāda are the main protagonists of this school. According to them, avidyā is one only. Since Brahman is pure consciousness, avidyā can never exist in it nor act on it. This is the opposing school propagated by

Vāchaspati Mishra. For him, the jīvas are the loci of avidyā and there is one avidyā for every jīva.

2.2 Post Shankara Advaita

Though Shankara wrote profusely, clearly enunciating the main doctrines of his school, there are certain places in his writings wherein the important aspects of certain doctrines are either vague or are capable of more than one interpretation. This has naturally resulted in the growth of quite a voluminous post-Shankara Advaita literature leading to different prasthānas or schools of thought.

2.2.1 'Vārttika-prasthāna' of Sureshvara (9th century A.D.) comes first in the series. This school gets its designation from the exposition contained in the 'vārttikās' or commentaries in verse, of Sureshvara on Sankara's Bhashya on the Brihadaranyaka and the Taittiriya Upanishads. According to this school, Brahman is the material cause of this world, and not māyā. The locus of avidyā is Brahman and not the jīvas. Avidyā is one only and not many. The mahāvākyas or the great Vedic dictums are capable of producing immediate cognition of the self as Brahman. Hence dhyānābhyāsa or practice of meditation on the meaning of those dictums is not necessary. The jīvas are but ābhāsas or fallacious appearances of Brahman in the individual minds. (This has earned this theory, the designation of Ābhāsavāda as opposed to Pratibimbavāda and Avacchedavāda of other schools.)

2.2.2 The 'Vivaraṇaprasthāna' of Padmapāda (9th cent. A.D.) and Prakāśātman (A.D .1200) comes next. The name is derived from the work Pañcapādikāvivaraṇa of the latter, it being a voluminous commentary on the Pañcapādikā of Padmapāda. Though this name suggests that it covers five pādas or sections of the Brahmasūtras , only the commentary on the first four sūtras is now available. The chief doctrines of this school are: Avidyā is a jaḍātmikā shakti (a force of material nature) and is the material cause of this world. It is bhāvarūpa, a positive entity, but not real. Māyā, prakṛti, avyakta, avyākṛta, tamas, shakti etc., are all its synonyms. It is called avidyā when āvaraṇa power is predominant and māyā, when vikṣepa power becomes dominant. Alternatively, it is māyā at the cosmic level and avidyā at the individual level. Avidyā rests on Brahman but acts on the jīvas. The jīvas are pratibimbas or reflections of Brahman in the antaḥkaraṇa (mind). The reflected images have no reality other than that of the original (bimba) Brahman. This theory is called Pratibimbavāda as contrasted with Ābhāsavāda .

2.2.3 The 'Bhāmatīprasthāna' of Vāchaspati Mishra (A.D. 840) is the third and the last of these major schools. Bhāmatī is his celebrated commentary on the Shāṅkarabhāshya of Brahmasūtras. This school is built round the Bhāmatī along with its subsidiary commentaries Kalpataru of Amalānanda (13th cent. A.D.) and Parimalā of Appayya Dīkṣita (16th cent. A.D.). The views of this school can be briefly summarised as follows:

Brahman is the material cause of the world, not as the locus of avidyā but as the object of avidyās supported by the jīvas. Māyā is only an accessory cause. Avidyā cannot abide in Brahman. It abides in the jīvas and is plural since the jīvas are plural. Vāchaspati advocates two varieties of avidyā: the mūlāvidyā or kāraṇāvidyā (primal nescience); the tūlāvidyā or kāryāvidyā (derivative nescience). It is the latter that is responsible for bhramasaṁskāras or error impressions. Also, Vāchaspati appears more inclined towards the Avacchedavāda or the theory of limitation with regard to the appearance of the jīvas. Just as a pot limits the infinite sky in itself, avidyā of the individual limits

Brahman and makes it appear like a jīva. Another point of importance in this school is that the mahāvākyas do not produce anubhava (immediate cognition). It is the mind seasoned by meditation that gives such experience. Mention may also be made here of Dṛṣṭisṛṣṭivāda, which advocates that the world is created simultaneously with its perception; and, Ekajīvavāda , which propounds that there is only one jīva which is in bondage and when it gets liberation, everything else disappears. Prakāśānanda (15th-16th cent. A.D.) is the chief exponent of these schools.

CHAPTER 3

INTRODUCTION OF MĀYĀ

Brahman is real. The world is unreal. The Jiva (individual soul) is none other than Brahman.

3.1 What is Māyā?

Māyā, literally meaning "illusion" or "magic", has multiple meanings in Indian philosophies depending on the context. In Vedic texts, māyā connotes a "magic show, an illusion, where things appear to be present but are not what they seem; the principle which shows "attribute-less Absolute" as having "attributes". Māyā also connotes that which "is constantly changing and thus is spiritually unreal" (in opposition to an unchanging Absolute, or Brahman), and therefore, "conceals the true character of spiritual reality".

In the Advaita Vedanta school of Hindu philosophy, māyā appearance is "the powerful force that creates the cosmic illusion that the phenomenal world is real." In this nondualist school, māyā at the individual level appears as the lack of knowledge (avidyā) of the real Self, Atman-Brahman, mistakenly identifying with the body-mind complex and its entanglements.

In Hinduism, the term Māyā has multiple meanings and connotations depending upon the contextual reference and reason is embedded in the interpretations of the world itself. According to ancient Hindu scriptures, the universal existence is comprised of two intertwined parts in general philosophical sense; one is invisible subtle world (the Sukshmā Sansār) represented by the Supreme

Consciousness (Brahman, God) along with the individual consciousness (Self, soul), and the other is the visible gross world (the Sthool Sansār) comprised of empirical or material or objects. While the seers and scholars visualize the former as real and permanent, the latter is considered unreal and impermanent but gives an illusion of representing real world. Due to this nature of the gross world, the ancient seers, scholars and the modern philosophers call it Māyāvi or illusionary world.

The aforesaid qualifications are based on deep philosophical analysis and observation; hence it appears to be a sustainable concept. Afterall the science represents only an intellectual and systematic study of the structure and behavior of the physical and natural world through experiment, observation and interpretation. A simple illustration could be given from the human attributes to appreciate and understand the logic of the existence of the subtle world. We don't physically see any human emotions but that does not mean they don't exist: For instance, love doesn't have a shape but a person in love is found to be extremely compassionate, caring and selfless. Similarly, when a person is under the influence of anger, he becomes irrational, agitated, aggressive and sometimes even violent. Here these emotions represent subtle existence that need a medium (physical being) for expression.

3.2 Māyā – Nature, Meaning and Connotation

Māyā has multiple tangible and intangible meanings and connotations in Hinduism, the literal meaning being illusion or magic. In Vedic literature, it connotes to extraordinary power and wisdom while in post-Vedic period, it refers to illusory state where things appear to be present and real but actually, they are not because they are not stable and permanent, and are constantly changing. Due to this attribute, they are considered as unreal in spiritual sense. In other words, Māyā is the power or precept that conceals the true nature of the spiritual reality under the veil of physical existence. According to Advaita philosophy, Māyā is an illusion that makes the world appear as duality.

The stated duality has been explained in a different way by the Samkhya school of Indian philosophy, which describes the universal reality into two aspects i.e., the ***Purusha and Prakriti***. Here Purusha is defined as the Supreme Self or the Subject, individual Self being only part of it, as the one who is conscious or knows, while the Prakriti, on a much broader canvas, encompasses everything else that is seen or known in the universe, including all that is material and psychological. This unmanifest **Prakriti, or Māyā**, which is otherwise absolute, pure and formless, is a pool of limitless potential comprising of three fundamental balancing forces called the gunas namely **Sattva, Rajas, and Tamas**. Prakriti manifests as the universe of tangible and intangible objects through the interplay of these gunas in various concentrations, proportions and forms.

Just as the illusion of a snake in a rope is not possible merely through ignorance without the sub-stratum rope, so also the world cannot be created merely by ignorance without the substratum, the Lord. Therefore the subtle causal condition is dependent on the Lord, and yet the Lord is not in the least affected by this ignorance, just as the snake is not affected by the poison. Know that the Prakriti is Māyā and the great Lord the ruler of Māyā.

The snake is not affected by its own poison. A magician is not affected by the magical illusion produced by himself, because it is unreal. Even so Brahman is not affected by Māyā. The world is only an illusion or appearance. Brahman appears as this universe, just as a rope appears as the snake. Therefore Brahman is unaffected by Māyā or the world illusion. No one is affected by his dream-creations or the illusory visions of his dream, because they do not accompany the waking state and the state of dreamless sleep. Similarly the Eternal Witness of all states of consciousness is not affected by the world or Māyā.

The Lord looks on Māyā and energizes her. Then she has the power of producing the world. In her own nature she is Jada or insentient.

Even though Brahman has no eyes or ears, or hands or feet, He is Omnipotent. He assumes different forms through Māyā. With respect to Brahman, the scripture alone is the authority, but not reason. The scripture declares that Brahman, though destitute of organs, possesses all capacities and powers, "Grasps without hands, moves swiftly without feet, sees without eyes and hears without ears". Though Brahman is devoid of all attributes, yet He is endowed with all powers through Māyā. There is no real change in Brahman but there is an apparent modification in Brahman on account of His inscrutable power of Māyā.

Brahman is endowed with all the attributes through Māyā, such as Omnipotence, Omniscience, etc., for qualifying Him to be the cause of the world.

In a broader sense, the Prakriti or Māyā or Nature is the divine and dynamic energy of Brahman (God). It comes into dynamic mode during the act of creation, as a manifestation of the latter's creative potential, of beings simultaneously subjecting them to the state of duality. As Hinduism has many schools of philosophical thoughts, some even believe that the Prakriti (Māyā) existed eternally as a separate entity along with Brahman and just like the latter, it is unborn, uncreated, independent and indestructible. However, whether as part of Him or independent, the most schools of Hinduism are in agreement of Brahman's (God) role in creation. With Māyā or Prakriti in play, the living beings are made to believe that what they experience through their senses is real and that they are independent of the objects and other beings they perceive through their senses. Therefore, Māyā, in effect, causes ignorance (avidya) and delusion, leading to duality responsible for the bondage in the empirical or material world. The ignorance-led Māyā is camouflage of the Absolute One and it projects as Many. Māyā is the veil that covers our true Self and real nature. The world around us is an illusion or Māyā, which is caused by the veiling power of Brahman.

According to Advaita Vedanta, the real nature of our Soul, the Atman, is divine, pure, perfect and eternally liberate. The Self does not have to become Brahman. Our true Self is one with Brahman. However, due to Māyā's impact, our true reality is conditioned, like a warped mirror, by time, space and causality. Our vision of reality is covered by that Māyā. Hence, we simply identify ourselves with the body, mind and ego rather than the Atman, the divine Self. This confusion creates more ignorance and pain in a domino effect. By identifying ourselves with the body, mind and ego, we suffer from thousands of miseries. Māyā is responsible for the appearance of our variegated universe. Thus, Māyā tries to affect our real nature in every moment. Followers of Advaita argue that Māyā a is fundamentally mysterious. Nobody knows why it exists and when it began. It is unreal or illusory in an absolute sense. Māyā is said to have two powers: (i) avarana-shakti, which covers Brahman and prevents Brahman's true nature from being known; and (ii) vikshepa-shakti, which conjures up the objects of the universe. By the former, it hides its own substratum from view and by the later, the unmanifest Māyā is made manifest as mind. This mind then plays games with its potentials that amount to projecting this universe with numerous names and forms. It is clearly bloomed in Ramana's words, "Ajñāna has two aspects: avarana (veiling) and vikshepa (multiplicity). Of these, avarana (veiling) denotes the veil hiding the Truth. That prevails in sleep. Multiplicity (vikshepa) is activity in different times. This gives rise to diversity and prevails in waking and dream states (jagrat and svapna). If the veil, i.e., avarana is lifted, the Truth is perceived." Thus, Māyā is a projection of Brahman that disappears when it is withdrawn. This Māyā projects this world just as ignorance of the substratum, namely the rope, projects the illusion of a snake.

Advaita Vedanta says that in Brahman, there is, as a lower order of reality, a Mithyā, anivacaniiya entity, called "Māyā". The Nama roopa is contained in Māyā in seed form. Brahma chaitanyam gets reflected in Māyā, to constitute an entity called "Iswara". Thus Iswara has the chaitanyam aspect and the matter aspect. In this combination, Iswara is omniscient (sarvajnah), omnipotent (sarvasaktimaan) and all pervading (sarvagatah). Therefore Ishwara has in himself the capacity to think, visualize and plan creation and the raw material for creation. Creation is the unfolding or differentiation of the nama roopa existing in seed form (avyakta or avyakrta nama roopa becoming vyakta or vyakrta nama roopa) and their superimposition on the changeless sub-stratum. The sub-stratum is real, the nama oopa are unreal. The differentiation and superimposition is done by Māyā under Isvara's guidance. When the differentiated Nama roopa are superimposed on Brahman, the Existence-Consciousness, the universe is manifested. The sub-stratum is real; the superimposed nama roopa is unreal. The substance, the essence, is the sub-stratum. The superimposed nama roopa are attributes. A rough comparison is the clay which is substance and the pot shape which is an attribute. But there is a difference between the comparison and the compared in other aspects. One of them is this - whereas clay, the substance is tangible and the pot shape, the attribute is intangible, Brahman, the substance is imperceptible and the nama roopa are perceptible. Nama roopa superimposed on Existence-Consciousness consist not only of the attributes contributing to the manifestation of what we regard as inanimate objects like shape, color, smell, taste, texture, weight, mass etc. but the attributes which contribute to the manifestation of bodies and minds of living beings, like shape, mass, weight, color, smell, taste and texture are the attributes contributing to the manifestation of the experienced universe as inanimate outside objects but the attributes of our bodies and minds, like the biological structure and functions and the mental faculties of cognition, emotions and thinking. Thus, the universe, the various worlds and the objects therein, like stars, planets, mountains, rivers etc. and bodies and minds of human beings, plants, animals, insects, gods and asuras are all the manifestation of the combination of Existence-Consciousness, the real and nama roopa, the unreal.. All the time what we encounter is this combination of the real and the unreal; what we perceive is the unreal part; we do not perceive the real part. In our state of ignorance we take the unreal part to be real. What lends existence to the unreal nama roopa is the real, the Brahman. But for Brahman providing the sub-stratum of Existence, the nama roopa cannot appear. Conversely without nama roopa, there will be no world for us to experience. Brahman, the sub-stratum, being avyavahaaryam (not accessible to transaction), transaction requires nama roopa. A combination of existence and nama roopa is required for experience and transaction. But for this combination, there will be no samsara or atma vicara or liberation from samsara. Iswara visualizes and plans the creation, keeping in mind the requirements of the karmas of the jivas and impels Māyā to unfold the nama roopa accordingly. Creation (srishti) is a cycle of projection and resolution of nama roopa. After the karma of the jivas pertaining to the janmas of jivas in a particular srishti is exhausted through enjoyment and suffering, Iswara makes Māyā withdraw the projected nama roopa unto Himself in his aspect as Māyā, there to remain, for a period, called "pralaya", in potential form, until karmas of jivas fructify for the next srishti. The srishti, sthiti laya (creation, maintenance, resolution) cycle is without a beginning or end. The Advaita concept of creation is called "vivarta vaada" indicating that creation is not real. The perceived world is Mithyā is. Iswara is Mithyā. Māyā is parinaami upaadaana kaaranam (transforming material cause) and Iswara is nimitta kaaranam (intelligent cause). Brahman does not undergo change when creation takes place; Remaining as the all-pervading Existence, Brahman, by Its mere presence, serves as the sub-stratum for the superimposition of nama roopa. And by its mere presence, it enables the antahkarana of living beings to acquire cidabhasa. When Sastra talks Brahman as the cause of the universe, we have to understand that Brahman's role in the manifestation of the world is confined to these two aspects.

3.3 Prakriti versus Māyā

Ishwara has been described as a magician (Māyāvi) in the Upanishads. Ramanuja interprets it as the power of Ishwara for creating the universe is as astonishing as the power of the magician. Māyā is that power of Ishwara which creates mysterious objects.

In Hinduism Māyā is used to denote both Prakriti or Nature and the deluding power. Prakriti is the dynamic energy of God. According to some schools of Hinduism, Prakriti exists eternally as a separate entity from God. Just like Him, it is unborn, uncreated, independent and indestructible. It either acts independently of Him or acts in unison with Him as a co-creator or partner.

According to other schools, Prakriti is the dynamic energy of God, either latent or created on purpose. It comes into existence during the act of creation, as a manifestation of His Will, to envelop the beings He creates and subject them to the state of duality. Whether it is independent of Him or dependent, all schools of Hinduism, with a few exceptions, recognize God as the Creator.

In His role as Ishwara, the Lord of the visible and invisible universe, God undertakes five different functions, namely, Creator, Preserver, Destroyer, Concealer and Bestower of grace. In His role as Concealer, He unleashes the power of Māyā, through Prakriti, to conceal Himself from what He creates and delude all the living beings (jivas) into thinking that what they experience through their senses is true and that they are independent of the objects and other beings they perceive through their senses. Māyā therefore causes ignorance and through ignorance perpetuates the notion of duality, which is responsible for our bondage and mortality upon earth.

When we know that Māyā is the power that blinds us, binds us and deludes us, we become aware of the extent of its influence and its role in our lives. Out of this awareness comes a sense of caution and discriminating, which ultimately leads to our salvation. But till we reach that stage, we remain in the grip of Māyā, like fish, caught helplessly in a net.

Shaivism recognizes Māyā as one of the bonds or malas (impurities). It is responsible for our animal (pashu) existence or beingness and becomingness. It causes in us ignorance and egoism and binds us to the objects we desire and seek. It makes us believe that the objective world in which we live and experience alone is true. It draws us outwardly and binds us to the things, we love or hate or we want to possess or get rid of. It is responsible for our experience of time and space which otherwise do not exist. It conceals our true nature and makes us believe that we are mere physical and mental beings. Through its powerful pull, it draws us forcefully into the objective reality of the world in which we live and binds us to things and events through our thoughts and desires.

Unlike the western religion, in Hinduism God is not separate from His creation. His creation is an extension of Him and an aspect of Him. This world comes into existence, when God expands Himself outwardly, like a web woven by a spider. In His subjective and absolute state, His creation is unreal and illusory, but in our objective and sensory experience and in our beingness it is very much real and tangible. It is a projection or reflection of Him, like the objects in the mirror and the mirror itself, different from Him somewhat, but also not so different, dependent but virtually distinct. He uses the concealing power of His own Māyā to draw Himself into Prakriti and conceal Himself in it as a limited and diluted being.

How the beings are subjected to delusion? It is through the senses and their activity. The Bhagavadgita explains the process thus, "By constantly thinking of the sense objects, a mortal being becomes attached to them. Attached thus he develops various desires, from which in turn ensues anger. From anger comes delusion, and from delusion arises confusion of memory. From confusion of memory arises loss of intelligence and when intelligence is lost the breath of life is also lost (2.60-63)." So, the sense first draws out and involve us with what we see and experience. Through this constant contact with the sense objects, we develop attachment with them. This attachment in turn causes desires. Because of the desires, we want to own and possess things, we develop likes and dislikes, attraction and aversion. We draw ourselves into situations and relationships we believe will lead to our happiness and fulfilment. We become so involved in the process and with Prakriti that we forget who we are and why we are here or what we need to do in order to be ourselves.

Māyā causes delusion in many ways. Under the influence of Māyā an individual loses his intelligence and power of discretion. He forgets his true nature. He loses contact with his true self and believes that he is the physical self with a mind and body that are subject to constant change, instability, and birth and death. In that delusion, he believes that he is doer of his actions, that he is responsible for his actions, that he is alone and independent, that he cannot live with or without certain things and so on, where as in truth he is an aspect of God, who has concealed himself, who is actually the real doer, and for whose experience all this has been created. Because of his ignorant thinking, he develops attachment with worldly objects and wants to possess them. He spends his life in the pursuit of unworthy objectives in the world considering them to be imperative for his success, survival, happiness and personal pride.

The world in which we live gives us an apparent illusion of stability, whereas in truth it is not. It is an illusion to believe that this world is the same always, or that the people we deal with are the same all the time. The world is therefore an illusion (Māyā), not because it does not exist in the physical sense, but because it is unstable, ever-changing, impermanent, unreliable and most important of all never the same. Ask yourself this question. Are the same person you were a minute ago?

The scriptures say that it would be unwise on our part to centre our lives around such an unstable world, because if you spend your precious life for the sake of impermanent and unreliable things, you are bound to regret in the end for wasting your life in the pursuit of emptiness. The real world lies beyond our ordinary senses where our existence would be eternal and where things would not change the way they do in this plane.

The philosophy is very simple but difficult to follow. After all what is illusion (Māyā)? It is something like a mirage which misleads you into wrong thinking and wrong actions. This world precisely does that. It offers you happiness but leads you into the darkness of suffering. It tempts you with many things and when you run after them you find them to be unreal and incapable of quenching your thirst for stability and permanence.

Māyā is such a device by which One Reality appears as many. It may be named as the inherent power found residing in the Supreme Brahman. As both the creation and dissolution of the world is a never-ending process and this timeless cycle is both beginningless and endless so, Māyā is beginningless and spontaneous. This Māyā is said to be eternal, since it has been existing from eternity and rests on the succession of bodies etc. without beginning or end. Though it manifests itself in all ordinary things which have a beginning in time, yet it itself has no beginning, as it is associated with the pure consciousness. Even after destruction, it remains in the Brahman in seed form. Hence, like Brahman, it is also eternal or beginningless (Anadi). Wherever name and form arises, there is Māyā. As tiny sparks come forth from fire, so does this varied world always come forth from Brahman, sustains in It and also dissolves back into It. Since the world is unceasingly being created and dissolved, the Māyā is also eternal for maintaining this cyclic process. This is illustrated by Shankara thus:

"It is the Self from which this moving and unmoving world continually proceeds like sparks of fire, in which it is merged like a bubble of water, and with which it remains filled during existence." Though Māyā has no beginning, it comes to an end to that soul who gains Self-Knowledge. Actually, in Advaita, Brahman and His Māyā are one and the same. But the world of Māyā is extremely different from the nature of Brahman. Māyā is the force that proficiently crates different varied, inert and changing worlds from the unchanging Brahman. Here, Māyā, thus, is an effect having a nature different from her cause – the Brahman.

The nature of Māyā is Anadi-Bhava or beginningless existence and is Anirvacaniya or inexpressible by speech. It is Sat-Asat-Vilakshana, distinct from existence and non-existence. It is Anadi-Santam, without beginning, but with an end. It is ended by Brahmajñānaṃ or Absolute Wisdom arrived at through intense meditation or Nididhyasana. Māyā differs from Brahman in that Brahman is Anadi-Anantam, beginningless and endless, whereas Māyā is Santam or removable. The origin of ignorance cannot be found out, but it is well known that the sages who have realized the Eternal Brahman free themselves from the effects of Māyā. One can only tell how to free oneself from Māyā, but one cannot say why Māyā creates a universe.

Māyā is a complex illusionary power, which causes the Brahman to be seen as the material world of separate forms. It absolutely depends on Him and cannot exist alone. But it acts on ignorant soul and creates countless tremendous things and events. He who is the ruler of this Māyā, is God/Brahman and he who is ruled by Māyā is the embodied soul. Shankara says, "Māyā called also the Undifferentiated is the power of the Lord. It is without beginning, is made up of the three Gunas and is superior to the effects (as their cause). She is to be inferred by one of clear intellect only from the effects She produces. She is neither existent nor non-existent nor partaking of both characters; neither same nor different nor both; neither composed of parts nor an indivisible whole nor both; She is the most wonderful and cannot be described in words.

Māyā is such a dynamic creative dynamism that hides Brahman from Brahman and creates the world. Ignorance (avidya) becomes synonymous with Māyā, since it is non-cognition of Brahman and identification with body, ego etc. It is not separate from Brahman and there is a relation of identity between the two. The question of relation has meaning only if we have two "distincts," but the world is not distinct from Brahman.

Māyā is material and unconscious. It is opposed to the nature of Brahman. It is neither real nor independent. All physical objects executed by Māyā are apparent by the senses. The senses are, in turn, perceived by the mind. The mind, in turn, is a movement that reveals in Consciousness. Consciousness is the ultimate reality that is not perceived by any other edifice. The objects observed by the senses seem to be constantly changing, while the senses seem to be stable and unchanging. On close inspection, the senses are realized to be constantly changing, while the mind, appears to be constant and static. Actually, the mind is seen to be unconscious and constantly changing. Misperception arises when the mind identifies with its own movement of thought and projects the belief that it is a separate self. The mind believes itself to be a perceiver who is separate from what it perceives. When the mind awakens to this misperception, the belief in being a separate self disappears. At last, the regularly moving mind can be perceived due to the static nature of Consciousness. Thus, the Māyā and its material creation are unconscious but Consciousness is static and ever-present.

Māyā has a technical significance as the creative power of Brahman. Though Māyā a is not real, it creates the universe as the reflection of Brahman. Before creation, there was only one Brahman. He created the universe through his power of Māyā or Prakriti. Prakriti is one, the eternal mode of Satva, Rajas and Tamas. It is dynamic and creates things through these Gunas. The Māyā creates universe by His power and rules over it. It is the regulator of Gunas. It is the creative self-power of the multiple and varied universe. It is associated with ignorance as well as false knowledge. It has got two powers – the power to cover or hide the Self and then to project the Universe. It created the subtle and the gross, the formless and with forms. Ether was born out of self, the air originated in ether, fire came out of air, the water was born in fire, the earth originated in water and finally from the earth came out the plants, etc. Space, time, nature, etc. are the coverings of Brahman. Brahman is everywhere. Just as the plants are born in the earth, hairs come out of body or the web comes out of the body of the spider, similarly, the world comes out of the perfection of the Brahman. The rivers, oceans, mountains, plants, human beings, gods, animals, birds, the four Vedas and Karmas, etc., all have their origin in Brahman. Again, in the stage of destruction, all living beings culminates in the earth, the earth disappears into water, water grips into fire, fire goes back to air, air absorbs into ether, ether culminates in sense organs, sense organs go back to subtle essences which culminates into Bhutadi, the Bhutadi goes back to Mahat, the Mahat disappears in Avyakta, the Avyakta goes to Akshar and the Akshar absorbs into Tamas and finally the Tamas disappears in Brahman.

Sankara expresses that, everything is due to the effect of Māyā —from Mahat down to the gross body. All these and Māyā itself are the not-Self— therefore, they are unreal, like the mirage in a desert. Thus, Māyā characterizes the conditional reality of our physical and mental appearance and the illusory reality for the Absolute Brahman. Māyā is a reflection of Brahman in the practical world. Its shelter is Brahman, but Brahman itself is untouched by the illusion of Māyā, just as a magician is not tricked by his own magic. For language is Māyā, it is unthinkable and it can make the impossible possible. The power of Māyā brings into view what is not there, like a magician makes his audience see a heavenly town in mid-air. On the transcendental level, only the Brahman is true. Māyā is Satya or truth for a worldly-minded man. It is nothing for a liberated sage or Jivanmukta who is identifying himself with Satchidananda Brahman.

Ramanuja's description of Prakriti differs from the explanation of Māyā put forward by Sankara. This distinction will be clear from the following:

3.3.1 Prakriti (According to Ramanuja):

1. Prakriti is real. It is not unreal and indeterminate.

2. The knowledge of Prakriti as the universe is true. No object is unreal. The universe is real.

3. The statements ostensibly denying the reality of the world means only this that there is one Brahman at the root of all multiplicity, not that the world does not exist.

4. Prakriti is the unconscious elements present in Ishwara. It exists in subtle seed form, and it is with this that Ishwara creates the Universe. It is the real or actual product of the unconscious element.

5. The unconscious element existing in God is susceptible to distortion (hence in Ishwara also) and this is real.

6. Prakriti itself appears in the form of its past remaining elements and the entire universe is pervaded by it.

7. Prakriti actually changes into the world.

3.3.2 Māyā (Sankara):

Vedanta posits a distinction between the relatively and the absolutely Real, and a theory of illusion to explain their paradoxical relationship. Sankara's resolution of the problem emerges from his discourse on the nature of Māyā, which mediates the relationship of the world of empirical, manifold phenomena and the one Reality of Brahman. Their apparent separation is an illusory fissure deriving from ignorance and maintained by 'superimposition'. Māyā, enigmatic from the relative viewpoint, is not inexplicable but only not self-explanatory. Sankara's exposition is in harmony with sapiential doctrines from other religious traditions and implies a profound spiritual therapy.

1. Māyā is indeterminate. It is neither real nor unreal.

2. Knowledge of Māyā as the universe is illusory, not real.

3. According to this statement of the Upanishads, multiplicity is unreal.

4. Māyā is the power of Ishwara. It does not exist in Ishwara in seed form. It is merely His desire or wish.

5. The power of the creation appears to be prakriti of the world only to those persons who see it as the world and not its fundamental Brahman nature.

6. The universe itself is not Māyā. Māyā is not transformed or changed, but it is only the magical power of Ishwara, which, due to ignorance, reflects Brahman in the form of the universe.

7. According to Vivartavada, Māyā is the object of intuition. The universe is the illusion of Brahman.

3.4 Māyā is of the nature of Adhyasa

To Shankara, all the objects of the world are the modification of Brahman, the original reality. Adhyasa is a serious mistake to superimpose on the subject, i.e., Atman whose nature is Intelligence. The object whose nature is insentiency covers the subject. Based on this view, he fans a theory known as Vivarta-Vada (theory of appearance) or Māyā - Vada or Anirvacaniya Khyati-Vada or superimposition (Adhyasa). The subject behind all objects is Atman or the Supreme Self whose nature is absolute consciousness. The object includes whatever of a non-intelligent nature, viz., body, sense, mind, prana and the objects of the senses, i.e., the manifested phenomenal universe. The deviation of experience or the duality is due to Māyā or illusion. In our waking, dreaming and in the sleeping state, we see plurality but it disappears when the real Knowledge is manifested. This wrong view is due to the effect of Māyā. Due to superimposition or Adhyasa, the Self is identified to be having name and form. The moment the Self gets associated with all these states and experiences as its own, the Self appears to be an individual entity. The cause of all duality is due to the ignorance in detecting the Real from the unreal. The body, senses, mind, intelligence or the ego are but Adhyasa on the Self. This unreal link of the Self with objects makes it appear to be the doer or the enjoyer who enjoys the happiness and suffers the miseries of the material world like the famous example of the rope and the snake. We see the super imposed snake, though snake is unreal but its existence depends upon the existence of the real rope. Henceforth, by the right knowledge of the snake, we can come across the Knowledge of the reality, here, the rope. In the same sense, the phenomenal world disappears instantly when the Self is realized we can come across the Knowledge of the reality, here, the Brahman. This is how Sankara explains the phenomenon of super imposition or Adhyasa.

3.5 Māyā is the bedrock and object of Brahman

Just as the imposition of the blue colour on the colour-less sky does not affect the sky itself or just as the magician is not biased by his magic, in the same way the Brahman is not prejudiced by Māyā. Māyā can be compared to a dense cloud shield that prevents us from seeing the sun remaining in the sky. When the cloud goes away, we become aware that the sun has been there all the time. Shankara states this clearly as "A ball of jaggery is sweetness itself in every particle of it. A slab of camphor is full of fragrance in every bit. Similarly, this wide world, attractive with trees, mountains, towns, gardens and temples, which has no reality of its own, is seen as existing and sentient only because of being pervaded by the substratum, the Self, which alone is Existence and pure Consciousness (just as jaggery is sweetness itself and camphor fragrance). Any eatable tastes sweet only if it contains jaggery (or sugar). Camphor gives fragrance to things coming into contact with it. So also, it is only because of the Self (Brahman) that everything in this world exists and all living beings acquire sentiency. Thus, the finite is the infinite hidden from our view through certain substratums. When we intuitively recognize the absolute the relative disappears. Our clouds or Māyā appearing as egotism, hatred, greed, lust, anger, ambition etc. are all pushed away when we meditate upon our real nature, when think in ways that manifest our true nature: that is, through truthfulness, purity, contentment, self-restraint and forbearance. This mental purification drives away the clouds of Māyā and allows our divine nature to shine forth.

3.6 Concept of Māyā in Vedas

In Vedas, the terms Māyā or Māyāva find a mention at several places with varying meanings and interpretations by the scholars and Indologists. To illustrate it, a few selective quotes and references are taken from these scriptures for the current discussion. In Rigveda itself, the term Māyā has been used in several hymns in the context of illusion, magic or power. The Rigveda also refers to Māyā bheda, i.e. breaching of Avidya (ignorance) in few Mantras, which essentially means the destruction of the illusion caused by Māyā that occurs during the course of learning the true Knowledge, i.e., the knowledge of Brahman.

Accordong to Rig veda X.177.1-3:

*पतंगमक्तमसुंरस्य मायया हृदा पंश्यंति मनंसा विपश्चितः ।
समुद्रे अंतः कवयो वि चंक्षते मरींचीनां पदमिंच्छंति वेधसंः ॥ (X. 177.1)*

*patamgámaktámásurasya māyáyā hṛdā́ paśyanti mánasā vipaścítaḥ ।
samudre' antaḥ kaváyo ví cakṣate márīcīnām padámicchanti vedhásaḥ ॥ (X. 177.1)*

पतंगो वाचं मनंसा बिभर्ति तां गंन्धर्वोऽवदद्गर्भे अन्तः ।

तां द्योतमानां स्वर्यं मनीषामृतस्य पदे कवयो नि पान्ति ॥ (X. 177.2)

patango vācam manasā bibharti tāṃ gandharvo 'vadad garbhe antaḥ |
tāṃ dyotamānāṃ svaryam manīṣām ṛtasya pade kavayo ni pānti || (X. 177.2)

अपंश्यं गोपामनिंपद्यमानमा च परां च पथिभिश्चरंतं ।
स सध्रीचीः स विषूंचीर्वसांन आ वंरीवर्ति भुवंनेष्वंतः ॥ (X. 177.3)

ápaśyam gopāmánipadyamānamā́ ca párā ca pathíbhiścárantam |
sá sadhrī́cīḥ sá víṣūcīrvásāna ā́ varīvarti bhúvaneṣvantaḥ || (X. 177.3)

Meaning:

The wise behold with their mind in their heart the Sun, made manifest by the illusion of the Asura; The sages look into the solar orb, the ordinary people desire the region of his rays.
The Sun bears the word in his mind; the Gandharva has spoken it within the wombs;
sages cherish it in the place of sacrifice, brilliant, heavenly, ruling the mind.
I beheld the protector, never descending, going by his paths to the east and the west;
clothing the quarters of the heaven and the intermediate spaces. He constantly revolves in the midst of the worlds.

OR, in other words,

I beheld the protector, never descending, going by his paths to the east and the west; clothing the quarters of the heaven and the intermediate spaces. He constantly revolves in the midst of the worlds. (Rigveda X.177.1-3)

Explanation: In the aforesaid hymn, symbolically a contrast has been created between the mind influenced by the light (Sun) and ignorance (illusion of Asura). The hymn is a call to discern the person's enemies or vices, perceive deception, and make good use of own mind to make distinction between that which is perceived and that which ordinarily remains unperceived.

The wise behold with their mind in their heart the Sun, made manifest by the illusion (Māyā) of the Asura; the sages look into the solar orb, the ordinary people desire the region of his rays.

Here the illusion does not imply that the material world does not exist or is merely imaginary; instead, it refers to its impermanent, transitory and misleading nature that tends to take the person away from the ultimate spiritual reality.

In Hindu mythology, Māyā is used in multiple contexts. For example, king Indra has been referred at places to using Māyā to conquer Vritra; deity Varuna's supernatural power is equated also with Māyā; then, both the Devas and Asuras are equipped with Māyāvi (magical) powers that they used against each other in conflicts and wars. The **Atharvaveda** (Book 8, Chapter 10.22) describes the primordial woman 12,2, whom Asura called Māyā and whose magical powers were exploited by them for self-gratification and sustenance. The contextual meaning of Māyā in Atharvaveda relates to the "power of creation", and term Virāj has been used in other texts also for the primeval being, Purusha, and some deities.

This Māyā consists of three gunas viz. sattva, rajas, and tamas. All that exists in the world consists of these three gunas. Brahman, after projecting the universe, remains hidden in it just as a seed after producing the tree remains concealed in the tree itself and not outside of it. That is to say "the cause produces the effect and remains concealed in the effect'.

The process of creation can be illustrated as under:

Brahman is the Lord of Māyā ►The same Brahman is known as the Creator, Preserver and Destroyer of the universe ► Creative aspect associated with Sattva is known as Brahma. ►Protective aspect associated with Rajas is known as Vishnu. ►Destructive aspect associated with Tamas is known as Siva. (Note: These three aspects are related to the phenomenal world and they have no bearing upon the attribute-less Brahman or the Ultimate Reality).

In **Puranas** and particularly in Vaishnavite literature, Māyā is often mentioned as one of the powers of Lord Vishnu. There is a legendary story in the Bhagavata Purana that once the sage Markandeya expressed his desire to Lord Vishnu to experience latter's Māyā. Consequently, Vishnu appeared as an infant on a fig leaf floating in a deluge and swallows the sage as only apparent survivor of the cosmic deluge. Markandeya perceives all creations of the universe, including his own hermitage, in His belly. Now the infant disgorges out the mesmerized sage, everything disappears and Markandeya realizes that he was in his hermitage all the time and had only experienced Vishnu's Māyā.

In Hindu texts, the material world (Māyā) has been described as mrigtrishna (mirage of the deer) at many places. In hot desert, the reflection caused by the sun rays often creates an impression of the water for the deer, he runs for it in vain, and ultimately dies exhausted. In the same manner, the Māyā creates illusion of happiness in the material world and people driven by sensory organs keep on chasing illusory happiness and end up without reaching the goal of life.

This aspect has been beautifully explained in the **Garuda Purana** also as under:

Chakradharo 'pi suratvam suratvalabhe sakalasurapatitvam,
Bhavtirum surapatirurdhvagatitvam tathapi nanivartate trishna.

(A king wishes to be the emperor of the whole world; the emperor aspires to be a celestial god; a celestial god seeks to be Indra, the king of heaven; and Indra desires to be Brahma, the secondary creator. Yet the thirst for material enjoyment does not get satiated.) (Garuda Purana: 2.12.14)

The modern age seer and scholar, **Swami Vivekanand** held that the Vedantin's description of Māyā in its current evolved form, is neither idealism nor realism, and nor a theory. It is a simple statement of facts about what we are and what we see around us. The following quote of Swami Vivekananda from the commentaries of Adi Shankara on Fourth Vyasa Sutra aptly describes the position:

"The Vedas cannot show you Brahman, you are That already. They can only help to take away the veil that hides truth from our eyes. The cessation of ignorance can only come when I know that God and I are one; in other words, identify yourself with Atman, not with human limitations. The idea that we are bound is only an illusion (Māyā). Freedom is inseparable from the nature of the Atman. This is ever pure, ever perfect, ever unchangeable."

Sri Ramakrishna once said:

" Māyā is nothing but the egotism of the embodied soul. This egotism has covered everything like a veil. 'All troubles come to an end when the ego dies'. If, by the grace of God, a man but once realizes that he is not the doer, then he at once becomes a jivanmukta. Though living in the body, he is liberated; he has nothing else to fear."

What has been so painstakingly captured in many Hindu scriptures but often explained in so complex or symbolic way, a fifteenth century saint and mystic poet Kabirdas put so well in his simple poem "Māyā Maha Thugni Hum Jaani". The translated text of the poem reads as under:

Kabirdas says that all this is a long and untold story of Māyā, which is the greatest illusory power."

According to Adi Shankara, the 'Yoga Māyā' is the Māyā formed by the union (yoga) of the three gunas viz. Sattva, Rajas and Tamas; therefore, the veil or illusion spread by the combination of gunas is called 'Yoga Māyā'.

The essence of all yogas is to get rid of desire to achieve equanimity through an equipoised mind. The living beings have ten senses in number, of which five are the organs of perception and the other five as the organs of action. In addition, the five subtle sensory experiences of touching, seeing, hearing, smelling and tasting also significantly matter, being accountable for the feelings of likeability and dislike towards the things. These sense organs along with the subtle senses are the instruments for the cause of uncontrolled desire, which incite to attachment and cravings for the object(s), which are the products of Māyā or Nature, that delude the being in turn. In essence, what we see around is the empirical realm owing to Māyā, while the absolute reality is hidden under the latter's veil. The Bhagavad Gita emphasizes the living beings to look beyond the mere appearance of things to explore the spiritual truth of the universe.

When these functions of the mind are inhibited through the force of conscious effort on the part of the discriminative consciousness, the play of phenomenal existence is stopped its further progress, and when the seed of the mind is burnt by spiritual knowledge, the tree of Samsara is cut off root and branch!

The restlessness of the individual is caused by the projecting forth of mental forces for purposes of acquiring objects of sense. So long as the objects are not obtained, there is the reign of agitation and irritation everywhere. There is only a temporary peace when the objects required are acquired, but the next moment the mind darts upon some other source of objective gratification and keeps the restlessness in continuity. Perfect quiescence comes only when the functioning of the imaginative mind is restrained and put an end to through meditation and Self-Knowledge. Only Brahma-Jnana can dispel the mental ignorance completely.

When true wisdom dawns the mind realizes its nature of Self-sufficiency and turns back to the Atma or the Source of Consciousness and rests as one with it in peace. This is the salvation of the individual, where the individual merges itself into the Infinite Consciousness and exists as the Absolute.

CHAPTER 4

MĀYĀ in upanishads

4.1 Māyā in Upanishads

According to Upanishads, The Supreme Being is believed, by the non-dualistic, Vedantist, to be associated with a certain power called Māyā or Avidya, to which the appearance of the universe is due; and it is urged by some that it is called Māyā or nescience, ignorance or illusion, because the world and its belongings stand in the way of our reaching to a knowledge of the ultimate truth-the eternal substratum of the world, the underlying principle of existence. The first step to the knowledge of the Supreme is the recognition of this permanent element.

Hinduism not being a dogmatic religion, independent concepts and theories exist but the larger consensus is that Māyā is the divine and dynamic energy of the God Himself. Though it is identified as the distracting and deluding force that pushes the soul into the whirlpool of Samsara but the God Himself appears to be Māyāvi too, who ostensibly creates it and its machinations to put Jiva in a constant struggle and test between the empirical and spiritual realities. With Moksha or liberation set as ultimate goal, the individual (Self) must be aware of the machinations of Māyā and knowledge to overcome it. Hence in the following paragraphs, let us briefly learn how Māyā binds living beings to the empirical world, conceals the truth and deludes them into the vicious cycle of births and deaths through her machinations, engaging a variety of factors such as sensory organs and subtle senses, diverse creation, desires and cravings, attachment to various objects, Karma, bondage, interplay of gunas, and so on.

As already mentioned earlier, we have ten sensory organs for perception and action as also five subtle senses which under the influence of Māyā are mostly used to perceive, know, relate and interact with the empirical world. They are difficult to control and tend to drag the being to Samsara instead of realizing soul and directing it to spiritual path. Another important perceptible occurrence is diversity in creation. People tend to be fascinated with the diverse nature of empirical world but are unable to perceive the underlying spiritual unity. Even as individuals, people are engrossed in diverse material possessions and accomplishments but fail to perceive the pure consciousness supporting Self.

The Self (Atman) is eternal, infinite, indestructible and without imperfections, and the physical body is just a clothing for it which is discarded at the death. As the Atman is different from the body and mind, it can be perceived only in a transcendental state when the mind and senses are inert and silent. In contrast, the most beings are driven by the body and mind which fall an easy prey to the desires and consequent cravings for the sensory objects. Hence, they most often engage in desire-ridden actions that lead to Karma and bondage. Similarly, under the influence of Māyā, ego and duality, the living beings develop the deeper attachment towards material possessions and inducements. Attachments lead to desire-driven actions, which is responsible for bondage in cycle of birth-death-rebirth. This is the reason why scriptures recommend practicing self-restraint, detachment and renunciation in life.

The seers pursued the path of Yoga, and came to the conclusion that the Supreme lord evolved the world with the help of His own Māyā. Here, it seems, the cause of the universe is consciousness one. He is Māyin. With the help of his own Māyā the Lord creates the universe. He can desire, so He, the Supreme Soul desired, May I be many, may I be born.

4.2 Māyā in Aitareya Upanishad

The Aitareya Upanishad is a Mukhya Upanishad, associated with the Rigveda. It comprises the fourth, fifth and sixth chapters of the second book of Aitareya Aranyaka, which is one of the four layers of Rig vedic text.

Aitareya Upanishad discusses three philosophical themes: first, that the world and man is the creation of the Atman (Universal Self); second, the theory that the Atman undergoes threefold birth; third, that Consciousness is the essence of Atman.

In **Aitareya Upanishad** also we find a version of Māyā, as His Creation (the worlds)

ॐ आत्मा वा इदमेक एवाग्र आसीन्नान्यत्किञ्चन मिषत् । स ईक्षत
लोकान्नु सृजा इति // I-i-1 //

oṃ ātmā vā idameka evāgra āsīnnānyatkiñcana miṣat . sa
īkṣata
lokānnu sṛjā iti (I-i-1)

स इमाँल्लोकानसृजत । अम्भो मरीचीर्मरमापोऽदोऽम्भः परेण दिवं
द्यौः प्रतिष्ठाऽन्तरिक्षं मरीचयः ।
पृथिवी मरो या अधस्तात्त आपः // I-i-2 //

sa imām̐ llokānasṛjata . ambho
marīcīrmaramāpo'do'mbhaḥ pareṇa divaṃ

dyauḥ pratiṣṭhā'ntarikṣaṃ marīcayaḥ .
*pṛthivī maro yā adhastātta āpaḥ (*I-i-2)

स ईक्षतेमे नु लोका लोकपालान्नु सृजा इति ॥ सोऽद्भ्य एव पुरुषं
*समुद्धृत्यामूर्छयत् ॥*I-i-3 ॥

sa īkṣateme nu lokā lokapālānnu sṛjā iti .. so'dbhya eva puruṣaṃ
*samuddhṛtyāmūrchayat (*I-i-3)

तमभ्यतपत्तस्याभितप्तस्य मुखं निरभिद्यत यथाऽण्डं
मुखाद्वाग्वाचोऽग्निर्नासिके निरभिद्येतं नासिकाभ्यां प्राणः ।
प्राणाद्वायुरक्षिणी निरभिद्येतमक्षीभ्यां चक्षुश्चक्षुष
आदित्यः कर्णौ निरभिद्येतां कर्णाभ्यां श्रोत्रं
श्रोत्रद्दिशस्त्वङ्निरभिद्यत त्वचो लोमानि लोमभ्य ओषधिवनस्पतयो
हृदयं निरभिद्यत हृदयान्मनो मनसश्चन्द्रमा नाभिर्निरभिद्यत
नाभ्या अपानोऽपानान्मृत्युः
*शिश्नं निरभिद्यत शिश्नाद्रेतो रेतस आपः ॥*I-i-4 ॥

tamabhyatapattasyābhitaptasya mukhaṃ nirabhidyata yathā'ṇḍaṃ
mukhādvāgvāco'gnirnāsike nirabhidyetaṃ nāsikābhyāṃ prāṇaḥ .
prāṇādvāyurakṣiṇī nirabhidyetamakṣībhyāṃ cakṣuścakṣuṣa
ādityaḥ karṇau nirabhidyetāṃ karṇābhyāṃ śrotraṃ
śrotraddiśastvaṅnirabhidyata tvaco lomāni lomabhya oṣadhivanaspatayo
hṛdayaṃ nirabhidyata hṛdayānmano manasaścandramā nābhirnirabhidyata
nābhyā apāno'pānānmṛtyuḥ
*śiśnaṃ nirabhidyata śiśnādreto retasa āpaḥ (*I-i-4)

Translation:

I-i-1: In the beginning this was but the absolute Self alone. There was nothing else whatsoever that winked. He thought, "Let Me create the worlds."

I-i-2: He created these world, viz. ambhas, marici, mara, apah. That which is beyond heaven is ambhas. Heaven is its support. The sky is marici. The earth is mara. The worlds that are below are the apah.

I-i-3: He thought, "These then are the worlds. Let Me create the protectors of the worlds." Having gathered up a (lump of the) human form from the water itself, He gave shape to it.

I-i-4: He deliberated with regard to Him (i.e. Virat of the human form). As He (i.e. Virat) was being deliberated on, His (i.e. Virat'') mouth parted, just as an egg does. From the mouth emerged speech; from speech came Fire. The nostrils parted; from the nostrils came out the sense of smell; from the sense of smell came Vayu (Air). The two eyes parted; from the eyes emerged the sense of sight; from the sense of sight came the Sun. The two ears parted; from the ears came the sense of hearing; from the sense of hearing came the Directions. The skin emerged; from the skin came out hair (i.e. the sense of touch associated with hair); from the sense of touch came the Herbs and Trees. The heart took shape; from the heart issued the internal organ (mind); from the internal organ came the Moon. The navel parted; from the navel came out the organ of ejection; from the organ of ejection issued Death. The seat of the procreative organ parted; from that came the procreative organ; from the procreative organ came out Water.

*(Note: All these creations of His, mentioned in the above hymns, are **Māyā**)*

According to Advaita Vedanta, Brahman is the Ultimate Reality. In ultimate sense Brahman is devoid of all qualities. It is indeterminate and non-dual. It is Nirvisesha and transcendent. Brahman is pure consciousness. Brahman associated with Māyā appears as qualified or Saguna or Ishvara who is the creator, preserver and destroyer of this universe. Brahman is the ground of the world which appears through Māyā. According to Sankara, Brahman is the efficient and as well as the material cause of the universe through Māyā. There is no causality in Brahman without Māyā. The world is an appearance. But from the phenomenal point of view, the world is quite real. It is practical reality so long as true knowledge does not dawn.

According to Advaita view, the self is pure consciousness and pure being. Jivatva is an appearance. It is phenomenal reality from the phenomenal point of view. Jivas are many but actually the plurality of the soul is an imposition. Pure self is only one. Therefore the Upanishad says : ***Tattvamasi***, the self is identified with Brahman. In true sense Brahman is an Absolute. Therefore it is said that Brahman is everything and everything is Brahman. Sankara criticizes Brahmapariamavada. The world is vivarta of Brahman. Appearance is Vivarta, Sankara does not declare the world to be an illusion. According to him, the world is not an illusion. It is ***Mithyā***.

ब्रह्म सत्यं जगन्मिथ्या जीवो ब्रह्मैव नापरः।

brahma satyam jagan-mithyä jivo brahmaiva näparah ||

(Verse 20 of the Brahma Jnana Vali Mala).

Brahman is real, the universe is mithyā (it cannot be categorized as either real or unreal). The jiva is Brahman itself and not different. This should be understood as the correct Sastra. This is proclaimed by Vedanta.

Also

अथ खलु क्रतुमयः *Chandogyopanishad,* // *3.14.1* //

All this is indeed Brahman.

Mithyā means the world is neither real nor unreal, but Mithyā. It appears to be real. The passages of the Upanishads mostly support Advaita view of Sankara, Sankara does not say that the world and Jivatva are mere dream. He says that there is a great difference between Svapna and Jagrat.

He who is one and infinite seems to make Himself many and finite; He who is unchangeable seems to change himself perpetually he who is absolute knowledge and holiness seems to make himself ignorant and unholy. Hence our philosophers call this power Māyā. It is most expressive term, indicating the incrustableness of a power whose nature can no more be understood than its existence denied. The Advaitin do not claim that the postulation of this incomprehensible power affords ny real explanation of the enigmas of the world; they candidly admit the final incomprehensibility of things, the mysteriousness of creation and gives this mystery a name, Māyā or Avidya. This term, A vidya when spoken of as the cause of the world, does not exactly mean ignorance, but rather 'knot-knowledge' i.e., something seemingly different from knowledge, which constitutes the essence of Divinity. Now God, as contemplated in Himself in His infinite and immutable essence, apart from Māyā, is the Nirguna Brahman, of whom or which nothing more can be said than that, it is Truth, Intelligence and Bliss, Sat, Cit, Ananda. As contemplated with reference of Māyā, as producing the world of finite objects by this mysterious power, God is

Ishvara, the Ruler, the Lord, what western theologians call the Personal God, the omniscitat and omnipotent Creator, Preserver and destroyer of the world, the Father, Guide, Instructor and Saviour of finite souls. The Advaitin do not say that these attributes of God, attributes which are called 'personal; are not true. What they say is that they are relatively true, true, that is, with reference to that mysterious power by which God seems to produce things different from him. These attributes imply a certain difference, a duality between God and the world; and duality is the result of Māyā. As Māyā is without beginning and without end, being the power of the Eternal Being, the Sagulna character of God is also eternal; he is eternally Ishvara Lord, as well as Brahman.

4.3 Māyā in Prashnopanishad

The Prashnopanishad is an ancient Sanskrit text, embedded inside Atharva Veda, ascribed to Pippalada sakha of Vedic scholars. It is a Mukhya (primary) Upanishad, and is listed as number 4 in the Muktika canon of 108 Upanishads of Hinduism.

The Prashna Upanishad contains six Prashna (questions), and each is a chapter with a discussion of answers. The chapters end with the phrase, prasnaprativakanam, which literally means, "thus ends the answer to the question".

16th shloka of the first Prashna in **Prashnopanishad** says the following about Māyā:

तेषामसौ विरजो ब्रह्मलोको न येषु जिह्ममनृतं न माया चेति ॥ 1.16॥

teshhaamasau virajo brahmaloko na yeshhu
jihmamanritam na maayaa cheti || 1. 16||

Meaning: To them belongs you stainless Brahma-world,
In whom there is no crookedness and falsehood, nor trick (Māyā)."

4.4 Māyā in Taittiriyopanishad

The Taittiriya Upanishad has three chapters: the Siksha Valli, the Ananda Valli and the Bhrigu Valli. The first chapter Siksha Valli includes twelve Anuvaka (lessons). The second chapter Ananda Valli, sometimes called Brahmananda Valli includes nine verses. The third chapter Bhrigu Valli consists of ten verses.

The Upanishad is one of the earliest known texts where an index was included at the end of each section, along with the main text, as a structural layout of the book. At the end of each Vallī in Taittiriya Upanishad manuscripts, there is an index of the Anuvakas which it contains. The index includes the initial words and final words of each Anuvaka, as well as the number of sections in that Anuvaka. For example, the first and second Anuvakas of Shiksha Valli state in their indices that there are five sections each in them, the fourth Anuvaka asserts there are three sections and one paragraph in it, while the twelfth Anuvaka states it has one section and five paragraphs. The Ananda Valli, according to the embedded index, state each chapter to be much larger than currently surviving texts. For example, the 1st Anuvaka lists pratika words in its index as brahmavid, idam, ayam, and states the number of sections to be twenty-one. The 2nd Anuvaka asserts it has twenty-six sections, the 3rd claims twenty-two, the 4th has eighteen, the 5th has twenty-two, the 6th Anuvaka asserts in its index that it has twenty-eight sections, 7th claims sixteen, 8th states it includes fifty-one sections, while the 9th asserts it has eleven. Similarly, the third Valli lists the Pratika and anukramani in the index for each of the ten Anuvakas.

Third Anuvaka in Taittiriyopanishad says that:

तस्माद्वा एतस्मात् प्राणमयात् । अन्योऽन्तर आत्मा मनोमयः । तेनैष पूर्णः ॥ 3 ॥

tasmādvā etasmāt prāṇamayāt | anyo'ntara ātmā manomayaḥ | tenaiṣa pūrṇaḥ || 3 ||

Meaning: Than that, verily,—than this one formed of Prāṇa,—there is another self within formed of Manas (mano-**māyā**). By him this one is filled.

Māyā, which resides in Brahman and is the material cause of the universe, is made up of three guṇas or principles. The guṇa of Tamas being the cause of the Annamaya, inertness is found to predominate in that kosha; there exists in it neither the kriyā-shakti nor the jñāna-shakti, neither the power of action nor the power of cognition. The guṇa of Rajas being the cause of the Prāṇamaya, the power of action inheres in the Prāṇamaya. The guṇa of Sattva being the cause of the three koshas from the Mano-maya upward, the power of cognition inheres in those three koshas. The cause of the Manomaya is Sattva mixed with Tamas; and therefore we find in it the Tāmasic qualities, such as attachment and hatred. The cause of the Vijñāna-maya is Sattva mixed with Rajas, and therefore we find in it the agency with reference to all Vedic sacrificial rites and all secular acts such as agriculture. The pure guṇa of Sattva is the cause of the Ānandamaya, and therefore, we find therein only joys of various kinds, termed love and so on. No doubt, the jñāna-shakti, the essence of cognition, is in itself only one; still it

appears threefold owing to a difference in its aspects or functions,—as the instrument (karaṇa-shakti), as the agent (kartṛ-shakti), and as enjoyment (bhoga-śakti). Manas is a product of jñāna-shakti, or essence of cognition in its aspect as an instrument; and formed of this Manas is the Manomaya, the aggregate of the vṛttis or states of mind such as desires, fancies, and the like. These states of mind are enumerated by the Vājasaneyins as follows:
"Desire, representation, doubt, faith, want of faith, firmness, want of firmness, shame, reflection, fear,-—all is mind."

4.5 Māyā in Shvetashvatara Upanishad

Shvetashvatara Upanishad is among the oldest texts that made explicit reference of the Brahman being the hidden reality, Māyā a (nature) as magic with the former as magician.

This Upanishad falls under the branch of Krishna Yajurveda. There are six chapters in it. The ground reason for the genesis of this world has been asked in its first chapter. In the third and fourth chapter, the topics like the genesis of the world, the omnipresence of this supreme entity of soul competent to generate, to maintain and to destroy and the significance of reckoning with this has been described.

ते ध्यानयोगानुगता अपश्यन् देवात्मशक्तिं स्वगुणैर्निगूढाम् ।
यः कारणानि निखिलानि तानि कालात्मयुक्तान्यधितिष्ठत्येकः ॥
1.3 ॥

te dhyānayogānugatā apaśyan devātmaśaktiṃ svaguṇair nigūḍhām /
yaḥ kāraṇāni nikhilāni tāni kālātmayuktāny adhitiṣṭhaty ekaḥ // 1.3 //

Meaning: The sages, absorbed in meditation through one-pointedness of mind, discovered the creative power, belonging to the Lord Himself and hidden in its own gunas. That non-dual Lord rules over all those causes - time, the self and the rest.

Finally, the sages found out through yoga that is to say through self-control and meditation, the ultimate cause of the universe. The discovery was that the attribute-less Brahman or Pure Consciousness, which is beyond time, space and causality, is the only Reality which through its own power of **Māyā** was the cause of the creation of the universe. **Māyā** is the power which belongs to Brahman and is not independent of it. Brahman and Māyā are inseparable as fire and its power to burn.

Brahman when associated with Māyā is called Saguna Brahman or with attributes (conceived as Isvara) which are the causes of creation, preservation and dissolution. Māyā is thus the material cause of the universe that is to say that Brahman creates the universe along with the various objects contained in it out of the raw material called Māyā. This is Brahman's lower aspect. But as Pure Consciousness, the higher aspect of Brahman (which is without any attribute, nirguna) is the entity which is the efficient cause of the creation of the universe. Thus Brahman is both the material and efficient cause of the universe i.e., both the raw material and the entity that creates the world. It is just like a spider weaving a web out of its own silk. The same spider is the cause of the silk produced out of its own body and is also the entity which weaves the web wherein it stays.

This non-dual Lord rules over all the secondary causes of the universe like time, the self-etc. The gist of this mantra is that Pure Brahman is not the cause of the universe; but associated with its power of Māyā it appears to be the creator, preserver and destroyer of the universe. Thus from the standpoint of the Absolute, there is no creation but from the standpoint of the universe Brahman with Māyā appears to create, preserve and dissolve the world.

क्षरं प्रधानममृताक्षरं हरः क्षरात्मानावीशते देव एकः ।
तस्याभिध्यानाद्योजनात्तत्त्व- भावात् भूयश्चान्ते विश्वमायानिवृत्तिः ॥
1.10 ॥

kṣaraṃ pradhānam amṛtākṣaraṃ haraḥ kṣarātmānāv īśate deva ekaḥ /
tasyābhidhyānād yojanāt tattvabhāvād bhūyaś cānte viśvamāyānivṛttiḥ // 1.10 //

Meaning: What is perishable, is Primary Matter (pradhana). What is immortal and imperishable, is Hara (the 'Bearer,' the soul). Over both the perishable and the soul the One God (deva) rules.

By meditation upon Him, by union with Him, and by entering into His being. More and more, there is finally cessation from every illusion (**Māyā**-nivrtti).

Prakriti (**Māyā**) is perishable and of changing nature. Its enjoyer, the jivatma, is imperishable and indestructible. It is one Brahman, which is called here as Hara, who rules over the perishable and imperishable both. Hara means the destroyer of ignorance. The word also signifies Siva or Rudra, one of the divine manifestations of Brahman in the phenomenal world. He is alone worth knowing and must be realized essentially. Pursuing this path, if somebody constantly meditates on Him, keeping himself always united with Him and realizing his identity with Him, eventually, he attains Him having known the unity between the individual self and the Supreme Self. Then he transcends the Māyā; his relation with this illusory world is cut off permanently. This identity is called in the scriptures as "I am Brahman" (ayam atma brahma, aham brhmaismi and other such mahavakyas).

छन्दांसि यज्ञाः क्रतवः व्रतानि भूतम् भव्यम् वेदाः यत् वदन्ति एतत्
विश्वम् अस्मान् च मायी सृजते।
तस्मिन् अन्यः मायया सन्निरुद्धः॥ ॥ 4.9 ॥

chhandaṁsi yajñāḥ kratavaḥ vratāni bhūtam bhavyam vedāḥ yat vadanti etat viśvam asmān ca māyī sṛjate| tasmin anyaḥ māyayā sanniruddhaḥ (4.9)

मायां तु प्रकृतिं विद्यान्मायिनं च महेश्वरम् ।
तस्यवयवभूतैस्तु व्याप्तं सर्वमिदं जगत् ॥ 4.10 ॥

māyāṁ tu prakṛtiṁ vidyānmāyinaṁ ca maheśvaram |
tasyāvayavabhūtaistu vyāptaṁ sarvamidaṁ jagat (4.10)

Meaning:

4.9. Sacred poetry(chandas), the sacrifices, the ceremonies, the ordinances, the past, the future, and what the Vedas declare— This whole world the illusion-maker (mayin) projects out of this. [Brahma]. And in that the other is bound up through that Māyā.

4.10. Now, one should know that Nature (Prakriti) is illusion (Māyā), And that the Mighty Lord (Maheshvara) is the illusion-maker (mayin). This whole world is pervaded. With beings that are parts of Him.

Human beings are infatuated with this magic creating bondage for self through illusions and delusions. The essence of Upanishadic wisdom is that the Māyā is a perceived reality, that has a tendency to crowd the true reality. Some cosmic realities as per Upanishads are as follows: Atman is conscious, Māyā is unconscious; Brahman is the figurative Upadana i.e, the principle, the cause while Māyā is the literal; Brahman and Atman is eternal, unchanging, invisible, absolute and resplendent consciousness while Māyā is prone to birth, change, evolution, replenishment and death with time under varying circumstances.

4.6 Māyā in Mandukya Karika

Gaudapada was a 6th century Hindu philosopher and scholar of the Advaita Vedanta philosophy, who authored the **Mandukya Karika** that included detailed commentaries on the Mandukya Upanishad, one of the ten such principal texts. While describing the nature of Brahman, Atman and Māyā, he insisted that the seeker must have true insight and accurate knowledge of the hidden truth for the liberation. He tried to explain in his Karika the correlation and interplay between Atman and Māyā as follows:

अनादिमायया सुप्तो यदा जीवः प्रबुध्यते ।
अजमनिद्रमस्वप्नमद्वैतं बुध्यते तदा ॥ 1.16 ॥

anādimāyayā supto yadā jīvaḥ prabudhyate .
ajamanidramasvapnamadvaitaṃ budhyate tadā ॥ 1.16 ॥

Meaning (1.16): When the individual Self, sleeping under the influence of Māyā that is beginningless, is awakened, then he realizes (Turiya that is) unborn, sleepless, dreamless and non-dual.

प्रपञ्चो यदि विद्येत निवर्तेत न संशयः ।
मायामात्रमिदं द्वैतमद्वैतं परमार्थतः ॥ 1.17 ॥

prapañco yadi vidyeta nivarteta na saṃśayaḥ .
māyāmātramidaṃ dvaitamadvaitaṃ paramārthataḥ ॥
1.17 ॥

Meaning (1.17): If a phenomenal world were to exist, it should, no doubt, cease to be. This duality is but an illusion (Māyā); in reality it is non-dual.

कल्पयत्यात्मनाऽऽत्मानमात्मा देवः स्वमायया
स एव बुध्यते भेदानिति वेदान्तनिश्चयः ॥ 2.12 ॥

kalpayatyātmanā''tmānamātmā devaḥ svamāyayā
sa eva budhyate bhedāniti vedāntaniścayaḥ ॥ *2.12* ॥

Meaning (2.12): The self-luminous Self, by Its own Māyā imagines Itself by Itself and It alone cognizes all objects. This is a settled fact of the Vedanta-texts.

अनिश्चिता यथा रज्जुरन्धकारे विकल्पिता ।
सर्पधारादिभिर्भावैस्तद्वदात्मा विकल्पितः ॥ 2.17 ॥

aniścitā yathā rajjurandhakāre vikalpitā |
sarpadhārādibhirbhāvaistadvadātmā vikalpitaḥ ||2. 17 ||

निश्चितायां यथा रज्ज्वां विकल्पो विनिवर्तते ।
रज्जुरेवेति चाद्वैतं तद्वदात्मविनिश्चयः ॥ 2.18 ॥

Niscitayam yatha rajjvam vikalpo vinivartate,
Rajjureveti cAdvaitam tadvadatmaviniscayah.(2.18)

प्राणादिभिरनन्तैश्च भावैरेतैर्विकल्पितः ।
मायैषा तस्य देवस्य यया संमोहितः स्वयम् ॥ 2.19 ॥

Pranadibhiranantaisca bhsvairetairvikalpitah,

Māyāisa tasya devasya yaya sammohitah svayam.(2.19)

Meaning: As the rope, whose nature is not really known, is imagined in the dark to be a snake, or a water-line, etc.; so also, is the Atman imagined. When real nature of the rope is ascertained, all illusions about it disappear with conviction that it is that one rope and nothing else; even so is the nature of the conviction regarding Atman. The Atman is imagined as Prana and other endless objects. This is due to Māyā of the luminous i.e. Brahman-Atman by which It is deluded.) (Mandukya Karika 2.17-19)

The various schools of Hindu philosophy have questioned, debated and tried to explain Māyā, each one in their own ways. The Samkhya school propounded its concept of duality through Purusha and Prakriti, with some texts and commentaries equating the latter with Māyā as the product of the interplay of three gunas in varying combinations and proportions. The realism-driven Nyaya school opined that neither the soul (Purusha) nor the material world (Prakriti) was an illusion, insight of which was later adopted and redefined by the Advaita Vedanta in a more plausible way. In Yoga school of thoughts, Māyā is the manifested world and the yogic perfection of the Brahman is the cause of the creation of Māyā.

4.7 Māyā in Mantrika Upanishad

The Mantrika Upanishad is a minor Upanishad of Hinduism. The Sanskrit text is one of the 22 Samanya Upanishads, is part of the Vedanta and Yoga schools of Hindu philosophy literature, and is one of 19 Upanishads attached to the Shukla Yajurveda. In the Muktika canon, narrated by Rama to Hanuman, it is listed at number 32 in the anthology of 108 Upanishads.

The Upanishad comprises 21 verses. It attempts a syncretic but unsystematic formulation of ideas from Samkhya, Yoga, Vedanta and Bhakti. It is therefore treated as a theistic Yoga text. Mantrika suggests the theory that the universe was created by Purusha and Prakriti together, and various active soul-infants drink from inactive Ishvara soul (God) who treats this as a form of Vedic sacrifice. This Upanishad interprets an exposition on Brahman (changeless reality) and Māyā (changing reality, metaphysical illusion). According to the Mantrika Upanishad, "the Brahman dwells in body as soul, and this soul as God changes dwelling thousands of time".

The Mantrika Upanishad is also called Chulika Upanishad.

भोग्यवस्तुजनकत्वेन मायां धेन्वा रूपयति--
गौरनादवती सा तु जनित्री भूतभाविनी ।
असिता सितरक्ता च सर्वकामदुघा विभोः ॥ 5॥

Bhogyavastujanakatvain mayam dhenva rupayati-
gauranādyantavatī sā janitrī bhūtabhāvinī .
sitāsitā ca raktā ca sarvakāmadudhā vibhoḥ (5)

Meaning:

5. The Lord's mighty Māyā, having both a beginning and end, the creatrix, brings beings into existence; white, black and red (She) fulfils all desires.

पिबन्त्येनामविषयामविज्ञातां कुमारकाः ।
एकस्तु पिबते देवः स्वच्छन्दोऽत्र वशानुगः ॥ 6॥

pibantyenāmaviṣayāmavijñātāṃ kumārakāḥ .
ekastu pibate devaḥ svacchando'tra vaśānugaḥ (6)

6. (The ignorant) experiences this non-objective Māyā a (whose real nature is) unknown (even) to sages like Kumara. The Lord alone freely following (Her) enjoys Māyā (as Her Lord and Companion).

पश्यन्त्यस्यां महात्मानः सुवर्णं पिप्पलाशनम् ।
उदासीनं ध्रुवं हंसं स्नातकाध्वर्यवो जगुः ॥ 8 ॥

paśyantyasyāṃ mahātmānaḥ suvarṇaṃ pippalāśanam .
udāsīnaṃ dhruvaṃ haṃsaṃ snātakādhvaryavo jaguḥ (8)

8. The magnanimous (sages) behold in (the sphere of) Māyā the bird eating the fruits (of Karmas). The priests who have completed their Vedic training have declared the Other to be detached.

4.8 Māyā in Sarva Sara Upanishad

The Sarvasara Upanishad is a Sanskrit text and is one of the 22 Samanya (general) Upanishads of Hinduism. The text, along with the Niralamba Upanishad, is one of two dedicated glossaries embedded inside the collection of ancient and medieval era.

The text exists in two versions, one attached to the Atharvaveda in many Sanskrit anthologies, and another attached to the Krishna Yajurveda in some anthologies such as the Telugu-language version. The two versions have some differences, but are essentially similar in meaning.

Sarvasara Upanishad defines and explains 23 Upanishadic concepts, while Niralamba Upanishad covers 29. These two texts overlap in some concepts, both refer to older Principal Upanishads (dated to 1st millennium BCE), but offer independent explanations suggesting that accepting a diversity of views were a part of its tradition.

कथं बन्धः कथं मोक्षः का विद्या काऽविद्येति ।
जाग्रत्स्वप्नसुषुप्तितुरीयं च कथम् ।
अन्नमयप्राणमयमनोमयविज्ञानमयानन्दमयकोशाः कथम् ।
कर्ता जीवः पञ्चवर्गः क्षेत्रज्ञः साक्षी कूटस्थोऽन्तर्यामी कथम् ।
प्रत्यगात्मा परात्मा माया चेति कथम् ।
आत्मेश्वरजीवः अनात्मनां देहादीनामात्मत्वेनाभिमन्यते
सोऽभिमान आत्मनो बन्धः । तन्निवृत्तिर्मोक्षः ।
या तदभिमानं कारयति सा अविद्या । सोऽभिमानो यया
निवर्तते सा विद्या । मन आदिचतुर्दशकरणैः
पुष्कलैरादित्याद्यनुगृहीतैः शब्दादीन्विषयान्-
स्थूलान्यदोपलभते तदात्मनो जागरणम् ।
तद्वासनासहितैश्चतुर्दशकरणैः शब्दाद्यभावेऽपि
वासनामयाञ्छब्दादीन्यदोपलभते तदात्मनः स्वप्नम् ।
चतुर्दशकरणो परमाद्विशेषविज्ञानाभावाद्यदा
शब्दादीन्नोपलभते तदात्मनः सुषुप्तम् ।
अवस्थात्रयभावाभावसाक्षी स्वयंभावरहितं
नैरन्तर्यं चैतन्यं यदा तदा तुरीयं चैतन्यमित्युच्यते ।
अन्नकार्याणां कोशानां समूहोऽन्नमयः कोश उच्यते ।
प्राणादिचतुर्दशवायुभेदा अन्नमयकोशे यदा वर्तन्ते
तदा प्राणमयः कोश इत्युच्यते ।
एतत्कोशद्वयसंसक्तं मन आदि चतुर्दशकरणैरात्मा
शब्दादिविषयसङ्कल्पादीन्धर्मान्यदा करोति तदा मनोमयः
कोश इत्युच्यते । एतत्कोशत्रयसंसक्तं तद्गतविशेषज्ञो
यदा भासते तदा विज्ञानमयः कोश इत्युच्यते ।
एतत्कोशचतुष्टयं संसक्तं स्वकारणाज्ञाने
वटकणिकायामिव वृक्षो यदा वर्तते तदानन्दमयः कोश
इत्युच्यते । सुखदुःखबुद्ध्या श्रेयोऽन्तः कर्ता यदा तदा
इष्टविषये बुद्धिः सुखबुद्धिरनिष्टविषये बुद्धिर्दुःखबुद्धिः ।

शब्दस्पर्शरूपरसगन्धाः सुखदुःखहेतवः ।
पुण्यपापकर्मानुसारी भूत्वा प्राप्तशरीरसंयोग-
मप्राप्तशरीरसंयोगमिव कुर्वाणो यदा दृश्यते
तदोपहितजीव इत्युच्यते । मन आदिश्च
प्राणादिश्चेच्छादिश्च सत्त्वादिश्च पुण्यादिश्चैते
पञ्चवर्गा इत्येतेषां पञ्चवर्गाणां धर्मीभूतात्मा
ज्ञानादृते न विनश्यत्यात्मसन्निधौ नित्यत्वेन
प्रतीयमान आत्मोपाधिर्यस्तल्लिङ्गशरीरं
हृद्ग्रन्थिरित्युच्यते तत्र यत्प्रकाशते चैतन्यं स
क्षेत्रज्ञ इत्युच्यते । ज्ञातृज्ञानज्ञेयानामाविर्भाव-
तिरोभावज्ञाता स्वयमाविर्भावतिरोभावरहितः
स्वयंज्योतिः साक्षीत्युच्यते ।
ब्रह्मादिपिपीलिकापर्यन्तं सर्वप्राणिबुद्धिष्ववशिष्टत-
योपलभ्यमानः सर्वप्राणिबुद्धिस्थो यदा तदा कूटस्थ
इत्युच्यते । कूटस्थोपहितभेदानां स्वरूपलाभहेतुर्भूत्वा
मणिगणे सूत्रमिव सर्वक्षेत्रेष्वनुस्यूतत्वेन यदा काश्यते
आत्मा तदान्तर्यामीत्युच्यते ।
सत्यं ज्ञानमनन्तं ब्रह्म । सत्यमविनाशि । अविनाशि
नाम देशकालवस्तुनिमित्तेषु विनश्यत्सु यन्न विनश्यति
तदविनाशि । ज्ञानं नामोत्पत्तिविनाशरहितं नैरन्तर्यं
चैतन्यं ज्ञानमुच्यते । अनन्तं नाम मृद्विकारेषु
मृदिव स्वर्णविकारेषु स्वर्णमिव तन्तुविकारेषु
तन्तुरिवाव्यक्तादिसृष्टिप्रपञ्चेषु पूर्णं व्यापकं
चैतन्यमनन्तमित्युच्यते ।
आनन्दं नाम सुखचैतन्यस्वरूपोऽपरिमितानन्द-
समुद्रोऽवशिष्टसुखस्वरूपश्चानन्द इत्युच्यते ।
एतद्वस्तुचतुष्टयं यस्य लक्षणं देशकाल-
वस्तुनिमित्तेश्वव्यभिचारी तत्पदार्थः परमात्मेत्युच्यते ।
त्वंपदार्थादौपाधिकात्तत्पदार्थादौपाधिक-
भेदाद्विलक्षणमाकाशवत्सूक्ष्मं केवलसत्ता-
मात्रस्वभावं परं ब्रह्मेत्युच्यते । माया नाम

अनादिरन्तवती प्रमाणाप्रमाणसाधारणा न सती नासती न सदसती स्वयमधिका विकाररहिता निरूप्यमाणा सतीतरलक्षणशून्या सा मायेत्युच्यते । अज्ञानं तुच्छाप्यसती कालत्रयेऽपि पामराणां वास्तवी च सत्त्वबुद्धिर्लौकिकानामिदमित्थमित्यनिर्वचनीया वक्तुं न शक्यते ।

नाहं भवाम्यहं देवो नेन्द्रियाणि दशैव तु ।
न बुद्धिर्न मनः शश्वन्नाहङ्कारस्तथैव च ॥ 1॥

katham bandhaḥ katham mokṣaḥ kā vidyā kā'vidyeti . jāgratsvapnasuṣuptiturīyaṃ ca katham . annamayaprāṇamayamanomayavijñānamayānandamayako śāḥ katham . kartā jīvaḥ pañcavargaḥ kṣetrajñaḥ sākṣī kūṭastho'ntaryāmī katham . pratyagātmā parātmā māyā ceti katham . ātmeśvarajīvaḥ anātmanāṃ dehādīnāmātmatvenābhimanyate so'bhimāna ātmano bandhaḥ . tannivṛttirmokṣaḥ . yā tadabhimānaṃ kārayati sā avidyā . so'bhimāno yayā nivartate sā vidyā . mana ādicaturdaśakaraṇaiḥ puṣkalairādityādyanugṛhītaiḥ śabdādīnviṣayān-sthūlānyadopalabhate tadātmano jāgaraṇam . tadvāsanāsahitaiścaturdaśakaraṇaiḥ śabdādyabhāve'pi vāsanāmayāñchabdādīnyadopalabhate tadātmanaḥ svapnam . caturdaśakaraṇo paramādviśeṣavijñānābhāvādyadā śabdādīnnopalabhate tadātmanaḥ suṣuptam . avasthātrayabhāvābhāvasākṣī svayaṃbhāvarahitaṃ nairantaryaṃ caitanyaṃ yadā tadā turīyaṃ caitanyamityucyate . annakāryāṇāṃ kośānāṃ samūho'nnamayaḥ kośa ucyate . prāṇādicaturdaśavāyubhedā annamayakośe yadā vartante tadā prāṇamayaḥ kośa ityucyate . etatkośadvayasaṃsaktaṃ mana ādi caturdaśakaraṇairātmā śabdādiviṣayasaṅkalpādīndharmānyadā karoti tadā manomayaḥ kośa ityucyate . etatkośatrayasaṃsaktaṃ tadgataviśeṣajño yadā bhāsate tadā vijñānamayaḥ kośa ityucyate . etatkośacatuṣṭayaṃ saṃsaktaṃ svakāraṇājñāne vaṭakaṇikāyāmiva vṛkṣo yadā vartate tadānandamayaḥ kośa ityucyate . sukhaduḥkhabuddhyā śreyo'ntaḥ kartā yadā tadā iṣṭaviṣaye buddhiḥ sukhabuddhiraniṣṭaviṣaye buddhirduḥkhabuddhiḥ . śabdasparśarūparasagandhāḥ sukhaduḥkhahetavaḥ . puṇyapāpakarmānusārī bhūtvā prāptaśarīrasaṃyoga-maprāptaśarīrasaṃyogamiva kurvāṇo yadā dṛśyate tadopahitajīva ityucyate . mana ādiśca prāṇādiścecchādiśca sattvādiśca puṇyādiścaite pañcavargā ityeteṣāṃ pañcavargāṇāṃ dharmībhūtātmā jñānādṛte na vinaśyatyātmasannidhau nityatvena pratīyamāna ātmopādhiryastalliṅgaśarīraṃ hṛdgranthirityucyate tatra yatprakāśate caitanyaṃ sa kṣetrajña ityucyate . jñātṛjñānajñeyānāmāvirbhāva-tirobhāvajñātā svayamāvirbhāvatirobhāvarahitaḥ svayaṃjyotiḥ sākṣītyucyate . brahmādipipīlikāparyantaṃ sarvaprāṇibuddhiṣvavaśiṣṭata-yopalabhyamānaḥ sarvaprāṇibuddhistho yadā tadā kūṭastha ityucyate . kūṭasthopahitabhedānāṃ svarūpalābhaheturbhūtvā maṇigaṇe sūtramiva sarvakṣetreṣvanusyūtatvena yadā kāśyate ātmā tadāntaryāmītyucyate . satyaṃ jñānamanantaṃ brahma . satyamavināśi . avināśi nāma deśakālavastunimitteṣu vinaśyatsu yanna vinaśyati tadavināśi . jñānaṃ nāmotpattivināśarahitaṃ nairantaryaṃ caitanyaṃ jñānamucyate . anantaṃ nāma mṛdvikāreṣu

mṛdiva svarṇavikāreṣu svarṇamiva tantuvikāreṣu tanturivāvyaktādisṛṣṭiprapañceṣu pūrṇaṃ vyāpakaṃ caitanyamanantamityucyate .
ānandaṃ nāma sukhacaitanyasvarūpo'parimitānanda-samudro'vaśiṣṭasukhasvarūpaścānanda ityucyate .
etadvastucatuṣṭayaṃ yasya lakṣaṇaṃ deśakāla-vastunimitteśvavyabhicārī tatpadārthaḥ paramātmetyucyate .
tvaṃpadārthādaupādhikāttatpadārthādaupādhika-bhedādvilakṣaṇamākāśavatsūkṣmaṃ kevalasattā-mātrasvabhāvaṃ paraṃ brahmetyucyate . māyā nāma anādirantavatī pramāṇāpramāṇasādhāraṇā na satī nāsatī na sadasatī svayamadhikā vikārarahitā nirūpyamāṇā
satītaralakṣaṇaśūnyā sā māyetyucyate . ajñānaṃ tucchāpyasatī kālatraye'pi pāmarāṇāṃ vāstavī ca sattvabuddhirlaukikānāmidamitthamityanirvacanīyā vaktuṃ na śakyate .
nāhaṃ bhavāmyahaṃ devo nendriyāṇi daśaiva tu .
na buddhirna manaḥ śaśvannāhaṅkārastathaiva ca (1)

Meaning:

1. What is Bandha (bondage of the Soul) ? What is Moksha (liberation) ? What is Avidya (nescience)? What is Vidya (knowledge) ? What are the states of Jagrat (waking), Svapna (dreaming) , Sushupti (Dreamless sleep), and the fourth, Turiya (Absolute) ? What are the Annamaya, Pranamaya, Manomaya, Vijnanamaya and Anandamaya Koshas (vestures or sheaths of the soul) ? What is the Karta (agent), what the Jiva (individual self), the Kshetrajna (knower of the body), the Sakshi (Witness), the Kutastha, the Antaryamin (Internal Ruler) ? What is the Pratyagatman (Inner Self), what the Paramatman (Supreme Self), the Atman, and also **Māyā?** -- the master of Self looks upon the body and such like things other than the Self as

Itself: this egoism is the bondage of the soul. The cessation of that (egoism) is Moksha, liberation. That which causes that egoism is Avidya, nescience. That by which this egoism is completely turned back is Vidya, knowledge. When the self, by means of its four and ten organs of sense beginning with the mind and benignly influenced by the sun and the rest which appear outside, perceives gross objects such as sound etc., then it is the Atman's Jagrat (wakeful) state. When, even in the absence of sound etc., (the self) not divested of desire for them, experiences, by means of the four organs, sound and the rest in the form of desires – then it is the Atman's state of Svapna (dream). When the four and ten organs cease from activity, and there is the absence of differentiated knowledge, then is the Atman's state of Sushupti (dreamless sleep).

4.9 Māyā in Brihadaranyaka Upanishad

The Brihadaranyaka Upanishad is one of the Principal Upanishads and one of the first Upanishadic scriptures of Hinduism. A key scripture to various schools of Hinduism, the Brihadaranyaka Upanishad is tenth in the Muktikā or "canon of 108 Upanishads".

इ॒दं वै॒ त॒न्म॒धु ड॒ध्य॒ङ्ङ् अथर्व॒णो॒ऽश्वि॒भ्यामुवाच । त॒दे॒तदृषिः
प॒श्यन्नवोचत्
रूप॒ꣳ-रूपं प्र॒तिरूपो बभूव, त॒दस्य रूप॒ं प्रतिच॒क्षणाय॒-
-न्द्रो माया॒भिः पुरु॒रूप ईयते, युक्ता॒ ह्य॒स्य ह॒रयः शता॒ द॒शे॒ति ।
अय॒ं वै॒ ह॒रयो, अय॒ं वै॒ दश च सह॒स्राणि ब॒हूनि चानन्ता॒नि च ।
त॒दे॒त॒द्ब्र॒ह्मापूर्व॒मनप॒रमनन्त॒रमबाह्य॒म् अय॒मात्मा॒ ब्र॒ह्म स॒र्वानुभूः ।
इ॒त्यनुशा॒सनम् (II-V-19)

ida̱ṃ va̱i ta̱nma̱dhu ḍadhya̱ṅṅ atharvaṇo̱'śvi̱bhyāmuvāca .
ta̱deta̱dṛṣiḥ

paśyannavocat rūpag̱-rūpaṃ pratirūpo babhūva, tadasya rūpaṃ praticakṣaṇāye-
-ndro māyābhiḥ pururūpa īyate, yuktā hyasya harayaḥ śatā daśeti .
ayaṃ vai harayo, ayaṃ vai daśa ca sahasraṇi bahūni cānantāni ca .
tadetadbrahmāpūrvamanaparamanantaramabāhyam ayamātmā brahma sarvānubhūḥ .
ityanuśāsanam (II-V-19)

Meaning: This is that meditation on things mutually helpful which Dadhyac, versed in the Atharva-Veda, taught the Ashvins. Perceiving this the Rishi said, '(He) transformed Himself in accordance with each form; that form of His was for the sake of making Him known. The Lord on account of **Māyā** (notions superimposed by ignorance) is perceived as manifold, for to Him are yoked ten organs, nay, hundreds of them. He is the organs; He is ten and thousands – many and infinite. That Brahman is without prior or posterior, without interior or exterior. This self, the perceiver of everything, is Brahman. This is the teaching.

4.10 Māyā in Kaivalya Upanishad

The Kaivalya Upanishad is an ancient Sanskrit text and one of the minor Upanishads of Hinduism. It is classified as a Shaiva Upanishad, and survives into modern times in two versions, one attached to the Krishna Yajurveda and other attached to the Atharvaveda. It is, as an Upanishad, a part of the corpus of Vedanta literature collection that presents the philosophical concepts of Hinduism.

The Upanishad extols Shiva, aloneness and renunciation, describes the inner state of man in his personal spiritual journey detached from the world. The text is notable for presenting Shaivism in Vedanta, discussing Atman (Self) and its relation to Brahman, and Self-knowledge as the path to kaivalya (liberation).

स एव **माया**परिमोहितात्मा शरीरमास्थाय करोति सर्वम् ।
स्त्र्यन्नपानादिविचित्रभोगैः स एव जाग्रत्परितृप्तिमेति ॥ 12॥

sa eva māyāparimohitātmā śarīramāsthāya karoti sarvam .
stryannapānādivicitrabhogaiḥ sa eva jāgratparitṛptimeti
(12)

Translation: With his self thus deluded by **Māyā** or ignorance, it is he who identifies himself with the body and does all sorts of things. In the waking state it is he (the Jiva) who attains satisfaction through the varied objects of enjoyment, such as women, food, drink, etc.

स्वप्ने स जीवः सुखदुःखभोक्ता स्वमायया कल्पितजीवलोके ।
सुषुप्तिकाले सकले विलीने तमोऽभिभूतः सुखरूपमेति ॥ 13॥

svapne sa jīvaḥ sukhaduḥkhabhoktā svamāyayā
kalpitajīvaloke .
suṣuptikāle sakale vilīne tamo'bhibhūtaḥ sukharūpameti
(13)

Translation: In the dream-state that Jiva feels pleasure and pain in a sphere of existence created by his own **Māyā** or ignorance. During the state of profound sleep, when everything is dissolved (into their causal state), he is overpowered by Tams or non-manifestation and comes to exist in his form of Bliss.

4.11 Māyā in Maitrayaniya Upanishad

The Maitrayaniya Upanishad is an ancient Sanskrit text that is embedded inside the Yajurveda. It is also known as the

Maitri Upanishad, and is listed as number 24 in the Muktika canon of 108 Upanishads.

The Maitrayaniya Upanishad is associated with the Maitrayanas school of the Yajurveda. It is a part of the "black" Yajurveda, with the term "black" implying "the un-arranged, motley collection" of content in Yajurveda, in contrast to the "white" (well arranged) Yajurveda where Brihadaranyaka Upanishad and Isha Upanishad are embedded.

अथान्यत्राप्युक्तं महानदीषूर्मय इव निवर्तकमस्य
यत्पुराकृतं समुद्रवेलेव दुर्निवार्यमस्य मृत्योरागमनं
सदसत्फलमयैर्हि पाशैः पशुरिव बद्धं
बन्धनस्थस्येवास्वातन्त्र्यं यमविषयस्थस्यैव
बहुभयावस्थं मदिरोन्मत्त इवामोदममदिरोन्मत्तं पाप्मना
गृहीत इव भ्राम्यमाणं महोरगदष्ट इव विपद्दष्टं
महान्धकार इव रागान्धमिन्द्रजालमिव ***माया****मयं स्वप्नमिव*
मिथ्यादर्शनं कदलीगर्भ इवासारं नट इव क्षणवेषं
चित्रभित्तिरिव मिथ्यामनोरममित्यथोक्तम् ॥ शब्दस्पर्शादयो
येऽर्था अनर्था इव ते स्थिताः । येष्वासक्तस्तु भूतात्मा न
स्मरेच्च परं पदम् ॥ 2॥

athānyatrāpyuktaṃ mahānadīṣūrmaya iva nivartakamasya
yatpurākṛtaṃ samudraveleva durnivāryamasya
mṛtyorāgamanaṃ
sadasatphalamayairhi pāśaiḥ paśuriva baddhaṃ
bandhanasthasyevāsvātantryaṃ yamaviṣayasthasyaiva
bahubhayāvasthaṃ madironmatta
ivāmodamamadironmattaṃ pāpmanā
gṛhīta iva bhrāmyamāṇaṃ mahoragadaṣṭa iva vipadṛṣṭaṃ
mahāndhakāra iva rāgāndhamindrajālamiva māyāmayaṃ
svapnamiva

mithyādarśanaṃ kadalīgarbha ivāsāraṃ naṭa iva kṣaṇaveṣaṃ citrabhittiriva mithyāmanoramamityathoktam .. śabdasparśādayo ye'rthā anarthā iva te sthitāḥ . yeṣvāsaktastu bhūtātmā na smarecca paraṃ padam (2)

Meaning: It has been said: 'As waves in great rivers, the past deeds are one's safeguard – like the coast line for the ocean. Rebirth is unavoidable – bound by good and bad results (of actions), as a beast by ropes. Like a prisoner, one in the clutches of Death is not free; dwells in the midst of many fears. He who is maddened by worldly pleasures is like one intoxicated. He is in the grip of sin and roams, like one bitten by a snake is he in the jaws of danger, as in darkness one is blinded by passion. As caught in a magic show one is in the midst of **Māyā**. He sees everything wrongly as in a dream, essenceless like the pith of plantain – like an actor dressed up for a moment – falsely attractive like a painted wall. It has been stated 'sense-objects' like sound are there, sources of trouble. Attached to them, the Self forgets the supreme place.

4.12 Māyā in Nrisimha Poorva Tapaniya Upanishad

The Nrisimha Tapaniya Upanishad is a minor Upanishadic text. It is one of the 31 Upanishads attached the Atharvaveda, and classified as one of the Vaishnava Upanishads. It is presented in two parts, the Purva Tapaniya Upanishad and the Uttara Tapaniya Upanishad, which formed the main scriptures of Narasimha sect of the Vaishnavas dated prior to the 7th century.

The text is notable for asserting a four-fold identity, that Atman (soul, self) is same as Om, Brahman (Absolute Reality) and Vishnu Man-Lion avatar, Nrisimha. The Upanishad opens with verses of the Rigveda. Its foundation of monism philosophy, as well its style is also found in other Vaishnava Upanishads such as those dedicated to Rama.

देवा ह वै प्रजापतिमब्रुवन्नानुष्टुभस्य
मन्त्रराजस्य नारसिंहस्य शक्तिं बीजं नो
ब्रूहि भगवन्निति स होवाच प्रजापतिर्माया वा
एषा नारसिंही सर्वमिदं सृजति सर्वमिदं रक्षति
सर्वमिदं संहरति तस्मान्मायामेतां शक्तिं
विद्याद्य एतां मायां शक्तिं वेद स पाप्मानं
तरति स मृत्युं तरति स संसारं तरति सोऽमृतत्वं
च गच्छति महतीं श्रियमश्नुते मीमांसन्ते
ब्रह्मवादिनो ह्रस्वा दीर्घा प्लुता चेति ॥

devā ha vai prajāpatimabruvannānuṣṭubhasya
mantrarājasya nārasiṃhasya śaktiṃ bījaṃ no
brūhi bhagavanniti sa hovāca prajāpatirmāyā vā
eṣā nārasiṃhī sarvamidaṃ sṛjati sarvamidaṃ rakṣati
sarvamidaṃ saṃharati tasmānmāyāmetāṃ śaktiṃ
vidyādya etāṃ māyāṃ śaktiṃ veda sa pāpmānaṃ
tarati sa mṛtyuṃ tarati sa saṃsāraṃ tarati so'mṛtatvaṃ
ca gacchati mahatīṃ śriyamaśnute mīmāṃsante
brahmavādino hrasvā dīrghā plutā ceti

Meaning: The devas requested Brahma to teach them the power of Anushtup Mantra Raja (The king of Chants set to anushtup meter) and also its root. Brahma told them:

This illusion (**Māyā**) which is the power of Narasimha is the one which creates everything, protects them and destroys them. Therefore you have to realize that this illusion is the power. The one who understands the power of this illusion, he crosses all sins and also attains deathlessness. He enjoys the wealth with fame. The experts in Brahmam argue among themselves whether this is short, long or extra-long. One who pronounces this with short ending, will burn away all sins and would attain deathlessness. He who pronounces this in long ending, would get wealth with fame and also attain deathlessness. He who pronounces it with extra-long ending would attain ethereal knowledge and also deathlessness. What follows is the explanation given by sages.

4.13 Māyā in Tejo-Bindu Upanishad

The Tejobindu Upanishad is a minor Upanishad in the corpus of Upanishadic texts of Hinduism. It is one of the five Bindu Upanishads, all attached to the Atharvaveda, and one of twenty Yoga Upanishads in the four Vedas.

The text is notable for its focus on meditation, calling dedication to bookish learning as rubbish, emphasizing practice instead, and presenting the Vedanta doctrine from Yoga perspective.

The Tejobindu is listed at number 37 in the serial order of the Muktika enumerated by Rama to Hanuman in the modern era anthology.

चिन्मात्रान्नास्ति माया च चिन्मात्रान्नास्ति पूजनम् ।
चिन्मात्रान्नास्ति मन्तव्यं चिन्मात्रान्नास्ति सत्यकम् ॥ 2.36 ॥

चिन्मात्रान्नास्ति कोशादि चिन्मात्रान्नास्ति वै वसु ।
चिन्मात्रान्नास्ति मौनं च चिन्मात्रान्नस्त्यमौनकम् ॥ 2.37 ॥

चिन्मात्रान्नास्ति वैराग्यं सर्वं चिन्मात्रमेव हि ।
यच्च यावच्च चिन्मात्रं यच्च यावच्च दृश्यते ॥ 2.38 ॥

cinmātrānnāsti māyā ca cinmātrānnāsti pūjanam .
cinmātrānnāsti mantavyaṃ cinmātrānnāsti satyakam (2.36)

cinmātrānnāsti kośādi cinmātrānnāsti vai vasu .
cinmātrānnāsti maunaṃ ca cinmātrānnastyamaunakam (2.37)

cinmātrānnāsti vairāgyaṃ sarvaṃ cinmātrameva hi .
yacca yāvacca cinmātraṃ yacca yāvacca dṛśyate (2.38)

Chapter 2, 36-38. **Māyā** is nothing without Chinmatra. Puja (worship) is nothing without Chinmatra. Meditation, truth, sheaths and others, the (eight) Vasus, silence, non-silence and indifference to objects – are nothing without Chinmatra. Everything is from Chinmatra. Whatever is seen and however seen – it is Chinmatra so far.

(Note: Whatever is Chit (consciousness) in the universe is only Chinmatra. This universe is Chinmaya only. You are Chit. I am Chit; contemplate upon the worlds also as Chit.)

4.14 Māyā in Yoga Tattva Upanishad

The Yogatattva Upanishad is an important Upanishad within Hinduism. It is one of eleven Yoga Upanishads attached to the Atharvaveda, and one of twenty Yoga Upanishads in the four Vedas. It is listed at number 41 in the serial order of the Muktika enumerated by Rama to Hanuman in the modern era anthology.

Two major versions of its manuscripts are known. One has fifteen verses but attached to Atharvaveda, while another very different and augmented manuscript exists in the Telugu language which has one hundred and forty-two verses and is attached to the Krishna Yajurveda. The text is notable for describing Yoga in the Vaishnavism tradition.

तेषां मुक्तिकरं मार्गं मायाजालनिकृन्तनम् ।
जन्ममृत्युजराव्याधिनाशनं मृत्युतारकम् ॥ 5 ॥

नानामार्गैस्तु दुष्प्रापं कैवल्यं परमं पदम् ।
पतिताः शास्त्रजालेषु प्रज्ञया तेन मोहिताः ॥ 6 ॥

teṣāṃ muktikaraṃ mārgaṃ māyājālanikṛntanam .
janmamṛtyujarāvyādhināśanaṃ mṛtyutārakam (5)

nānāmārgaistu duṣprāpaṃ kaivalyaṃ paramaṃ padam .
patitāḥ śāstrajāleṣu prajñayā tena mohitāḥ (6)

Meaning: 5-6. Kaivalya, the supreme seat, is the path which gives them emancipation, which rends asunder the snare of **Māyā**, which is the destroyer of birth, old age and disease and which enables one to overcome death. There are no other paths to salvation. Those who go round the net of Shastras are deluded by that knowledge.

4.15 Māyā in Annapurna Upanishad

The Annapurna Upanishad is a Sanskrit text and one of the minor Upanishads of Hinduism. It is classified as a Samanya Upanishads and attached to the Atharvaveda.

The text is structured into five chapters, as a discourse between yogin Nidagha and Vedic sage Ribhu. The first chapter presents a series of questions such as "Who am I? How did the universe come about? what is the meaning of birth, death and life? what is freedom and liberation?" The text then discusses its answers, after attributing the knowledge to goddess Annapurna.

The text is notable for describing five types of delusions, asserting the Advaita Vedanta doctrine of non-duality and oneness of all souls and the metaphysical Brahman, defining spiritual liberation as being unattached to anything and freedom from inner clingings. The text describes Jivanmukti – achieving freedom in this life, and the characteristics of those who reach self-knowledge.

केवलं साक्षिरूपेण विना भोगो महेश्वरः ।
प्रकाशते स्वयं भेदः कल्पितो मायया तयोः ।
चिच्चिदाकारतो भिन्ना न भिन्ना चित्त्वहानितः ॥ IV-33 ॥

kevalaṃ sākṣirūpeṇa vinā bhogo maheśvaraḥ .
prakāśate svayaṃ bhedaḥ kalpito māyayā tayoḥ .
ciccidākārato bhinnā na bhinnā cittvahānitaḥ (4.33)

Meaning: Alone as the Witness, without participation, the great Lord shines by Himself. Through **Māyā** is set up the difference between them. Spirit is other than Its form; as It does not dwindle, the Spirit is non-different (from all objects).

सिद्धान्तोऽध्यात्मशास्त्राणां सर्वापह्नव एव हि ।
नाविद्यास्तीह नो माया शान्तं ब्रह्मेदमक्लमम् ॥ V-112 ॥

siddhānto'dhyātmaśāstrāṇāṃ sarvāpahnava eva hi .
nāvidyāstīha no māyā śāntaṃ brahmedamaklamam (5.112)

Meaning: The repudiation of the objective manifold is the doctrine of the Shastras setting forth the Spirit. Here is neither avidya nor **Māyā**; this is the tranquil Brahman, unfatigued.

CHAPTER 5

MĀYĀ IN BRAHMA SUTRAS

5.1 Maharshi Bādarāyaṇa: The Author of 'Brahma Sutras'

Maharshi Bādarāyaṇa (महर्षि बादरायण) was an Indian philosopher and sage who was the reputed author of the Brahma Sutras, the source text for the Hindu philosophical school of Vedānta. Estimates of his lifetime vary very widely from around fifth century BCE to third or fourth century CE.

Badarayana is recognized as the compiler, Sutrakara, of the Brahma Sutras (an exposition on Brahman) also called Vedanta Sutra, Sariraka Mimamsa Sutra and Uttara Mimamsa Sutra. Brahma Sutra is the most authoritative exposition of the Vedanta. But it was not the first. Badarayana cites the views of the earlier scholars such as Audulomi, Kaskrtsna, Badrai and Asmarthya.

His work on Brahma Sutras is variously dated from 500 BCE to 450 CE. The Brahma Sutras of Bādarāyaṇa, also called the Vedanta Sutra, was compiled in its present form around 400–450 CE, but the great part of the Sutra must have been in existence much earlier than that. Estimates of the date of Bādarāyana's lifetime differ between 200 BCE and 200 CE.

Bādarāyana is regarded as having written the basic text of the Vedanta system, the Vedānta sūtra a.k.a. Brahmasūtra. He is thus considered the founder of the Vedānta system of philosophy.

According to Bādarāyana, the Veda is eternal and the shastra is the great authority. No amount of reflection logical argumentation can lead to the discovery of metaphysical truth. Sutra admits two sources of knowledge: **(i) pratyaksham (perception) and (ii) anumanam (inference).** The revealed shruti is self-evident and is called pratyaksham. By Shruti, Bādarāyana means the Upanishads, and by smriti he means the Bhagavadgita, the Mahabharata and the Code of Manu. In any theory of knowledge, inference is based on perception; so also Smriti is based on Shruti. Bādarāyana makes a distinction between two spheres of existence: the thinkable and the unthinkable. The thinkable consists of the region of prakriti with the elements, the mind, intellect, and egoity, whereas the unthinkable is Brahman. With regard to the knowledge of the latter the only means is the shastras. Any reasoning which is not in conformity with the Veda is useless for Bādarāyana. Reasoning proceeds from characteristic marks. But of Brahman we cannot say that it is characterized by this or that to the exclusion of other attributes. Reasoning, therefore is subordinate to intuitional knowledge, which can be obtained by devotion and meditation.

(This book is humbly dedicated to Maharshi Bādarāyaṇa, The Author of 'Brahma Sutras')

5.2 Māyā in Brahma Sutras

Adhikarana VII: (Brahma Sutras 21-22) refutes the objection that Brahman in the form of the individual soul is subject to pleasure and pain by showing that though Brahman assumes the form of the individual soul, yet He transcends the latter and remains untainted by any property of Jiva whom He controls from within. Though the individual soul or Jiva is no other than Brahman Himself, yet Brahman remains the absolute Lord and as such above pleasure and pain. Jiva is a slave of Avidya. Brahman is the controller of Māyā. When Jiva is freed from Avidya, he becomes identical with Brahman.

Brahma-Sutra 1.1.13

विकारशब्दान्नेतिचेन्न प्राचुर्यात् *(1.1.13)*

vikāraśabdānneticenna prācuryāt (1.1.13)

Meaning: If (it be objected that the term Anandamaya consisting of bliss can) not (denote the Supreme Self) because of its being a word denoting a modification or transformation or product (we say that the objection is) not (valid) on account of abundance, (which is denoted by the suffix '**Māyā**').

Brahma-Sutra 1.1.14

तद्धेतुव्यपदेशाच्च *(1.1.14)*

Taddhetuvyapadeśācca (1.1.14)

Meaning: And because he is declared to be the cause of it (i.e. of bliss; therefore '**Māyā**' denotes abundance or fullness).

Brahma-Sutra 2.1.26

देवादिवदपि लोके *(2.1.26)*

devādivadapi loke (2.1.26)

Meaning: (The case of Brahman creating the world is) like that of gods and other beings in the world (in ordinary experience).

We see also that in the world gods and sages create particular things such as palaces, chariots, etc., by force of will, without external aid. Why cannot the Omnipotent Creator create the world by His will-power (Sat Sankalpa) or His in finite power of **Māyā**?

Brahma-Sutra 2.1.30

सर्वोपेता च तद्दर्शनात् ॥ 2.1.30 ॥

sarvopetā ca taddarśanāt || 2.1.30 ||

Meaning: And (Brahman is) endowed with all (powers), because it is seen (from the scriptures).

This Sutra gives proof of Brahman's being endowed with **Māyā** Shakti, the power. Various scriptural texts declare that Brahman possesses all powers. "The great Lord is the Māyin (the ruler of **Māyā**)"

Brahma-Sutra 2.1.31

विकरणत्वान्नेति चेत्, तदुक्तम् ॥ 2.1.31 ॥

vikaraṇatvānneti cet, taduktam || 2.1.31 ||

Meaning: If it be said that because (Brahman) is devoid of organs (it is) not (able to create, though endowed with powers), (we say) this has (already) been explained.

As Brahman is devoid of organs. It cannot create. Moreover, It is described as "Not this, not this", which precludes all attributes; so how can It possess any powers? This Sutra replies that it has already been explained in 2. 1. 4. and 2. 1. 25 that with respect to Brahman the scripture alone is authority and not reason. The scripture declares that Brahman, although devoid of organs, possesses all capacities. "Grasping without hands, moving swiftly without feet" etc. Though Brahman is without attributes, yet on account of **Māyā**, It can be taken to possess all powers.

Brahma-Sutra 2.1.38

सर्वधर्मोपपत्तेश्च *(2.1.38)*

Sarvadharmopapatteśca (2.1.38)

Meaning: And because all the qualities (required for the creation of the world) are reasonably found (only in Brahman) He must be admitted to be the cause of the universe.

There is no real change in Brahman but there is an apparent modification in Brahman on account of His inscrutable power of **Māyā**.

Brahma-Sutra 3.2.1

संध्ये सृष्टिराह हि *// 3.2.1 //*

saṃdhye sṛṣṭirāha hi || 3.2.1 //

Meaning: In the intermediate stage (between waking and deep sleep, there is a real) creation, because (the Sruti) says so.

The question is raised whether the creation which one experiences in the dream state is as real as this world of ours, or merely **Māyā**, false, as compared with this waking world. This Sutra, which gives the view of the opponent, holds that it is just as real, for the Sruti declares, "There are no chariots, nor horses to be yoked to them, nor roads there, but he himself creates the chariots, horses, and roads. For he is the agent". Moreover, we do not find any difference between the experience of the waking state and that of the dream state. A meal taken in dream has the effect of giving satisfaction even as in the waking state. Therefore the creation of the dream state is real and springs from the Lord Himself, even as He creates ether etc.

Brahma-Sutra 3.2.2

निर्मातारं चैके, पुत्रादयश् च ॥ 3.2.2 ॥

nirmātāraṃ caike, putrādayaś ca || 3.2.2 ||

Meaning: And some (Sakhas or recensions) (state the Self or the Supreme Lord to be) the creator (of objects of desires while we are asleep) and (objects of desires there stand for) sons etc.

A further argument is given by the opponent that the creation even in dreams is by the Lord Himself. "He who is awake in us shaping objects of desire while wp are asleep . . . that is Brahman". Sons etc. are the objects of desire that He creates. So, as in the case of the waking state, even in dreams the Lord Himself creates, and hence the world of dreams is also real. Therefore the dream world is not false but real like this Vyavaharika (phenomenal) world of ours.

Brahma-Sutra 3.2.3

मायामात्रं तु, कार्त्स्न्येनानभिव्यक्तस्वरूपत्वात् ॥ 3.2.3 ॥

māyāmātraṃ tu, kārtsnyenānabhivyaktasvarūpatvāt || 3.2.3 ||

Meaning: But (the dream world is) mere illusion (**Māyā**), on account of its nature not being manifest with the totality (of attributes of the waking state).

'But' discards the view expressed by the two previous Sutras. The nature of the dream world does not agree in toto with that of the waking world with respect to time, place, cause, and non-contradiction, and as such that world is not real like the waking world. There can be no appropriate time, place or cause in the dream state. Inside the body, there is not enough space for objects like chariots, horses, etc., and in a dream the soul does not leave the body; for if it did, then one who dreams of having gone to America would find himself there on waking while he went to sleep in India. Nor is the midnight proper time for an eclipse of the sun seen in a dream, nor can we conceive a child's getting children in a dream to be real. Moreover, even in dreams we see objects seen being transformed, as for example, when we see a tree turn into a mountain. "He himself creates the chariots etc.", only means that objects which have no reality appear to exist in dreams just as silver does in a mother-of-pearl. The argument that the dream world is real because it is also a creation of the Supreme Lord, like this waking world, is not true, for the dream world is not the creation of the Lord but of the individual soul. "When he dreams . . . himself puts the body aside and himself creates (a dream body in its place)". This text clearly proves that it is the Jiva that creates in dreams and not the Lord.

CHAPTER 6

MĀYĀ IN SRIMAD BHAGAVAD GITA AND THE MOKSHA GITA

6.1 Māyā in Srimad Bhagavad Gita

The Bhagavad Gita is one Hindu text which not only embodies the supreme spiritual mystery but also contains the essence of all the four Vedas and other scriptures. This is one treaty where a person can find solution of the most of his doubts and queries on Hindu spiritualism. In His discourse to deluded Prince Arjuna in Kurukshetra, Shri Krishna declares Māyā as God's divine energy as interplay of three gunas, which is difficult but not impossible to overcome by any devoted seeker.

Bhagavad Gita (BG), 7.14:

दैवी ह्येषा गुणमयी मम माया दुरत्यया।
मामेव ये प्रपद्यन्ते मायामेतां तरन्ति ते॥ 7.14॥

daivī hyeṣhā guṇa-mayī mama māyā duratyayā
mām eva ye prapadyante māyām etāṁ taranti te (7.14)

Meaning: My divine energy Māyā, consisting of the three modes of nature, is extremely difficult to overcome. However, those who surrender unto me cross over it easily.) (BG: Chapter 7, Verse 14)

Commentary:

Some people claim that Maya is Māyā (non-existent). They say that the material energy Māyā is a perception created due to our ignorance, but if someone attains spiritual knowledge, Māyā will cease to exist. The soul (Brahman) itself is the Ultimate Reality, and once we understand that, all illusions shall dispel. However, this theory is negated by the Bhagavad Gita in this verse. Shri Krishna has already stated that Māyā is an extension of His energy and not an illusion.

6.2 Māyā is not just illusion – it is also the agency that brings about illusion

The word "Māyā" is common in yogic philosophy. Though often translated as illusion, Maya is also the agency that brings about illusion.

The above-mentioned verse in Bhagavad-Gita (7.14) refers to Māyā as an agency when declaring it to be Krishna's energy. It is energy in the sense that it executes the supreme energetic person's will. Its purpose is not to keep us in illusion, but to teach us the futility of the illusion of living separate from Krishna. Once this futility sinks in, we re-position ourselves as his loving servants, for that is our constitutional position as his eternal parts.

The illusions we face during our life-journey serve a positive educational purpose. They are like the wrong options in a multiple-choice test. The presence of such options impels students to internalize their lessons, thereby becoming intelligent enough to choose the right option.

As long as we equate Māyā with just illusion, we tend to underestimate the power of those illusions and overestimate the power of our intelligence to see through them. But human intelligence pitted against the divine illusory energy is eminently a battle of unequals – we will, sooner or later, end up deluded. The above-mentioned verse conveys this mismatch by deeming Maya formidable, even insurmountable.

When we see Māyā as Krishna's illusory energy, we realize the necessity, indeed the indispensability. of internalizing the lesson that we can become safe only by absorbing ourselves in Krishna's loving service.

Of course, we can and should use our intelligence for understanding the nature of illusion. But this understanding is essentially a matter of the heart, not the head – it centers on redirecting our heart's love from the world towards Krishna by voluntary surrender to him, as the verse recommends. Only by such surrender can we go beyond the illusory energy's illusions.

BG 7.15:

न मां दुष्कृतिनो मूढा: प्रपद्यन्ते नराधमा: |
माययापहृतज्ञाना आसुरं भावमाश्रिता: || 7.15||

na māṁ duṣhkṛitino mūḍhāḥ prapadyante narādhamāḥ
māyayāpahṛita-jñānā āsuraṁ bhāvam āśhritāḥ || 7.15||

Meaning: Four kinds of people do not surrender unto Me—those ignorant of knowledge, those who lazily follow their lower nature though capable of knowing Me, those with deluded intellect (Māyā), and those with a dominating nature.

BG 7.25:

The concept of Yoga as power to create Māyā gave rise to compound term 'Yoga Māyā', which finds mention in Hindu texts, including **Shrimad Bhagavad** Gita (7.25).

नाहं प्रकाश: सर्वस्य योगमायासमावृत: |
मूढोऽयं नाभिजानाति लोको मामजमव्ययम् || 7.25||

nāhaṁ prakāśhaḥ sarvasya yoga-māyā-samāvṛitaḥ.
mūḍho 'yaṁ nābhijānāti loko mām ajam avyayam. (7.25)

Meaning: I am not manifest to everyone, being veiled by My divine 'Yoga Māyā' energy. Hence, those without knowledge do not know that I am without birth and changeless.

Commentary: The Supreme Energetic Shri Krishna has infinite energies. Amongst these, 'Yoga Māyā', the souls, and Māyā are the main ones. God descends in this world by virtue of His 'Yoga Māyā' energy and reveals His divine pastimes, His divine abode, His divine bliss and love on the Earth plane. However, the same 'Yoga Māyā' power keeps His divinity veiled from us. We are unable to feel His presence, although He is seated in our hearts. Even in the present, if we are fortunate enough to see the Lord in His personal-form, we cannot recognize Him. Until we are eligible for His divine vision, the 'Yoga Māyā' keeps God's divine form concealed from us. And only by God's grace, the 'Yoga Māyā' bestows upon us the divine vision that allows us to recognize and see God.

Shri Krishna explains to arjuna that the 'Yoga Māyā' energy of Brahman serves as a veil to make Him invisible to the ignorant people, who can see and believe His finite form known by birth but are unaware of His (Brahman) highest state which is immutable and unsurpassable. This can be learnt only through the embodiment of truth, knowledge and bliss.

The concept of Māyā discussed in the current piece is largely derived from the philosophy of the Advaita Vedanta school. The Vedanta school itself is divided into many sub-schools on the principles of Advaita and Dvaita, and their derivatives, in that the former believes in oneness of the Brahman (God) and Atman (soul) while the latter considers Brahman and Atman as distinct entities. According to the Vedanta concept, the perceived world is not what it appears to be and Māyā is one that manifests and perpetuates this false sense of duality among beings. According to the Advaita philosophy, we experience two realities; one is Vyavaharika (empirical reality) and the other Paramarthika (absolute, spiritual reality). Māyā is illusory because it has potential to create bondage to the empirical world, and thus, it hinders realization of the truth, which is unitary Self and its relation with the Supreme Soul, or Brahman. As per Advaita concept, Māyā is cause of the manifestation of the material world, whereas Brahman, which supports Māyā, is the principal force behind creation cause of the world.

One brilliant example of empirical reality and its nemesis is quoted in the Sabha Parva of the epic Mahabharata. Duryodhana visits the Māyā sabha (hall of illusion) in the Indraprastha on the occasion of the Rajsuya Yagya by Pandavas, and becomes confused and envious after experiencing its glamour and grandeur; in turn, Queen Draupadi ridicules him watching his predicament. This episode infuriates Duryodhana who feels insulted and resolves to take revenge against the cousin Pandavas and Draupadi for belittling him through this outlandish display of power and wealth. Needless to mention, the episode becomes the main cause for the subsequent ugly events leading to the Mahabharata war. In this episode, the Māyā sabha symbolizes the world, Duryodhana the egoistic individual (Jiva) and Draupadi personifies Māyā instigating the state of confusion, delusion, confusion and emotional agony of the Kaurava prince. The great story of Mahabharata vindicates how human beings fall prey to miseries and destruction for their desires and cravings under the influence of Māyā.

BG 9.7, 9.8:

सर्वभूतानि कौन्तेय प्रकृतिं यान्ति मामिकाम्।
कल्पक्षये पुनस्तानि कल्पादौ विसृजाम्यहम् || *BG, 9.7||*

sarva-bhūtāni kaunteya prakṛitiṁ yānti māmikām
kalpa-kṣhaye punas tāni kalpādau visṛijāmyaham || BG, 9.7||

प्रकृतिं स्वामवष्टभ्य विसृजामि पुनः पुनः।
भूतग्राममिमं कृत्स्नमवशं प्रकृतेर्वशात् || *BG, 9.8||*

prakṛitiṁ svām avaṣhṭabhya visṛijāmi punaḥ
bhūta-grāmam imaṁ kṛitsnam avaśhaṁ prakṛiter vaśhāt || BG, 9.8||

Meaning BG 9.7, 9.8:

At the end of one kalpa, all living beings merge into My primordial material energy. At the beginning of the next creation, O son of Kunti, I manifest them again. Presiding over My material energy, I generate these myriad forms again and again, in accordance with the force of their natures. Controlling My own Prakriti, I send forth, again and again, all this multitude of beings, helpless under the sway of māyā.

Commentary:

At that time, all the souls within the material creation also go and rest in the body of God, in a state of suspended animation. Their gross and subtle bodies merge back into the source, māyā. However, the causal body still remains. After dissolution, when God creates the world again, the material energy unwinds in the reverse sequence *prakṛiti—mahān—ahankār—pañch tanmātrā—pañch mahābhūta*. Then, the souls that were lying in a state of suspended animation with only causal bodies are again placed in the world. In accordance with their causal bodies, they again receive subtle and gross bodies, and the various life forms are created in the universe. These life forms vary in nature amongst the different planes of existence. In some planetary systems, fire is the dominant element in the body, just as in the earth plane, the dominant bodily elements are earth and water. Hence, the bodies vary in their subtleness and the functions they can perform. Shree Krishna thus calls them myriad life forms.

BG 18.66:

सर्वधर्मान्परित्यज्य मामेकं शरणं व्रज।
अहं त्वां सर्वपापेभ्यो मोक्षयिष्यामि मा शुचः ॥ 18.66॥

Sarva-dharman parityajya mam ekam sharanam vraja,
Aham tvam sarva-papebhyo mokshayishyami ma shuchah.
(18.66)

Meaning: Abandon all varieties of dharmas and simply surrender unto me alone. I shall liberate you from all sinful reactions; do not fear.) (BG: Chapter 18, Verse 66)

In the Bhagavad Gita, Shree Krishna has declared egoism and ignorance as demoniac attributes which are captivated by the mind and body of the people under the influence of Māyā. Ego is one attribute, which is characterized by the attitude of irrational ownership and doership among individuals by taking control on the body and mind. Similarly, due to ignorance, people tend to assume that the enjoyment of the sensory objects in material world is the real aim and truth of life and they verily indulge in all such activities, which prevent them in experiencing own spirituality and essential nature of Self. The ego and ignorance add to the cause of duality and delusion. It is this state of ignorance and egoism, which is the cause of most human sufferings and major obstacle in the path of liberation.

If Māyā is the macrocosm, the attributes like egoism, ignorance and delusion undoubtedly manifest as the microcosm of the living beings. The deluded person is unable to see things in correct perspective and often mistakes one for another ultimately making own life miserable. This is the reason why scriptures insist on knowledge (Jnana yoga) for overcoming delusion and confusion of the mind. The true knowledge purifies the mind and body, induces desireless actions and meaningful contemplation about the Self: As a result, the person gradually overcomes ignorance to perceive the real purpose of life and hidden Self. Three gunas are considered as the dynamic modes of Māyā and their combination in various proportion reflects how the person is inclined and conducts in both worlds i.e. empirical and spiritual realms.

Karma and bondage are two other major derivatives of the machinations of Māyā that determine the present and future destiny of soul. Karma literally relates to action, work or deed but at spiritual level Hinduism relates it to the principle of cause and effect where intent and actions of an individual (cause) influence the future of that individual (effect). This aspect has been beautifully explored in Bhagavad Gita, where Lord Krishna Himself revealed that good intent and good deed contribute to good Karma leading to future happiness and peace, while bad intent and bad deed contribute to bad Karma that inflict future pain and suffering. As per Bhagavad Gita, Karma is also closely linked with the concept of rebirth as also the nature and quality of future life by leaving its imprints on the Self (Atman). According to the scriptures and even common Hindu belief, the selfish or desire-ridden actions under the influence of Māyā bind men to their consequences and this bondage leads to the vicious cycle of birth and death.

Impermanence and constant change are among the most striking features of the material or empirical world. They are also considered as the essential machinations of Māyā and no living being is spared of their effect. This impermanence and changes are also the cause of gradual decay and death of the mortal body. The attributes of impermanence and mutability enable Māyā to have an important role in the transmigration of the soul, which is otherwise eternal, permanent, indestructible and immutable. The state of beingness is reflected through the materiality of the body and mind at the gross and/or subtle levels through the desires and cravings, which ultimately lead to the Karma and bondage of the soul. This is the reason why Shree Krishna insisted on selfless actions and eschewing all desires and cravings to achieve a stable mind that paves the path of liberation.

Both the soul and Māyā are the subtle energies of the Universal Consciousness, known as Brahman in Hinduism or God in common parlance. While the individual soul in its purest form is same as Brahman, the former has ultimate destiny of merger with the latter through the process of Moksha or liberation but the mechanics are veiled through Māyā, which is the chief cause of the material world. The Hindu scriptures appropriately put forth the principles and processes whereby this cosmic union could be achieved by overcoming: Desires through detachment and renunciation;

egoism through contemplation about Self; demoniac attributes through divine qualities; ignorance through knowledge; impact of three gunas through practicing purity; duality through realizing Self; delusion through discernment; and Karma and bondage through selfless action. Nonetheless, it also true that the absolute truth of our existence may remain beyond our reach in most cases due to various limitations, but people could still wisely strive for the true knowledge for attaining relative peace and harmony in life.

6.3 Concept of Māyā in the Moksha Gita (Chapter 3)

Moksha Gita is the essence of Vedanta and all Upanishads. It is the "Song of Salvation". A study of Moksha Gita is to guide a sincere aspirant in the path of Jnana-Yoga. According to the Moksha Gita (authored by Swami Sivananda), the Chapter 3 says:

मायां नामेश्वरस्याहुरुपाधिं ब्रह्मणस्तु सा ।
स्वकीयेन विभर्त्यद्धा लीलामाश्चर्यकारिणी ॥ 3.1 ॥

māyāṃ nāmeśvarasyāhurupādhiṃ brahmaṇastu sā .
svakīyena vibhartyaddhā līlāmāścaryakāriṇī (3.1)

Meaning: Māyā is the Upadhi (limiting adjunct) of Ishwara. She is an illusory power of Brahman. She keeps up the Lila of Ishwara through Her three Gunas, viz. Sattwa, Rajas and Tamas (Purity, passion and darkness).

The Ultimate Reality is the support for the world even as the Sun is the support for the mirage. The world is the dazzling of Eternal Consciousness. The nihilists are wrong in saying that nothing exists at all. The world-phenomenon cannot be based on Nothing-less or Emptiness. An appearance demands a Reality as its corollary. The world is an expression of Brahman through Māyā even as the body is an expression of Atman through mind. The Prana, the mind and the senses are the operative organs of the active self which is agitated by the Vikshepa-Shakti or the distracting power of Māyā. The Brihadaranyaka Upanishad says that the one Brahman alone puts on all names, forms and does all actions in its own Being. Thus the whole universe is to be understood as a sport of the one Absolute which seems to play in Itself by revealing Itself in multifarious forms.

Māyā is the cosmic aspect of the power that hides Reality's essence. It is the limiting adjunct of Ishwara or the highest manifestation of the Absolute. The cosmic force of mentation limits the Infinitude of Brahman and makes it appear as the Cosmic person or Ishwara. Brahma, Vishnu and Shiva are the three aspects of this Ishwara even as the same Mr. Ramesh may be a Collector, a Magistrate and a Minister all at once. The differences in the Person are due to his different functions and powers, but the being is one. The power of veiling the Reality particularizes its being by a special mode of objectification and makes it hail as the Ishwara or the God of the universe. The absolute nature of non-duality is split up into the quality of relativity the reason for which is not known. Even Ishwara, therefore, has an element of non-being in him, because he is limited to relative existence by Māyā. But Ishwara is the Lord of Māyā and not its slave as the Jiva is. He puts on the cloak of Māyā, and yet is conscious of the Absolute Condition of Existence. This is the difference between the Omniscient Ishwara and the ignorant Jiva or the earthly individual.

The qualities of Sattwa, Rajas and Tamas, light, activity and darkness, form the essence of Māyā and it is these qualities that play the havoc of the world-phenomenon. Sattwa illumines, Rajas distracts and Tamas clouds the understanding of the individual. The appearances of Ishwara and Māyā correspond to all further miniatures of the same in the planes of greater ignorance where they get more and more separated until in the earthly plane they are totally cut off as the physical entities which constitute the diverse nature of the world. In logical language, Ishwara is a degeneration of Brahman caused by the self-limiting power of objectification or the force of Māyā, the reason for the appearance of which is an eternal enigma.

सेयं मायाऽसती नैव यतो नः प्रतिभासते ।
सतीयं नापि यज्ज्ञानोदये नश्यति सत्वरम् ॥ 3.2 ॥

seyaṃ māyā'satī naiva yato naḥ pratibhāsate .
satīyaṃ nāpi yajjñānodaye naśyati satvaram (3.2)

एवं माया हि तच्छब्दवाच्या नैव प्रकीर्त्यते ।
सैषाऽनिर्वचनीयं हि भानं किञ्चन कथ्यते ॥ 3.3 ॥

evaṃ māyā hi tacchabdavācyā naiva prakīrtyate .
saiṣā'nirvacanīyaṃ hi bhānaṃ kiñcana kathyate (3.3)

Meaning: 3.2 & 3.3. Māyā is not non-existent because it appears; neither is it existent because it is destroyed by the dawn of knowledge. Māyā is not That. It is an indescribable appearance.

The root-meaning of the word "Māyā" indicates its non-existent nature. But we cannot account for the existence of a non-existent appearance. Even appearance is after all not non-existent, for a non-existent thing never is, and an appearance is something which is. Otherwise one could not talk of and speculate over appearances. Māyā is therefore not non-existent because it appears to us, and it is not even existent for it is non-enduring. This mystery eludes all reason and logic and cannot be determined its nature by any metaphysics. The greatest philosophers began to hide themselves within the conviction that the human mind is not all-knowing and therefore it cannot answer trans-empirical questions. Somehow Māyā exists. Why it cannot be said. And somehow Māyā disappears. Why it cannot again be said. It is an illusion that has deceived even the wisest of men and has led astray even the ablest of geniuses. Only Self-Knowledge or intuitive illumination can solve the why and how of Māyā.

Māyā is not that. It is not Brahman and yet, it is the Power of Brahman. It is a deceptive and indescribable appearance, which not only makes the individual forget the Unity of Brahman but in addition to it, presents an unreal distractive phenomenon of diversity. Intellect which is rooted in egoism is the distracting factor in the individual and the Anandamaya-Kosha or the sheath of ignorance is the veiling factor. Māyā is, therefore, a beginningless play of cosmic imaginative force which apparently divests the Eternal Nature of its Indivisibility and makes it put on a variety of forms in its own being and further gives way to the descension into strong attachment of such egoistic centres of consciousness to their particular forms and experiences. Māyā is termed in many ways, appearance, power, force, phenomenon, and the like, which all go to point to its unreal character and its untrustworthy behavior. Every thought, therefore, is an activity in the realm of Māyā, for all thoughts spring from individual consciousness which is itself the effect of the diversifying nature of Māyā. All individuals, right from the supreme Ishwara, down to the insignificant creature of the Netherlands are within the boundaries of

Māyā, differing only in the degree or the extent to which each is influenced by it.

सा माया वर्णनातीता सदसद्भ्यां विलक्षणा ।
अनिर्वाच्योच्यते नूनमनादिर्भावरूपयोः ॥ 3.4 ॥

अनादिरपि सान्तेयमृषेरेवात्मवेदिनः ।
शुद्धसत्त्वस्वरूपां तां मायामाहुर्मनीषिणः ॥ 3.5 ॥

sā māyā varṇanātītā sadasadbhyāṃ vilakṣaṇā .
anirvācyocyate nūnamanādirbhāvarūpayoḥ (3.4)

anādirapi sānteyamṛṣerevātmavedinaḥ .
śuddhasattvasvarūpāṃ tāṃ māyāmāhurmanīṣiṇaḥ (3.5)

Meaning, 3.4 & 3.5: Māyā is Indescribable (Sat-Asat-Vilakshana Anadi Bhava Rupa Anirvachaniya Māyā). She is neither Sat nor Asat. Māyā is Anadi Santam. She is beginningless but has an end only for the sage who has realized the Self. Māyā is Shuddha Sattwa or pure Sattwa.

Māyā is neither Sat nor Asat, neither real nor unreal, neither is, nor is not. It transcends human comprehension, it stands above all ratiocination, it controls even the reasoning capacity of the individual. The degree of intelligence of a person is proportional to what extent he is freed from the stupefying influence of Māyā. It is hard to withdraw oneself from its clutches for it originates from and is based on the Eternal Brahman Itself. That which is based on the Infinite Reality must therefore be a hideous power difficult to win victory over. To extricate oneself from the hypnotic effect of this Divine Illusion the individual has to dehypnotize himself into the consciousness of Self-Illumination and absoluteness.

Māyā is Shuddha-Sattwa and is not preponderated by Rajas or Tamas. That is the reason why Ishwara or the Cosmic Lord is uncontrolled and unaffected by the hypnotizing power of Māyā. Ishwara who is the Infinite limited by Māyā is midway between the Indivisible Brahman and the multiple universe. Hence Ishwara is conscious of the Eternal Reality as well as of the diverse world of nature. He is in a sense, the mediator between Jiva and Brahman. Here is the necessity of the Jivas for developing the devotion to God, for a sudden jumping into the Infinite Brahman is hard for the ignorant Jivas, without the help of the Universal Controller, Ishwara. Ishwara is the Personal God, the object of religious worship, and Brahman is the Absolute Truth, the object of philosophical quest.

मायां विजित्य यो मर्त्य आत्मज्ञानं तु विन्दते ।
स एव प्रभवेत्तस्या ज्ञातुमुत्थानसंलयौ ॥ 3.6 ॥

māyāṃ vijitya yo martya ātmajñānaṃ tu vindate .
sa eva prabhavettasyā jñātumutthānasaṃlayau (3.6)

Meaning: He who gets knowledge of the Self having overcome Māyā, the illusory power, will alone know what Māyā is, how it arises and is destroyed.

One who acquires Infinite Knowledge does not find any mystery in the appearance of Māyā. The spiritual seeker overcomes Māyā through meditation on Brahman and negation of worldly propensities. The Truth-centered Sage possesses the wealth of imperishable wisdom and is ever in unison with the One Whole Being of Brahman. The terrible sport of Māyā appears as Satya or real to a worldly person, as Anirvacaniya or indescribable to an aspirant, and Tuccha or mean to a Jnani.

Knowledge of the Self is the resting in the awareness of the unlimitedness of Consciousness and Bliss in one unchangeable mass. When this stupendous state of Truth is experienced, Māyā flees away from that Light of Enlightenment. Where there is Light there cannot be darkness. When Avidya is destroyed, Vidya shines by itself. When the clouds are no more, the sun shines in his pristine greatness. When ignorance is removed, Knowledge at once reveals itself. When egoism is disintegrated, the Absolute alone hails supreme.

The why, what and how of Māyā can be known only by one who has transcended Māyā and has entered the Glory of the Self. Others can merely speculate over it, but cannot solve the riddle, for the instrument or the mechanism of human knowledge is centered in his psychological organ which is a modification of Māyā itself. Darkness cannot destroy darkness. Ignorance cannot remove ignorance, for they both are not contradictory forces. Man's highest faculty of knowledge is the intellect which is itself a creature of self-limitation and hence it is impossible for the human being to determine the nature of the Power that supersedes him in extent and subtlety. It is only the intuitional light which comprehends in itself the totality of existence that can step above Māyā and behold the majesty of the Self. Only then can the illusoriness of Māyā and the eternity of Brahman be realized in completeness. Intellect should give way to the higher religious experience not based on the ego. Real religion begins when the intellect stops working. That is the religion of Self-realization where the entire Brahman is experienced and Māyā is totally negated.

विषया पञ्च भूतानि तन्मात्राण्यवधारय ।
उत्पादीनीति मायाया विकारा वेति तत्त्वतः ॥ 3.7 ॥

viṣayā pañca bhūtāni tanmātrāṇyavadhāraya .

utpādīnīti māyāyā vikārā veti tattvataḥ (3.7)

Meaning: The five elements, the five Tanmatras (subtle or root elements) and the various objects of the world are all products or modifications of Māyā.

The five rudimentary principles of sound, touch, colour, taste and smell and the five gross elements of sky, air, fire, water and earth are born of the Vikshepa-Shakti or the distracting power of Māyā, which projects thereby the world of objective existence. Constant change within itself is the natural tendency of the force of Māyā. Māyā does not rest in itself. It is a vigorous active agent whose sole purpose is to transform itself into the phenomenon and Noumenon (a thing as it is in itself, not perceived or interpreted, incapable of being known, but only inferred from the nature of experience), through evolution and involution of diverse bodies. Disintegration and integration are the two aspects of the destructive and constructive powers of Māyā. Individuals are thrown into Being or Becoming by this gigantic Power according to the extent of the process of development undergone by each individual.

The five-fold functioning of breath, the five sense-organs and the five organs of action are again the further modifications of the subtle root-elements. Mind, intellect, sub-conscious and ego are the four-fold functions of the psychic mechanism which is the product of the Sattwa-portion of the subtle elements. The macrocosm and the microcosm are thus closely related as the original and the duplicate. The physical sheath or the body is the materialized effect of the psychic being and thus the entire universe with its individuals is a modification of Māyā.

धूमेन मनुजैः सत्ता यथाग्नेरनुमीयते ।
तथा सत्ता च मायायास्तन्नानाव्यक्तिभिर्नतु ॥ 3.8 ॥

dhūmena manujaiḥ sattā yathāgneranumīyate .
tathā sattā ca māyāyāstannānāvyaktibhirnanu (3.8)

Meaning: Just as you can infer the existence of fire through smoke, so also you can infer the existence of Māyā through Her various manifestations.

The existence of Māyā is inferable through the universal workings of nature. The main action of Māyā is diversification and unification. The existence of Māyā is felt by the perception of something which cannot belong to the Eternal Reality. Birth, growth, change, decay and death are the common phenomena which are seen in the daily life of every individual. These five-fold modifications are the essence of egoistic life. Creation, preservation, destruction, love, hatred, exhilaration, pain, are certain factors in the evolution of the universe. Such activities as these cannot belong to what is absolutely permanent. Activity is a struggle to overcome the existing defect. An untainted being which has no reason to wish for anything else, which is in itself full and perfect, changes not and acts not, for there is no purpose whatsoever in modifying itself into something else. It is ever satisfied in itself and is eternally in joyous repose. Therefore, the bustle of universal life and the daily cry and strife of individuals must be Māyā.

Moreover the existence of individuality itself proves the existence of Māyā. Individuality is not permanent, for it is limited and finite. A finite being cannot be everlasting. Therefore, individuality is a negation of Absoluteness. Hence, individual existence must be Māyā.

The people of the world struggle to obtain external objects, because their egoistic personalities are not allowed their existence independent of the other objects of the universe.

They strive hard and feel the necessity to relate themselves to the manifold entities that exist apart from themselves, thus proving the unreality of their individual independence. Therefore, life as different personalities in the world is Māyā. Thought, speech and action are non-eternal and are mere expulsions of consciousness-rays, and therefore, the multitudinous appearance of degrees of reality also is a phase of Māyā.

माया मनोमयी प्रोक्ता या सृजत्यसकृद्भ्रमान् ।
नानारूपांश्च सर्वत्र सर्वं व्याप्नोति निश्चितम् ॥ 3.9 ॥

यदा ते निहतं चित्तं सविचारविवेचनैः ।
तदाप्रभृति माया त्वां पीडयत्येव नो दृढम् ॥ 3.10 ॥

māyā manomayī proktā yā sṛjatyasakṛdbhramān .
nānārūpāṃśca sarvatra sarvaṃ vyāpnoti niścitam (3.9)

yadā te nihataṃ cittaṃ savicāravivecanaiḥ .
tadāprabhṛti māyā tvāṃ pīḍayatyeva no dṛḍham (3.10)

Meaning, 3.9 & 3.10: Māyā is of the nature of mind. Māyā generates different degrees of illusions. Māyā pervades everywhere. If your mind is destroyed by discrimination and Vichara, then Māyā will not afflict you.

Māyā is centered in the individual consciousness in the form of mind. Whatever Māyā does, that the mind also does. Mind is miniature- Māyā. The veiling and distracting activity of Māyā is undertaken by the mind in the form of nescience and egoism. Nescience is seated in the innermost sheath or the Anandamaya kosha of the soul and the ego is seated in the intellect. The mind projects the physical body even as Māyā projects the cosmos. The activity of the universe is going on in the human body too. The Chandogya Upanishad says that the space within the heart contains the earth and the heaven, the sun, moon, stars, lightning, clouds, wind, fire, etc., in the same way as the outer space contains. Whatever is found in the external universe is found exactly in the miniature cosmos or the human body. Jiva is therefore a degraded copy of Ishwara. And Atman, therefore, is Brahman.

There are different degrees in the manifestation of Māyā or illusion. The power of disfiguring Reality is not of the same degree everywhere. Māyā is more manifest and works more powerfully in inanimate beings than animate, more in brute nature than in refined, more in Tamas and Rajas than in Sattwa, more in the uncivilized than in the civilized, more on earth than in heaven, more in man than in the celestial, more in an aspirant than in a saint, more in the sleeping and dreaming states than in the waking, more in gross forms than in subtle. Māyā is manifest in a progressive evolutionary basis on one hand and as a steady concealing of Reality on the other hand. In other words the whole process of appearance is in the domain of Māyā.

Māyā pervades in every quarter and cranny. There is nothing on earth or in heaven which is not controlled by the play of Māyā. The universal change drags together with it the entirety of the individuals also and each individual is compelled by the cosmic change to change itself in the same manner befitting the cosmic process of Māyā. Nothing here, not even a piece of straw, can be excluded from the operation of the law of Māyāic evolution. Māyā is the ruling power which borrows its strength from Brahman.

When the mind is destroyed, Māyā also is swept away from the vision of the individual. When the eye-sight is corrected, the appearance of two moons vanishes. When sun sets, there is no more the dance of the mirage. The whole universe is the perception by the mind of the Absolute Brahman in varieties of forms due to the fluctuations caused by desire for objective gain. Hence, the destruction of the mind is the brushing aside of the entire phenomena and that ends in the experience of the light of the Self.

विषयान् भोक्तुकामं तन्मायाबीजं स्मृतं मनः ।
अतो मनो निहन्तव्यं तत्प्रणाशाय सुव्रतः ।
अधिगत्य परां शान्तिं ब्रह्मज्ञानं तदैष्यसि ॥ 3.11 ॥

viṣayān bhoktukāmaṃ tanmāyābījaṃ smṛtaṃ manaḥ .
ato mano nihantavyaṃ tatpraṇāśāya suvrataḥ .
adhigatya parāṃ śāntiṃ brahmajñānaṃ tadaiṣyasi (3.11)

Meaning: This mind whichever hankers after sensual objects is the seed of Māyā. If the mind is annihilated Māyā will vanish. You will attain the state of quiescence. Brahma-Jnana will dawn in you.

The seed of Māyā is the mind which sends forth branches of its objectifying force through the channels of the organs of sensing. The mind hankers after the objects of the senses, including the intellect and the ago. The craving for objects is the effect of the desire of the individual consciousness to flow with the process of self-multiplication and self-preservation as laid in the scheme of the workings of Māyā. The very meaning of phenomenal existence is preservation of the egoistic individuality and reproducing oneself into manifold forms. The senses are projected by the mind of the individual in order to effect this process of Māyā. The functions of the mind day and night are in accordance with Māyā's law of diversification and preservation of the diversified forms through attachment to such forms and further through an additional external urge to reproduce oneself and strive to maintain individual life. This whole mad process of the mind constitutes the life of man on earth.

When these functions of the mind are inhibited through the force of conscious effort on the part of the discriminative consciousness, the play of phenomenal existence is stopped its further progress, and when the seed of the mind is burnt by spiritual knowledge, the tree of Samsara is cut off root and branch!

The restlessness of the individual is caused by the projecting forth of mental forces for purposes of acquiring objects of sense. So long as the objects are not obtained, there is the reign of agitation and irritation everywhere. There is only a temporary peace when the objects required are acquired, but the next moment the mind darts upon some other source of objective gratification and keeps the restlessness in continuity. Perfect quiescence comes only when the functioning of the imaginative mind is restrained and put an end to through meditation and Self-Knowledge. Only Brahma-Jnana can dispel the mental ignorance completely.

When true wisdom dawns the mind realizes its nature of Self-sufficiency and turns back to the Atma or the Source of Consciousness and rests as one with it in peace. This is the salvation of the individual, where the individual merges itself into the Infinite Consciousness and exists as the Absolute.

CHAPTER 7

THE CONCEPT OF MITHYĀ

The dictionary definition of the word 'Mithyā' gives: (i) contrarily, incorrectly, wrongly, improperly; (ii) falsely, deceitfully, untruly; (iii) not in reality, only apparently; (iv) to no purpose, fruitlessly, in vain. Mithyā means "false belief", and it is an important concept in Hinduism. Mithyā cannot be easily defined as 'indefinable', 'non-existent', 'something other than real', 'which cannot be proved, produced by avidya or as its effect', or as 'the nature of being perceived in the same locus along with its own absolute non-existence'.

Mithyā is variously rendered in English as 'unreal', 'dependently real', 'seemingly real', 'relatively real', etc. The most popular definition of Mithyātvam, 'unreality', as given in the Advaitasiddhi is: 'That which appears in a locus where it does not belong in the three periods of time'. Thus, in the rope-snake analogy, the snake appears in the rope where it does not belong in the three periods of time. The rope is not the locus for the snake to exist. Yet it is apprehended there due to ignorance of the locus, rope. When the true knowledge of the rope arises, the snake is known to have not been there. Similarly, the world (and samsara) is imagined to be present in the substratum, locus, Brahman. When by the help of the Scripture and the Preceptor the knowledge of Brahman arises, the world will be known to have not been there. In the sequel a study of the application of the above definition of 'Mithyā' is taken up with the Bhagavadgita as the source for the definition.

Everybody lives in myth. This idea disturbs most people, for conventionally, myth means falsehood. Nobody likes to live in falsehood.

But there are many types of truths, subjective as well as objective. Some logical, some intuitive, some cultural, some universal. Some depend on evidence, others on faith. Myth is truth which is subjective, intuitive, cultural and grounded in faith.

Myth is essentially a cultural construct, a common understanding of the world that binds individuals and communities together. This understanding may be religious or secular.

Ideas such as heaven and hell, angels and demons, fate and freewill, sin, Satan and salvation are religious myths.

Ideas such as sovereignty, nation-state, human rights, women's rights, animal rights and gay rights are secular myths.

Secular or religious, myths are truths that we live by.

If myth is an idea, mythology is the vehicle of that idea. Mythology constitutes stories, symbols and rituals that make a myth tangible. Stories, symbols and rituals are essentially languages—languages that are heard, seen and performed. Together they construct the truths of a culture. The story of the Resurrection, the symbol of the crucifix and the ritual of baptism establish the idea that is Christianity. The story of independence, the symbol of the national flag and the ritual of the national anthem reinforce the idea of a nation state.

7.1 Introduction to Mithyā in Ancient Hindu Texts

7.1.1 Muktika Upanishad (2.14) says:

*जन्मान्तशताभ्यस्ता मिथ्या संसारवासना ।
सा चिराभ्यासयोगेन विना न क्षीयते क्वचित् ॥ 2.14॥*

*janmāntaśatābhyastā mithyā saṃsāravāsanā .
sā cirābhyāsayogena vinā na kṣīyate kvacit (2.14)*

Translation: The false impression (Mithyā) of worldly life is got in a hundred lives and cannot be destroyed without long practice. So avoid desire of enjoyment as a distance with effort and practice the three (destruction of impressions, cultivation of knowledge and destruction of the mind).

7.1.2 Varaha Upanishad says:

जीवेश्वरादिरूपेण चेतनाचेतनात्मकम् ॥ 2.53b॥

jīveśvarādirūpeṇa cetanācetanātmakam (2.53b)

*ईक्षणादिप्रवेशान्ता सृष्टिरीशेन कल्पिता ।
जाग्रदादिविमोक्षान्तः संसारो जीवकल्पितः ॥ 2.54॥*

*īkṣaṇādipraveśāntā sṛṣṭirīśena kalpitā .
jāgradādivimokṣāntaḥ saṃsāro jīvakalpitaḥ (2.54)*

Translation, 2.53b-2.54: The creation, sentient as well as non-sentient from Ikshana (thinking) to Pravesha (entry) of those having the forms of Jivas and Ishvara is due to the creation or illusion (Mithyā) of Ishvara; while the Samsara (worldly existence) from the waking state to salvation is due to the creation of Jiva.

त्रिणाचिकादियोगान्ता ईश्वरभ्रान्तिमाश्रिताः ।
लोकायतादिसाङ्ख्यान्ता जीवविश्रान्तिमाश्रिताः ॥ 2.55 ॥

triṇācikādiyogāntā īśvarabhrāntimāśritāḥ .
lokāyatādisāṅkhyāntā jīvaviśrāntimāśritāḥ (2.55)

Translation: So, the Karmas ordained in the sacrifice (called) Trinachaka (so called after Nachiketas of Katha Upanishad) to Yoga are dependent upon the illusion (Mithyā or Bhranti) of Ishvara; while (the systems from) Lokayata (atheistical system) to Sankhya rest on the illusion of Jiva.

दीर्घस्वप्नमिदं यत्तद्दीर्घं वा चित्तविभ्रमम् ।
दीर्घं वापि मनोराज्यं संसारं दुःखसागरम् ।
सुप्तेरुत्थाय सुप्त्यन्तं ब्रह्मैकं प्रविचिन्त्यताम् ॥ 2.64 ॥

dīrghasvapnamidaṃ yattaddīrghaṃ vā cittavibhramam .
dīrghaṃ vāpi manorājyaṃ saṃsāraṃ duḥkhasāgaram .
supterutthāya suptyantaṃ brahmaikaṃ pravicintyatām
(2.64)

Translation: This mundane existence which is an ocean of sorrow, is nothing but a long-lived dream, or an illusion (Mithyā) of the mind or a long-lived reign of the mind. From rising from sleep till going to bed, the one Brahman alone should be contemplated upon.

7.1.3 According to Patanjali Yoga Sutra (1.8)

विपर्ययो मिथ्याज्ञानमतद्रूपप्रतिष्ठम् ॥ 1.8 ॥

viparyayo mithyājñānamatadrūpapratiṣṭham (1.8)

Translation: Indiscrimination (Viparyayo) is false knowledge (Mithyā), which is not based in real nature of its object.

7.1.4 Bhagavad Gita (3.6 & 18.59)

कर्मेन्द्रियाणि संयम्य य आस्ते मनसा स्मरन् ।
इन्द्रियार्थान्विमूढात्मा मिथ्याचारः स उच्यते ॥ 3.6 ॥

karmendriyāṇi saṃyamya ya āste manasā smaran .
indriyārthānvimūḍhātmā mithyācāraḥ sa ucyate (3.6)

Translation: Those who restrain the external organs of action, while continuing to dwell on sense objects in the mind, are certainly in delusion (Mithyā) themselves and are to be called hypocrites.

यदहङ्कारमाश्रित्य न योत्स्य इति मन्यसे ।
मिथ्यैष व्यवसायस्ते प्रकृतिस्त्वां नियोक्ष्यति ॥ 18.59 ॥

yadahaṅkāramāśritya na yotsya iti manyase .
mithyaiṣa vyavasāyaste prakṛtistvāṃ niyokṣyati (18.59)

Translation: If, motivated by pride, you think, "I shall not fight," your decision will be in vain (Mithyā). Your own nature will compel you to fight.

7.2 Mithyā in Advaita Vedanta

In Advaita Vedanta the world is held to be 'Mithyā'. The unobjective and non-subjective consciousness as the only reality cannot be established unless the world is proved false.

So, the concept of falsity (Mithyā) occupies a unique position in Advaita philosophy.

As per Hinduism, Mithyā is a construct of the mind, which is inexplicable. According to Advaita, Brahman is the only reality. Everything else is non-real and is superimposed on it. The concept of adyasa (superimposition), which is in general linked with the concept of non-real is defined by Shankara in his commentary on Brahma Sutras as appearance elsewhere with a nature like recollection of what was seen before and cognition of something that does not exist.

The common example given for Mithyā in Hindu religion are that of a rope in the dark perceived as a snake and a piece of shiny sea shell mistaken for silver. The nature of such an illusion is inexplicable (anirvacaniya) and is in reality identifiable with the underlying substratum.

To hold that the world is illusory or false (Mithyā) does not mean that it is absolutely unreal. The Advaitins contend that the third category of indeterminability is either real or unreal. The world is not real just because it has a physical reality nor it is non-real because it is beyond physical reality.

The concept of non-real reality is discussed elaborately in many Advaitic texts like Nyaya Rama Dipavali, Tattva Pradipika, Tarka Sangraha of Anandagiri, Advaita-siddhi of Madhusudana Saraswati, Pramanamala and other texts of Anandabodha.

The Advaita-siddhi, Madhusudana Saraswati gives twenty-six inferential arguments regarding Mithyā:

The general **five definitions** of Mithyā are:

(i) Not being the locus of either reality or unreality (this definition is attributed to Padmapada).

(ii) What is eternally negated in the same locus where it is cognized (Mithyā is an entity which appears in a place.

(iii) What is contradicted by knowledge (illusory cognition is sublated where knowledge of underlying substratum arises).

(iv) The locus of which is equally the locus of its eternal negation (attributed to Chitsukha). To put it differently, an object which is invariably absent where it seems to be present is called Mithyā.

(v) That which is other than reality (attributed to Anandabodha).

Mithyā parallels the concepts of Avidya in the Vedanta school of Hinduism, and Aviveka in its Samkhya school.

Ignorance begets aviveka (lack of correct, discriminative knowledge) states Samkhya school of Hinduism. One engages in deeds, good and bad, due to aviveka, earns punya or becomes a victim of sin and is reborn. Aviveka also means lack of reason or imprudence or indiscretion. Avidya is related concept in Vedanta school of Hinduism. Avidya and aviveka give dukkha i.e., suffering.

Madhusūdana Sarasvatī in his Advaita-siddhi gives five definitions of Mithyā, meaning false or indeterminable. False is something that appears and is later negated or contradicted; the unreal is never an object of experience, the concept of unreal is self-contradictory. Falsity is defined as – not being the locus of either reality or unreality, it is distinct from both reality and unreality.

In practice, Mithyā has three means, –

(i) that which does not exist in three divisions of time, past, present and future;
(ii) that which is removable by knowledge; and
(iii) that which is identical with the object of sublation.

Madhusudana Sarasvati was an unparalleled dialectician in the Vedantic school of thought in sixteenth century. A Madhva intellectualist, famous for his Nyayamrita, has praised Madhusudana's Bhaktirasayanam who again raises several charges against his definitions of 'Mithyā'. It is said that in his classic work Advaitasiddhi, Madhusudana cleared all the fallacies posed by Madhvas and successfully defeated them. All his five definitions on Mithyā are free from error which conveyed the gist that Mithyā never exists but appears to exist. It does not exist in all the three periods in the locus in which it appears. Similarly, the world does not exist in the absolute sense. It appears to be real as long as Brahman is known. Once Brahman is known, the world, to the knower of Brahman never existed either in the past nor exists in the present and will not exist in future. Thus, the falsity (Mithyā) of any object lies in its nonexistence in the locus where its presence is imagined. Madhusudana originates many of his views from *Sarvajnatma's Samksepa-Sariraka*. He equates Eka Jiva Vada and drshti-srshti Vada in his Siddhantabindu. This is actually the traditional Vivarana which claims that the Absolute is both the locus as well as the object of ignorance which can be directly experienced in the state of deep-sleep. This view is also expressed by Vidyaranya in his Pancadasi. In this view, the Jiva himself is the material and proficient cause of the universe through his own nescience. All the objects perceived are illusory like things seen in dream. The delusion that there are many Jivas is only due to there being many bodies. The single Jiva can attain liberation by the realization of the self with hearing, reflection, devotion to Guru and the scriptures. Madhusudana, being a strict follower of Advaita, was also a great devotee of Lord Krishna. Madhusudana Sarasvati, the great Advaitin of the sixteenth century, was also a protagonist of the bhakti discipline. His Bhakti-rasayana is a most esteemed text in which one can discern an attempt to bring about a synthesis between Advaitism and the bhakti cult from the aesthetic point of view." He states in Gudartha Dipika, that a Jivan mukta is attracted to Hari who is also a Shiva bhakta. He says that the para bhakti is identical to Atma-jnanam. It is as same as the realization of all Mahavakyas like aham brahmasmi, so'ham etc. and becoming all this.

Mithyā is other than real but not real, Mithyā is identical with sublatability. Mithyā may also be understood as that which is negated even where it is found to exist. The followers of the Advaita School contend that the world-appearance is negated by Brahman-knowledge and hence it is illusory. To the followers of Vishishtadvaita, Mithyā is the apprehension of an object as different from its own nature.

The Advaita School considers Mithyā to mean falsity of the world. Disappearance (nivritti) is the necessary presupposition of Mithyā because what is falsely perceived ceases to exist with the dawn of right knowledge. But, Mithyā or falsity of the world, cannot be easily defined as indefinable or non-existent or something other than real or which cannot be proved or produced by avidya (or as its effect) or as the nature of being perceived in the same locus along with its own absolute non-existence. The opponents of the Advaita do not accept the contention that Atman is simply consciousness and cannot be the substratum of knowledge, and they insist that existence as the logical concomitant of the absence of non-existence and vice versa, with these two being mutually exclusive predicates, must be admitted. The opposite of unreality must be reality.

According to Advaita anything which is both cognized and sublated is Mithyā. Mithyā is negated even where it is found. The illusoriness of the world is itself illusory. Once Brahman-knowledge arises both the cognizer and the cognized disappear.

in Advaita Philosophy, Reality is one without a second and that is Brahman, the great. The non-duality of reality cannot ho established, if the world cannot bo shown false (Mithyā). This is why the concept of falsity (Mithyā). is so important in Advaita literature. Now, falsity does not mean unreality. The false is that which is other than reality and unreality . Reality is consciousness as such.

The proof of unreality is impermanence, the permanent one is the Sole Reality. Mithyā is apparent reality; at the level of ultimate truth, when, through the understanding of the Mithyā of all limiting adjuncts (upadhis) of name and form i.e., those that pertain to the individual body-mind (tvam) and as well to the lordship of Brahman (tat), everything is seen to be not another to pure Awareness, the distinctions of Jiva and Ishvara no longer apply, and it is the param Brahman, the very essential of the Lord Itself, that is the final reality. In Advaita the method to reveal the unreality (Mithyā) of things involves the idea of change and permanence i.e., what deviates and what persists.

Mithyā means 'illusoriness'. Advaita maintains that Brahman alone is real, the plurality of the universe is because the universe is illusory, the universe can be cognized; whatever that is cognized is illusory. The universe is different from the real as well as the real, the universe is indeterminable. Vedanta Desika refutes this contention because there is no such entity which is neither real nor unreal. The universe which is different from Brahman is inseparably related to Brahman. Badarayana (Brahma Sutra III.ii.28) declares that between the Jiva and Brahman there is difference as well as non-difference like the relation of light to its substratum or source on account of both being luminous, one being limited and the other all-pervading, the all-pervading is real and immortal. Rishi Damano Yamayana (Rig Veda X.xvi.4) insists that all should know about that part of the body which is immortal; the immortal part of the body is the Atman or Brahman, it is called a part because without it there cannot be life in one's body. Vachaspati of the Bhamati school states that whereas illusion conceals, mithyātva signifies 'concealment', the real nature of the cognized object is concealed resulting in non-apprehension of difference between the real and the unreal objects. If the term anirvacaniya is defined by the Advaita as the nature of being different from sat and asat in essence, which is the nature of Mithyā, then the element of difference must be real. Even though there is no bar on the validity of the experience of difference, but the fact remains that difference cannot be an attribute of objects. Madhvacharya concludes that difference is not something that falls outside the content of an object or what is generally considered to constitute its essence which in perception is the sum total of its distinction from others. The perception of an object is the same as the perception of its difference from all others.

The whole world is a mere notion, mere idea. Upanishads says it as the creation of Maya, taken place in Sankalpa matra (wishes) or Kalpana matra (ideas) or Akasa matra (sky). It exists in name and forms only.

Chandogya Upanishad says:

यथा सोम्यैकेन मृत्पिण्डेन सर्वं मृन्मयं विज्ञातँ स्याद्वाचारम्भणं विकारो नामधेयं मृत्तिकेत्येव सत्यम् ॥ 6.1.4॥

yathā somyaikena mṛtpiṇḍena sarvaṃ mṛnmayaṃ vijñātag̃ syādvācārambhaṇaṃ vikāro nāmadheyaṃ mṛttiketyeva satyam (6.1.4)

Translation: Just as through a single clod of clay all that is made of clay would become known, for all modifications is but name based upon words and the clay alone is real.

Explanation: To make it more perfect, the name and form of a clay pot does not exist when the pot is broken. But the substratum (clay) still exists on which the pot depends. There never goes a pot apart from clay. In this context, it is wiser to say that the "clay is satyam" and "pot is Mithyā."

7.3 Jagat Mithyā

Brahman is satyam as the rope and this universe is Mithyā like the vivarta of Brahman. This snake of Vivarta (alteration) is covered unto the rope by Mithyā. If we get knowledge of the rope, the illusion (Mithyā) of snake in the rope will vanish. Sri Adi Shankaracharya, the great master of Advaita who lived in the early part of the 8th Century said, "*Brahma satya jagat mithya, jivo brahmaiva naparah*". It means Brahman (name of the Ultimate Reality) is the only truth, the world is illusory, and there is ultimately no difference between the individual Self and the Brahman.

Mithyā means neither true nor false. The world cannot be false because we all clearly see and perceivee it. Shankaracharya says that the world is not true either, because it is constantly changing and everything that the world has to offer is temporary, transient and impermanent.

A fine dining experience gives us joy. Try doing it continuously for a few days and one would start nauseating. A trip to a nice resort is highly relaxing. After just a few days the charm of the place wears out. Eagerly awaited vacation trip to some place, after hectic running around and visiting various tourist sites for days, finally the heart cries "Home! Sweet Home!!" and longs for the comfort of the home.

That's why Shankara calls this world as Mithyā which means anything in this world can only give temporary happiness and not permanent happiness.

We forget the happenings in our dream very quickly. The experience we have in the waking world also we do forget but slowly over the time. This is what is conveyed by the adage "And, this too, shall pass away". This temporariness, irrelevance, impermanence of everything related to the outer world and the similarity of the experience with the dream world is what made Shankara term the world as neither false nor real, but illusory and need not be given any importance apart from what is required practically to transact.

In saying "Jivo brahmaiva naparah", Shankara is conveying that the realization of the individual Self, Atman, Life Energy in its purest form (without the ego) is nothing but realizing the Brahman, the Almighty Energy. The same opinion is echoed by the ancient Greek aphorism "Know Thyself" which is inscribed in the Temple of Apollo at Delphi. These sayings assert that one learns more by studying oneself (Svadhyaya) by making the mind calm and quiet and directing the single-pointed concentration inwards.

To achieve the goal of Brahman, Shankara proposes "Sadhana Chatushtaya", the four-fold qualifications namely; (i) Viveka (Reasoning), (ii) Vairagya (Dispassion), (iii) Shad Sampath (Six Treasures) and (iv) Mumukshutva (Burning Desire). Shad Sampath (Six Treasures) are Sama (Control of the mind), Dama (Control of the senses), Uparathi (Internal dispassion), Titiksha (Endurance), Shraddha (Faith) and Samadhana (Focus and Concentration).

Should Sadhana Chatushtaya be used only to pursue the goal of Self-Realization, Moksha or can it be used to pursue any other goal as well? Does that mean one cannot have the ambition to achieve anything in this world just because world is Mithyā?

For example, the same Shankara's principles could be very well applied by a professional also to become a better professional and succeed in achieving the desired goals in one's profession. Viveka means doing the necessary thinking, reasoning and meticulous planning. Vairagya means being dispassionate and disinterested in everything that is not connected with the goal. Shad Sampath is controlling the mind (Sama), controlling the action (Dama), internal dispassion towards distractions (Uparati), enduring the obstacles (Titiksha), believing or having faith and confidence in one's abilities (Sharaddha) and having complete focus and concentration towards the goal (Samadhana). Finally, the Mumukshatva is having the burning desire to attain the goal.

The one idea used in one field could very well be used in another field if applicable. Arjuna in the Mahabharata was a warrior by profession. Krishna preaches Advaita through

Bhagavad-Gita and does not ask him to run away, rather instills confidence in him to fight the battle valiantly to succeed, but all the time having the clear knowledge and understanding of Advaitic principles.

Vedantic literature also talks about four Ashramas that are mentioned in mentioned in Jabala Upanishad (4.1) and Yajnavalkya Upanishad (1.1). They are Brahmacharya (student life), Grihastha (household life), Vanaprastha (retired life) and Sanyasa (renounced life).

Grihastha is the married life and this stage represents most intense physical, sexual, emotional, occupational, social and material attachments. A human being is supposed to love the family, live the life cheerfully and fulfill one's responsibilities as a parent, spouse, caretaker, breadwinner for the family, etc. Everyone is encouraged to pursue Artha (wealth) and Kama (desires) vigorously without crossing the boundaries of Dharma (righteousness). In this stage, Vedanta urges everyone to fully indulge in the world and enjoy all the worldly pleasures without violating any ethics or morality.

Swami Vivekananda concurs by saying, "Fulfill your desire for power and everything else, and after you have fulfilled the desire, will come the time when you will know that they are all very little things; but until you have fulfilled this desire, until you have passed through that activity, it is impossible for you to come to the state of calmness, serenity, and self-surrender".

Interestingly this is exactly what Socrates says, "The unexamined life is not worth living", urging us to indulge in the worldly things so that we can have a deep comprehension of the world, clearly understand and realize the transient and momentary happiness they provide. It was the same poverty-stricken Socrates while striding through the city's busy central marketplace, looking at the mass of several things for sale, he would harrumph provocatively, "How many things I have no need of! ". That's the sign of the wise who have developed Vairagya (dispassion).

Definitely, a Grihastha can fully engage with the world, accepting and discharging one's responsibilities and at the same time be firmly grounded in Advaitic principles just like Arjuna did or king Janaka did. For such a Grihastha there comes a stage to move on to the next Ashrama which is Vanaprastha where the only responsibility or goal that remains is the pursuit of Brahman or Self-Realization.

7.4 More on Mithyā

Lord Krishna in the Gita does not consider the world as a falsehood (Mithyā) or illusion but as his yoga-maya. And as it is his creation, he does not consider it false, nor mukti from it the aim of human endeavour. Thus, he enjoins Arjuna to follow his dharma and fight and conquer the enemy. And this injunction makes his stance very clear. For if the world were an illusion (Mithyā), there would be no sense in participating in a national war that would be extremely violent and sanguinary. And even the fighting would be an illusion, fit to be discarded immediately in an awakening as if from a bad dream.

Nor is Sri Krishna's mukti an escape or palayana. The only moksha in his eyes is sayujya, or a complete union with the Divine (Brahman) in each thought, feeling, sense and action. Nirvana, according to the Gita is not the ending of all desire or one's response to the constant changes in the world but a Brahma-nirvana, one where only the Brahman exists and wills and acts, a true monism with Sri Krishna as Purushottama, above all purushas and prakritis.

The only Mithyāchara, wrong behaviour, is Arjuna's recoil at the prospect of killing those whom he identifies as his family, friends, teachers and companions. And his rejection is wrong at every level of dharma that Sri Krishna points out, right from his dharma as a Kshatriya who has to stand up for what is righteous and for those who have been oppressed by the asuric (demonic) forces.

Then, how does Sankara consider the world as illusion, Mithyā? This is the question that often confronts the seeker. It might be pertinent here to realize that figuring out what Sankara meant when he spoke these words is well-nigh impossible now, so coloured has his perception become to us in present times. For Sankara has become identified with the illusionists. But that may not have been his own position or understanding.

Mithyā is that which is both cognized and sublated (Sublated means that which as a smaller entity is assimilated into a larger entity). For example, if we consider modern physics, the Newtonian order is assumed or sublated into the Einsteinian paradigm. Once one understands Einsteinian physics, one realizes that everything that Newtonian principles posit is more completely satisfied with the Special and General Theories of Relativity and then some. And once the Newtonian framework is absorbed by the Einsteinian substratum, it may be seen as Mithyā. Newton is not false or unreal yet, but dependent on a larger, more universal principle or conditioned by it. This is the understanding of Mithyā, that which is neither real, nor unreal, *shadasad vilakshana*.

The Advaitic understanding allows for the existence of various levels. And confusion happens when we start mixing these levels. It is as if we told a child that his 3-D math is Mithyā before he has graduated into a 4-D frame of reference and mastered the new rules and principles of Arithmetic and geometry. It is as if we told a fifth grader that his calculations are Mithyā because they are not based on differential calculus that he has not learnt yet.

The illusoriness of the world is itself an illusory understanding. And once Brahma-knowledge arises, both the cognizer and the cognized disappear. Sri Aurobindo explains Advaita beautifully in his own manner thus, "There are several forms of Indian philosophy which base themselves upon the One Reality, but they admit also the reality of the world, the reality of the Many, the reality of the differences of the Many as well as the sameness of the One (Bhedabheda). But the Many exist in the One and by the One, the differences are variations in manifestation of that which is fundamentally ever the same. This we actually see as the universal law of existence where oneness is always the basis with an endless multiplicity and difference in the oneness....Through this we can look back into one of the fundamental secrets of existence, the secret which is contained in the one reality itself. The oneness of the Infinite is not something limited, fettered to its unity; it is capable of an infinite multiplicity. The Supreme Reality is an Absolute not limited by either oneness or multiplicity but simultaneously capable of both, for both are its aspects, although the oneness is fundamental and the multiplicity depends upon the oneness.

There is possible a realistic as well as an illusionist Adwaita. The world is a manifestation of the Real and therefore is itself real. The reality is the infinite and eternal Divine, infinite and eternal Being, Consciousness-Force and Bliss.

This Divine by his power has created the world or rather manifested it in his own infinite Being. But here in the material world or at its basis he has hidden himself in what seem to be his opposites, non-Being, inconscience and Insentience. This is what we nowadays call the Inconscient which seems to have created the material universe by its inconscient Energy; but this is only an appearance, for we find in the end that all the dispositions of the world can only have been arranged by the working of a supreme secret intelligence. The Being which is hidden in what seems to be an inconscient void emerges in the world first in Matter, then in Life, then in Mind and finally as the Spirit.

As Vedanta says, "Understanding Mithyā is much simpler if we come to the heart: that which depends upon something else for its being or existence, which has no existence by itself but is conditioned (or determined) by something other than itself, is Mithyā; Satyam, obviously, is that which is self-existent, independent and unconditioned."

Vedanta is a vast field. Eventually, one has to realize that its precepts are not fixed mathematical formulae but descriptions of the yogi's anubhava, which are individualized to some extent due to the nature of their adhara. It is only very vast yogis such as Sri Krishna or Sri Aurobindo who can hold the various accounts in their vishhva-dharana. And yet, no individual account is incorrect or Mithyā, even if it gets sublated into the larger vision of a more complete or poorna Vedanta.

7.5 Story of Ramakrishna and Advaita Vedanta of Totapuri

There is a fascinating story about the Advaita practices of Ramakrishna, probably the most famous Indian saint of the nineteenth Century. At the time of the story, Ramakrishna was already a master of dualistic mysticism, fully steeped in the meditation of the Goddess Kali. Nevertheless, he agreed to receive the Advaita teachings from a wandering, naked, ash-besmeared master of nondualism named Totapuri.

Totapuri regarded all forms of worship, so dear to Ramakrishna, as childish and ridiculous. He instructed Ramakrishna the basics of Advaita Vedanta, saying:

"Brahman is the only Reality, ever pure, ever illumined, ever free, beyond the limits of time, space, and causation. Though apparently divided by names and forms through the inscrutable power of maya, that enchantress who makes the impossible possible, Brahman is really One and undivided. When a seeker merges in the beatitude of samadhi, he does not perceive time and space or name and form, the offspring of maya. Whatever is within the domain of maya is unreal. Give it up. Destroy the prison-house of name and form and rush out of it with the strength of a lion. Dive deep in search of the Self and realize It through samadhi. You will find the world of name and form vanishing into void, and the puny ego dissolving in Brahman-Consciousness. You will realize your identity with Brahman, Existence-Knowledge-Bliss Absolute."

He also taught Ramakrishna the practice of formless meditation (technically different than nondual meditation, but nevertheless a major step in that direction), but that first night as Ramakrishna sat to meditate, he was immediately lost in dualistic absorption of the Goddess Kali. When he reported this failure to Totapuri the next day, his teacher picked up a tiny shard of glass from the ground and stuck it into the skin between Ramakrishna's eyes, ordering him to concentrate on that spot. So, Ramakrishna sat in meditation, and when Kali arrived again, he – in his own metaphor –

picked up the "sword of nondual wisdom and cut her down with it." She instantly disappeared and Ramakrishna was thrust into a nondual absorption that lasted several days. He thanked Totapuri, saying, "If you had not come, I would have lived my whole life with the hallucination. My last barrier has fallen away."

But Totapuri himself had not yet finished expanding the depths of his own nondual awareness. Several months after his teaching of Ramakrishna, Totapuri contracted a severe case of dysentery. His incapacitation made it impossible to meditate, and so – in the classic style of an Advaitin monk – he grew disgusted with the limitations of his body. In his view the body was nothing more than an illusion (Mithyā) or obstacle on his path, and now it was being more of an obstacle than usual. A free soul cares nothing for the body. So, one night, Totapuri strode into the Ganges determined to drown his body and be rid of this annoying object. But the tide was out and he ended up walking all the way across to the other side unharmed. Dumbfounded, he looked back at the Kali Temple gleaming in the moonlight and experienced a sudden, deep awakening. He saw the power of the absolute not just in the formless, but now also in the form of the temple, the goddess, the river, even his body. Thus, Totapuri experienced the elimination of the distinction between form and the formless, and went to a much deeper level of nondual awareness. As the Heart Sutra maintains, the perfection of wisdom lies in the realization that emptiness and form are one, not two.

The mystics are not satisfied with a situation analogous to quantum physics, where the observer and the observed cannot be separated, but can still be distinguished. They go much further, and in deep meditation they arrive at a point where the distinction between observer and observed breaks down completely, where subject and object fuse into a unified undifferentiated whole. Thus, the Upanishads say,

"Where there is a duality, as it were, there one sees another; there one smells another; there one tastes another . . . But where everything has become just one's own self, then whereby and whom would one see, then whereby and whom would one smell, then whereby and whom would one taste?"

This, then, is the final apprehension of the unity of all things. It is reached- so the mystics tell us-in a state of consciousness where one's individuality dissolves into an undifferentiated oneness, where the world of the senses is transcended and the notion of 'things' is left behind.

CHAPTER 8

THE BRAHMAN: AN INTRODUCTION

8.1 Introduction to Brahman

Sanskrit Brahman (an n-stem, nominative bráhma, from a root bṛh- "to swell, expand, grow, enlarge") is a neuter noun to be distinguished from the masculine brahmán—denoting a person associated with Brahman, and from Brahmā, the creator God in the Hindu Trinity, the Trimurti. Brahman is thus a gender-neutral concept that implies greater impersonality than masculine or feminine conceptions of the deity. Brahman is referred to as the supreme self. It is the unchanging reality amidst and beyond the world. Brahman is a concept that cannot be exactly defined.

In Hinduism, Brahman connotes the highest universal principle, the ultimate reality in the Universe. In major schools of Hindu philosophy, it is the immaterial, efficient, formal and final cause of all that exists. It is the pervasive, infinite, eternal truth, consciousness and bliss which does not change, yet is the cause of all changes. Brahman as a metaphysical concept refers to the single binding unity behind diversity in all that exists in the Universe.

Brahman is a key concept found in the Vedas, and it is extensively discussed in the early Upanishads. The Vedas conceptualize Brahman as the Cosmic Principle. In the Upanishads, it has been variously described as Sat-Chit-Ananda (truth-consciousness-bliss) and as the unchanging, permanent, highest reality.

Brahman is discussed in Hindu texts with the concept of Atman, (Self), personal, impersonal or Para Brahman, or in various combinations of these qualities depending on the philosophical school. In dualistic schools of Hinduism such as the theistic Dvaita Vedanta, Brahman is different from Atman (Self) in each being. In non-dual schools such as the Advaita Vedanta, the substance of Brahman is identical to the substance of Atman, is everywhere and inside each living being, and there is connected spiritual oneness in all existence.

Brahman means the concept of the transcendent and immanent ultimate reality, Supreme Cosmic Spirit in Hinduism. The concept is central to Hindu philosophy, especially Vedanta.

Ishvara, (lit., Supreme Lord), in Advaita, is identified as a partial worldly manifestation (with limited attributes) of the ultimate reality, the attribute-less Brahman. In Visishtadvaita and Dvaita, however, Ishvara (the Supreme Controller) has infinite attributes and the source of the impersonal Brahman.

Devas, are the expansions of Brahman/God into various forms, each with a certain quality. In the Vedic religion, there were 33 devas, which later became exaggerated to 330 million (33 crores or 33 Koti) devas. In fact, devas are themselves regarded as more mundane manifestations of the One and the Supreme Brahman. and 33 crore devas originally meant 33 types of divine manifestations.

Brahman is a concept present in Vedic Samhitas, the oldest layer of the Vedas dated to the late 2nd millennium BCE. The concept Brahman is referred to in hundreds of hymns in the Vedic literature. The diverse reference of Brahman in the Vedic literature, starting with Rigveda Samhitas, convey different senses or different shades of meaning". There is no one single word in modern Western languages that can render the various shades of meaning of the word Brahman in the Vedic literature. The concept Brahman is discussed in the Vedas along four major themes: (i) as the Word or verses (Shabda-brahman), (ii) as Knowledge embodied in Creator Principle, (iii) as Creation itself, and (iv) as a Corpus of traditions.

The concept of Brahman in the Upanishads expands to metaphysical, ontological and soteriological themes, such as it being the "primordial reality that creates, maintains and withdraws within it the universe", the "principle of the world", the "absolute", the "general, universal", the "cosmic principle", the "ultimate that is the cause of everything including all gods", the "divine being, Lord, distinct God, or God within oneself", the "knowledge", the "Self, sense of self of each human being that is fearless, luminous, exalted and blissful", the "essence of liberation, of spiritual freedom", the "universe within each living being and the universe outside", the "essence and everything innate in all that exists inside, outside and everywhere". According to **Dr. S. Radhakrishnan**, the sages of the Upanishads teach Brahman as the ultimate essence of material phenomena that cannot be seen or heard, but whose nature can be known through the development of self-knowledge (*atma jnana*).

The Upanishads contain several mahā-vākyas or "Great Sayings" on the concept of Brahman:

First mahā-vākya:

अहं ब्रह्म अस्मि (aham brahmāsmi), Brihadaranyaka Upanishad (1.4.10). "I am Brahman"

Second mahā-vākya:

अयम् आत्मा ब्रह्म (ayam ātmā brahma), Brihadaranyaka Upanishad (4.4.5). "The Self is Brahman"

Third mahā-vākya:

सर्वं खल्विदं ब्रह्म (sarvam khalvidam brahma), Chandogya Upanishad (6.2.1). "All this is Brahman"

Fourth mahā-vākya:

तत्त्वमसि (tat tvam asi), Chandogya Upanishad (6.8.7). "Thou art that" ("You are Brahman")

8.2 Brahman as the Ultimate Reality

What is ultimate reality? Anything that is real in-itself is real in an ultimate sense. This ultimate reality is to be distinguished from other forms of reality. If there are things which are necessarily related and have a nature only in relation to other things, they cannot constitute ultimate reality. They have a lower kind of reality. This is known as 'prātibhāsika-satya' (apparent truth, illusory appearance), as explained earlier in this book under the heading of Sankara's three degrees of reality. Similarly, if there are things which do not exist of themselves, but are caused, to exist through the activity of something else, they too are not ultimate reality. The 'world' as we know it is the name of that whole collection of things in space or in time that are not self-existent and that come under the domination of the law of causality. This is called (as mentioned earlier in this book) 'vyāvahārika-satya', which is illustrated by this world of our day-to-day experience. This world appearance has a much higher degree of reality and lasts till one gets ātma-jñāna or brahma-jñāna, realization of Truth. It is satya or true for all purposes of vyavahāra i.e., day-to-day existence or practical life.

Reality, on the other hand, is beyond thought. It may be thought or it may not be thought, it may be known or it may not be known. It is independent of every subjective activity. May be, nothing exists in this sense. May be, reality in its **ultimate** and concrete form is subject-object or it is of the stuff of experience, so that nothing can possibly exist without relation to experience. This degree of reality is called, 'pāramārthika-satya', the highest Truth and the only truth that really exists. It is Brahman or Ātman, which is nirguṇa (without attributes) and nirākāra (without forms), hence incapable of being described except in a negative way ('neti, neti'—'not this, not this').

Brahman is the Great, the ultimate truth. This is beyond which nothing can be greater; it is the highest truth, the Absolute. A measure of its greatness is provided by the world. The world which is limitless in time and limitless in space is still contained within Brahman. It is contained not as a real part, -for Brahman has no parts. It is contained as a mere appearance is contained in the ground. A mere appearance may appear great in time and in space. But its greatness is as nothing in comparison to the greatness of the ground. The greatness of the latter is qualitatively different. What is great in time and space can have a greater. But what is great out of time and space cannot have a greater even in conception. It is the true infinite. All finite and all conceivable wholes are nothing in comparison to the infinite. The great world is therefore only an infinitesimal part of the greatness of Brahman.

The causality of Brahman is only an outside character of Brahman. It is called its *tatastha lakshana*. By knowing that

Brahman is the cause, we know nothing about the own nature of Brahman. Besides, the cause is inferred only from the effect. We invariably go from the effect to the cause, not vice-versa. It is because we are confronted with a world that we go from the world to its metaphysical cause. To say therefore that Brahman is the cause of the world is to give merely an accidental or an outside description of Brahman. All we can say is that the being of Brahman is in a sense necessary being, because without it the world would not appear and would not be the world it is. The world demands an ultimate metaphysical cause, but it says nothing definitely about the nature of this cause. All it says is that the cause must transcend time, space and causality, which are the defining characters of empirical facts.

We have, for the present at least, conceived metaphysical causality on the analogy of clay and pots made of clay. This sort of cause is called vivarta upadana. Brahman is the unchanging ground, while the world is a changing appearance only. The ground is the truth. It is uncreated and unborn. The world is created, and it also passes. The reality of the latter consists in name and form only, while the reality of the former is substantial. It is the same kind of relation which we find between the real and the illusory. The former is the reality of the latter. We conclude that Brahman is the reality' of the world.

This Supreme Cosmic Spirit or Absolute Reality called Brahman is said to be eternal, genderless, omnipotent, omniscient, and omnipresent, and ultimately indescribable in human language. It can be at best described as infinite Being, infinite Consciousness and infinite Bliss. Brahman is regarded as the source and essence of the material universe. It is pure being. Brahman manifests as Hiranyagarbha, the "world soul", which also can take many forms or manifestations of the thousands of gods.

In accordance with his principles, Sankara regards the creation by and from Brahma from both an esoteric and an exoteric standpoint. On the one hand, he remarks, the creation of the phenomenal world as described in terms of empirical thought by the Vedas and Upanishads has no absolute reality at all; it is intended to teach parabolically that the Self of all things is Brahma. On the other hand, the world of experience cannot be ignored altogether; it is a fact of consciousness, though only of unenlightened consciousness, and accordingly an explanation of its process must be found, Creation consists in a division of Brahma by himself into a boundless variety of "names and forms," intelligible existence which constitute the empiric world and possess determinate principles of being, formal and material potentialities (shakti) that never vary throughout all the world's successive cycles.

If Brahman was not at the core of our being, as the core of our being, we could not possibly become one with Brahman. All talk of "becoming" is of course not really accurate if we think of it as becoming something we are not.

Brahman and Shakti (Power) are in reality one. Sri Ramakrishna often used the simile of fire and its power to burn. Fire is the Purusha and the burning power is the Prakriti. It is not amiss to say that Prakriti is the Effect of the presence of Brahman–is Brahman Itself. The Upanishad recapitulates this, saying:

"This is the truth of Brahman in relation to nature: whether in the flash of the lightning, or in the wink of the eyes, the power that is shown is the power of Brahman. This is the truth of Brahman in relation to man: in the motions of the mind, the power that is shown is the power of Brahman. For this reason should a man meditate upon Brahman by day and by night."

Wherefore: "Brahman is the adorable being in all beings. Meditate upon him as such. He who meditates upon him as such is honored by all other beings."

"He who attains to knowledge of **Brahman**, being freed from all evil, finds the Eternal, the Supreme", says Kena Upanishad.

All truth is a two-edged sword. It tells us what IS and what IS NOT. The truth about the Self and Brahman also tells us what is not the Self or Brahman. Those of us who are clinging to the unreal will find this painful or at least uncomfortable. But we have to let go of the unreal to lay hold of the Real. If we do not like this fact we need not bother with Real, but keep on whirling around in our little hamster wheel we call life. But the wise listen and act upon it.

That which one seeks is not an abstraction but a positive reality known. Perhaps the most heartening thing that can be said about That Which Is the fact that it is The Goal. Its attainment is not only possible, it is inevitable. The entire field of relative existence, however much we have damaged or corrupted it, and it in turn has damaged or corrupted us, has a single purpose: the attainment of Brahman and the consequent liberation of the questing spirit (atman). This is what everything is all about. So no wonder we have made such a mess of things–literally. Not knowing either their or our purpose, what else could be the result?

"Shake off this fever of ignorance. Stop hoping for worldly rewards. Fix your mind on the Atman. Be free from the sense of ego," counsels Lord Krishna. "You dream you are the doer; you dream that action is done, you dream that action bears fruit. It is your ignorance; it is the world's delusion that gives you these dreams." "Seek this knowledge and comprehend clearly why you should seek it: such, it is said, are the roots of true wisdom: ignorance, merely, is all that denies them." "When men have thrown off their ignorance, they are free from pride and delusion. They have conquered the evil of worldly attachment. They live in constant union with the Atman. All craving has left them. They are no longer at the mercy of opposing sense-reactions. Thus they reach that state which is beyond all change."

8.3 Brahman as Existence or Being

Long ago, the Rigveda proclaimed: "The One Being the wise diversely speak of." All philosophy proceeds from this, all religion is based on this. We, moreover, hear such declarations as "Truth, Knowledge, Infinity is Brahman," "Consciousness, Bliss, is Brahman," "All this is, verily, Brahman," "This Self is Brahman," "Immortal, Fearless, is Brahman," and the like. And we are further aware of assertions like "That from which these beings are born, That by which, after having been born, they live, That into which they re-enter and with which they become one—know That, the Brahman." Omnipresence, omniscience and omnipotence are said to be the characteristics of God. These serve the purpose of defining the twofold nature of Brahman, the Reality—its essential nature (Swarupa-lakshana) and accidental attribute (tatastha-lakshana). The former is the independent and imperishable truth of Brahman, the latter is its superimposed dependent quality which is subject to change in the process of time.

Being is truth in the transcendent sense without reference to anything else. It does not pay heed to the difficulty of man that he cannot transcend the limitations of relativistic consciousness and so naturally takes the value and meaning of the relative order to be the truth. The highest value of truth is equated with pure being, for non-being can have no value.

Brahman is that which is permanent in things that change. It is without name and form, which two are the characteristic natures of the world of appearance, and is essentially existence-absolute. Existence can never change, never perish, though things in which also it is, perish. Hence existence is the nature of Reality and is different from the things of form and name. Existence is second-less and has no external relations or internal differentiations. It is unlimited by space, time and individuality. It is related to nothing, for there is nothing second to it. It has nothing similar to it, nothing dissimilar, for That alone is. The whole universe is a spiritual unity and is one with the essential Brahman. It has no difference within or without. Brahman is alike throughout its structure, and hence the knowledge of the essence of any part of it is the knowledge of the Whole. The knowledge of the Self is the knowledge of Brahman. Everything that is, is the one Brahman, the Real of real, *satyasya satyam*. By knowing it, everything becomes known. "Just as by the knowledge of a lump of earth, everything that is made of earth comes to be known, all this modification being merely a name, a play of speech, the ultimate substratum of it all being the earth, similarly, when Brahman is known, all is known." "Where there is an apparent duality, there is subject-object-relation; but where the Atman alone is, how can there be any relation or interaction of anything with anything else?" "There is knowledge, and yet, there is no perception or cognition, for that knowledge is indestructible, it is unrelated consciousness-mass". It is the eternal objectless Knower, and everything besides it is a naught, an appearance, a falsity.

Brahman is Existence which is infinite Consciousness of the nature of Bliss.

Brahman is Existence, Consciousness, Infinitude.

Brahman is Consciousness, Bliss.

That which is Infinitude is Bliss and Immortality.

These sentences give the best definition of the highest Reality. Brahman is Consciousness—*prajnanam brahma*. It is the ultimate Knower. It is imperceptible, for no one can know the knower, no one can know That by which everything else is known. "There is no seer but That, no hearer but That, no thinker but That, no knower but That." It is the eternal Subject of knowledge, no one knows it as the object of knowledge. This limitless Self-Consciousness is the only Reality. The content of this Consciousness is itself. This is the fullness of perfection and infinitude. "Brahman is Infinite, the universe is Infinite, from the Infinite proceeds the Infinite, and after deducting the Infinite from the Infinite, what remains is but the Infinite." This sentence of the Upanishad seems to pile up infinities over infinities and arrive at the bewildering conclusion that after subtracting the Whole from the Whole, the Whole alone remains. The implied meaning here is the changeless and indivisible character of the Infinite Reality, in spite of forms appearing to be created within it. The Infinite is non-dual and there can be no dealings with it.

This Bhuma (earth) is the Essential Brahman where one sees nothing else, hears nothing else, understands nothing else. It is Bliss and Immortality, the plenum of felicity. This is the Complete Being.

The Brihadaranyaka Upanishad (II. 3. 1) says that Brahman has two forms, "the formed and the formless, the mortal and the immortal, the existent and the moving, the real and the beyond." There is a contrast between Brahman and the name-and-form world, the former being the beyond, the inexpressible, the foundationless, the unconscious, the unreal in relation to the latter which is empirically experienced as the being, expressible, founded, conscious, real. Logically, attribute or quality itself becomes an unsound concept when it is extended to the Absolute. A thing has an attribute only in relation to another thing. There is no meaning in saying that a substance has an attribute when that substance alone is said to exist. The nature of a self-existent absolute principle is indeterminable. Every attribute limits it and creates a difference in non-difference. Brahman cannot be said to have any intelligible attribute, for Brahman is the entire existence and has nothing second to relate itself to. Sat (being) is an idea in relation to asat (non-being), chit (consciousness) in relation to Jada (inertness), Ananda (bliss) in relation to duhkha (pain), Ananta (infinitude) in relation to alpa (limitedness), prakasha (light) in relation to tamas (darkness). Every qualitative concept involves relations, and every thought creates a duality. To think Brahman is to reduce Brahman to the world of experience. Thought is possible only in an individualized state, but Brahman is not an individual, and is unapproachable by an individual. Brahman cannot even be conceived of as light, for it has nothing to shine upon. Not even is it consciousness, for it is conscious of nothing. Consciousness or light in the absolute condition cannot be called as consciousness or light, for such conceptions are dualistic categories. Being as it is in itself is nothing to the individual. It is not an object of knowledge. Truth is independent, unrelated, self-existent; but there is no such thing as an independent, unrelated, self-existent quality. The only recourse to be taken is to admit the failure of the intellect in determining the nature of Reality and resort to negative propositions.

Brahman is "One and limitless, limitless to the east, limitless to the south, limitless to the west, limitless to the north, and above and below, limitless in every direction; for its directions like east exist not, no across, no below, no above; this Paramatman is incomprehensible, infinite, unborn, not to be reasoned about.

Brahman is established on its own Greatness, or, rather, not on greatness at all. It is the division-less, partless, mass of plenitude—on what can it establish itself? The Self-existent Brahman is supported by nothing, for everything is supported by it. It is childish to say that it has established fame, though its Name is "Great Fame". "Here, on earth, people call cows and horses, elephants and gold, servants and wives, fields and houses as constituting greatness"; but Brahman is not of the greatness of this type, because here greatness is dependent on an external object. The greatness of Brahman lies in its own Being, and not on anything second.

Brahman alone, the Greatest, is this whole universe.

—Mund. Up., II. 2. 11.

"Verily, that Great, unborn Self, undecaying, undying, immortal, fearless, is Brahman." The whole of Reality is not exhausted in this world-process. "Encompassing the whole universe He extends beyond it to infinity. Whatever is here is this Purusha alone, whatever was and whatever will be. He is the Lord of immortality. Such is His greatness yet the Purusha is greater still. All beings are one-fourth of Him, His three-fourths hail as the immortal beyond the dust of the earth" (Rigveda, X. 90). "Unmoving, it is swifter than the mind", for the Real which is the Self is presupposed by all forms of thought. "The senses fall back in trying to reach it." "Ahead of others running, it goes standing." "It moves, and it moves not"; it is other than what is static and kinetic. "It is far, and it is near; it is within all this, and it is outside all this." It is the Self, the being of all. "Sitting, it goes far. Lying, it moves everywhere." "It is manifest and hidden." Such metaphorical definitions of Reality point to the central meaning of its absoluteness of character. That which does everything does nothing in particular. All speculations about the nature of the Ultimate Principle finally lend themselves to the unanimous conclusion that it is eternal, infinite, unconditioned, non-dual, absolute, existence. "It is without an earlier and without a later, without an inside and without an outside, the Being of the Self of all, the Experiencer of everything." Yajnavalkya describes the Supreme Being thus: "An Ocean, the One, the Seer, without duality it is. This is the State of Brahman. This is the supreme goal. This is the supreme prosperity. This is the supreme abode. This is the supreme bliss. On a part of this bliss other creatures are living." "It does not become greater by good action, nor inferior by bad action."

8.4 Pancha Koshas and the Brahman

Man in essence is the all-pervading immortal soul. He identifies himself, on account of delusion and ignorance, with the five illusory Koshas or sheaths, the (i) Annamaya, (ii) Pranamaya, (iii) Manomaya, (iv) Vijnanamaya, (v) Anandamaya and thinks that he himself is subject to the various changes. He identifies himself with the Annamaya Kosha or the physical body and when the physical body is burnt, he thinks himself burnt. He regards himself black. He becomes attached to his son, wife, cattle, wealth, house, etc., on account of ignorance (Avidya) and thinks himself to be the owner of them. He thinks that he is a student, a householder, an ascetic and so on. The body is a product of five elements. It is entirely distinct from the real Self. The ignorant man is bound to Samsara by mere delusion, by the false ideas of 'I' and 'mine'.

He identifies himself with the Pranamaya Kosha and thinks 'I am hungry, I am thirsty, I did this action.' The Pranamaya Kosha is quite foreign to the real Self. He identifies himself with the Manomaya Kosha and regards himself as the thinker and thinks 'I am angry, I am lustful, I am greedy.' The Manomaya Kosha is entirely distinct from the real Self of man. He identifies himself with the Vijnanamaya Kosha and regards himself as the cognizer and thinks 'I am intelligent, I know everything, I am the enjoyer.' He identifies himself with the Anandamaya Kosha and feels 'I am happy.' Both the Vijnanamaya and the Anandamaya Koshas are quite foreign to the real Self of man.

Just as there is a set of five vessels, one within the other, just as there are the layers of an onion, so also are these Koshas lying one within the other. There is the singlet closet to the body. Over this there is the shirt, over the shirt there is the waist-coat, over the waist-coat there is the coat, over the coat there is the over-coat. Even so the Atman is enveloped by these five sheaths.

The teacher first gives an exposition of the five Koshas to his disciple, gives him an insight into the nature of the Koshas and then points out that **Brahman** which is beyond the Koshas is identical with the man's innermost Atman within, just as one points out the star by pointing out first the end of the tree's branch. In Arundhati Nyaya one big star is shown first to the man, then a small, then a smaller star and finally the smallest star. Even so, the instructions given takes the mind from the gross to the subtle, from the subtle to the subtler and eventually from the subtler to the subtlest of although Atman or the Self which is encased within the five sheaths (koshas).

The human mind which is tainted by various kinds of Vasanas and impurities that have accumulated in this beginningless Samsara can realise the subtle Atman within, only by some appropriate process or method, and it is this appropriate process which the teacher describes in his masterly discourses. The illumined teacher enables his disciples to rise above the level of effects by explaining the grand truth that the **Self and Brahman are identical**.

Man naturally identifies himself with the Koshas. His intellect becomes pure through meditation. He develops the faculty of true discrimination between the real and the unreal, between the permanent and the impermanent. When he acquires this faculty of discrimination, he abandons the first Kosha and recedes to the one next behind. He resolves by meditation each Kosha into what is behind it, till he reaches the innermost Atman behind the Koshas and then holds on to that Atman alone. Step by step he abandons one Kosha after another and dissolves all of them and eventually attains knowledge of **unity with Brahman** and becomes liberated from the round of births and deaths. The main object of the Shrutis also is to impart a knowledge of **Brahman** as the means of attaining the highest goal or the final emancipation (Moksha).

In order to transport man by the ship of Brahma-Vidya to the farthest shore of the great ocean (Koshas), the Sruti says, '**This Atman is Brahman; Thou art That.**'

Just as a rope becomes a serpent, only on account of ignorance, so by Avidya or ignorance alone Atman becomes the man of five Koshas and appears to suffer along with the Koshas. The Annamaya Kosha constitutes the gross physical body. The Pranamaya, the Manomaya and the Vijnanamaya Koshas constitute the Linga Sarira or subtle body (astral body). The Anandamaya Kosha constitutes the causal body (Karana Sarira).

The physical body is formed of the essence of food. The subtle body is formed of uncompounded elements. The casual body is formed of Samskaras or Moola Ajnana (primitive ignorance). The Anandamaya Kosha is the cause for the subtle and gross bodies or the remaining four sheaths.

Birth and death are the Dharmas (attributes) of the Annamaya Kosha. Hunger and thirst are the Dharmas of the Pranamaya Kosha. Moha (delusion) and Shoka (grief) are the attributes of the Manomaya Kosha. The Atman is ever pure and unattached. He is absolutely free from the six waves of the ocean of Samsara, viz., birth, death, hunger, thirst, delusion and grief.

The physical body operates during the waking state. The subtle body functions during the dreaming state; and the causal body operates during deep-sleep state. During deep-sleep it is the thin veil of Anandamaya Kosha that separates the individual soul from the supreme Soul or **Brahman**.

The Shruti shows with the help of knowledge that **the individual soul is identical with the Brahman** who is within and beyond the five sheaths from the Annamaya (food sheath) down to the Anandamaya (the blissful sheath) and goes on to extract the kernel within, by divesting it of the five sheaths formed of ignorance, just as by threshing the many chaff-coverings of Kodrava one brings to view the grain within.

The Shruti represents, for the sake of contemplation, the five parts of the Annamaya Kosha in the form of a bird in the case of sacrificial fire. The sacrificial fire, arranged in the form of a hawk, a heron, or some other bird, has a head, two wings, a trunk and a tail. So also here, every Kosha is represented to be made up of five parts.

The Pranamaya Kosha or the vital sheath made of Prana, etc., ought to be figuratively understood as the molten copper poured into a crucible. The Pranamaya and the other three Koshas are not made up of a head, etc. It is better to imagine that these Koshas also are fashioned after the mould of the physical body, just as the molten metal poured into a mould takes the form of that mould. This will help the meditation and discrimination of the four Koshas.

The Annamaya Kosha is permeated by four Koshas, the Pranamaya and the rest. The Pranamaya Kosha is permeated by three Koshas, the Manomaya by two Koshas and the Vijnanamaya by one Kosha.

In order to lead the mind which has lost its longing and attraction for sensual objects to the inner being, which is behind the Annamaya Kosha or food-sheath, the Shruti explains the nature of Prana and the Pranamaya Kosha or the vital sheath. Distinct from the food-sheath or the gross physical body which has been described above, there is the inner Self made of Prana, falsely imagined to be the Atman like the gross body. The Pranamaya Kosha is also falsely identified with the real Self or Atman. This Self, formed of Prana fills the Self which is formed of food-essence, just as the air fills the bellows.

The Pranamaya Kosha is more subtle than the gross physical sheath. The vital forces of the Pranamaya Kosha perform the different functions of the body, viz., digestion, circulation of blood, deglutition, excretion, etc., and manipulate the physical body from within. The whole physical body is pervaded by the Pranamaya sheath. The Pranamaya sheath contains the five Karma Indriyas or organs of action, viz., organ of speech, hands, feet, organ of generation and anus. The different limbs of the physical body have their corresponding parts in the Pranamaya Kosha. Pranamaya Kosha, along with the mental and intellectual sheaths, forms the subtle body of Linga Sarira (astral body).

The Pranamaya Kosha is the self that abides in the Annamaya Kosha. **This physical body is mistaken for the pure Atman by false identification on account of ignorance.** The Shruti wants you now to give up the idea that the body is the Self and take up the idea that the Pranamaya Kosha is the Self. The mind is taken from the gross body to the subtle Pranamaya sheath. When the idea that the Pranamaya is the Self is deeply ingrained, the illusion that the Annamaya is one's own self vanishes. Then you begin to feel that the Annamaya is the body and the Pranamaya is one's own self that abides in the physical body.

The Manomaya Kosha is made up of Vrittis (Sankalpas or thoughts). It is subtler than the Pranamaya Kosha. It controls the Pranamaya Kosha. So it is the inner self of the Pranamaya Kosha.

Mind or Manas is that inner sense or internal organ or instrument consisting of Sankalpa and Vikalpa. It is the seat of volition. Just as the Annamaya Kosha is made of food-stuff, so also the Manomaya Kosha is formed of mind-stuff.

Manomaya self is the inner self of the Pranamaya. It permeates the Pranamaya Kosha. The Pranamaya Kosha is filled by the Manomaya Kosha. The Manomaya Kosha contains the organs of knowledge (Jnana Indriyas), viz., ear, skin, eye, tongue and nose. The real senses are within. What you see outside the physical eyes, etc., are mere instruments.

The Manomaya Kosha is more subtle and expansive than the Pranamaya Kosha. The Pranamaya Kosha is more subtle and expansive than the Annamaya Kosha.

The Manomaya Kosha or the mental sheath resides within the Pranamaya Kosha like the bladder of a football. Through the functioning of the Manomaya Kosha only you say, I think, I imagine. For the sake of contemplation, it is said to be of human form made up of five members, viz., head, right wing, left wing, trunk and tail. Just as the water assumes the shape of the vessel in which it is kept, just as the melted metal puts on the form of the mould into which it is poured, so also the human form of the Manomaya sheath follows that of the Pranamaya.

The Shruti leads the aspirant, who has withdrawn himself from the Pranayama and the Manomaya, still farther within, beyond even the Manomaya Kosha.

Vijnanamaya is the determinative knowledge (Nishchaya). This determinative knowledge (Adhyavasaya) is an attribute (Dharma) of the intellect (Buddhi). It is the determinative faculty which guides the mind and comes to right conclusion or determination. When the mind is in a doubting condition whether to do an action or not, Vijnanamaya renders help by coming to a determination 'I must do this.' The sacrificial rites are performed by one, only after ascertaining their nature from right sources of knowledge. Vijnana is the source of all sacrificial rites.

Vijnana or knowledge performs sacrifices, because a man who has knowledge performs sacrifices with faith, etc. Therefore, knowledge is said to be the doer. The Buddhi which determines gives sanction and the mind and the senses work through the gross body. Therefore Vijnana is the real agent.

The Shruti says that the Anandamaya self is also an effect. The Shruti teaches of the Self in his aspect as the enjoyer by Avidya or ignorance as he identifies himself with the Upadhi or Antahkarana or inner sense which is of four-fold nature (mind, intellect, memory and egoism). The Anandamaya is made up of the latent impressions of love and other forms of happiness. The Anandamaya is the seed-body or causal body (Karana Sarira). This body functions during deep-sleep the sum total of all causal bodies of all individual souls constitutes the Upadhi or Māyā of Ishvara.

Love, which springs up at the sight of a beloved son and the like is the head, as if it were Anandamaya self, because of its pre-eminence or prominence. It is the Anandamaya self who feels 'I am happy', 'I am the enjoyer'.

Moda is the joy of exultation produced by the acquisition and possession of a beloved object. Pramoda is the same joy intensified or raised to a high pitch. Love, joy (Moda) and delight (Pramoda) are reflections of bliss manifested in the Sattvic states of mind.

All living creatures are endowed with Manomaya, Vijnanamaya and Anandamaya selves, one abiding within another. The internal permeates the external self which lies outside. All of them are formed of Akasa and other elements of matter. All of them exist only by ignorance. They are set up by Avidya. They are all possessed of supreme Soul or **Brahman** who is everywhere, who is All, who is the cause of Akasa and all the rest, who is eternal, changeless, self-existent, who is existence, knowledge and infinity and who is beyond the five sheaths. He is indeed the Self of all. **He alone is verily the Atman**.

The philosophers of the materialistic school and the common people take the physical body as the Atman. They are not aware of the distinction between the body and the Atman. A knowledge of the five Koshas and the study of the Shrutis will open the eyes of these ignorant persons. The perceiver is distinct from the thing perceived. The sense of sight is distinct from colour and object of perception. The perceiving consciousness is the Self. The consciousness is distinct from the body which is made up of matter.

The **Supreme Brahman** has been described as Satyam, Jnanam, Anantam. A description of the five sheaths beginning with Annamaya has been given in order to realise the Supreme Brahman which is beyond the five sheaths. The supreme Brahman which lies within the five sheaths is also the Self of them all. This non-dual Brahman forms the support or the ultimate basic reality that underlies all duality produced by Avidya or ignorance. As the Anandamaya leads ultimately to unity, there is the supporting **Brahman**, one without a second, who is the ultimate basis of duality caused by ignorance, who is the tail, the support of the Anandamaya.

The five Koshas of man are described in order to destroy the veil of ignorance. Resolve each Kosha into that which precedes it in evolution, each effect into its immediate cause, till the ultimate cause is reached. Eventually you will be led to the **knowledge of Brahman**, who is beyond cause and effect, who is neither the cause nor the effect. You will realise the oneness of the individual soul and the supreme Soul.

Māyā is the illusory power of Brahman. This is the material cause of the universe. It is made up of the Gunas, viz., Sattva (purity), Rajas (passion) and Tamas (darkness). Tamas is the cause of the Annamaya Kosha. So inertness predominates in this Kosha. It is not endowed with Kriya

Shakti (power of action) or Jnana Shakti (power of cognition). Rajas is the cause of the Pranamaya Kosha. It is endowed with Kriya Shakti (power of action). The cause of the Manomaya Kosha is Sattva mixed with Tamas. Therefore the Tamasic qualities, hatred etc., are present in the mind. The cause of the Vijnanamaya is Sattva mixed with Rajas. Therefore we find in it the agency. Man as mind and intellect (Buddhi) is a product of Jnana-Shakti. Through Jnana-Shakti man gets knowledge as how to possess the desired objects. Through Kriya Shakti he exerts and possesses the objects.

May you all abandon the identification with these illusory sheaths which is set up by Avidya or ignorance through discrimination and enquiry! May you all attain the Supreme Brahman by transcending the five sheaths!

CHAPTER 9

THE BRAHMAN IN UPANISHADS

9.1 Brahman in Upanishads

The Upanishads teach us the truth of the unity of the atman and Brahman. Therefore that truth is known as advaita, “not two,” meaning that there is no separation of the atman and Brahman at any time. If Brahman was not at the core of our being, as the core of our being, we could not possibly become one with Brahman. All talk of “becoming” is of course not really accurate if we think of it as becoming something we are not. Rather, it is the becoming aware of, becoming established in, our eternal unity with Brahman.

9.2 Brahman in Taittirīya Upanishad

‘सत्यं ज्ञानं अनंतं ब्रह्म’ (तैत्तिरीयोपनिषत्, 2.1.1)

satyaṃ jñānam-anantaṃ brahma. (taittirīya Upanishad, 2.1.1)

Meaning: Brahman is truth, knowledge, and infinite. He who knows that Brahman as existing in the intellect, lodged in the supreme space in the heart, enjoys, as identified with the all - knowing Brahman, all desirable things simultaneously.

These are not separate attributes. They form the very essence of Brahman. According to Shankara, Brahman is the only, the supreme and the most perfect reality.

From that Brahman, which is the Self, was produced space. From space emerged air. From air was born fire. From fire was created water. From water sprang up earth. From earth were born the herbs. From the herbs was produced food. From food was born man. That man, such as he is, is a product of the essence of food. Of him this indeed, is the head, this is the southern side; this is the northern side; this is the Self; this is the stabilizing tail.

ब्रह्म सत्यं जगन्मिथ्या जीवो ब्रह्मैव नापरः ।

Brahma Satyam, Jagat Mithya, Jivo Brahmaiva naparah.

(Verse 20 of the Brahma Jnana Vali Mala).

Meaning: Brahman (the Absolute) alone is real; this world is unreal; and the jiva or the individual soul is non-different from Brahman. This is the quintessence of his philosophy.

9.3 Brahman in Katha Upanishad

The Katha Upanishad is one of the mukhya (primary) Upanishads, embedded in the last eight short sections of the Kaṭha school of the Krishna Yajurveda. It is listed as number 3 in the Muktika canon of 108 Upanishads.

The Katha Upanishad consists of two chapters (Adhyāyas), each divided into three sections (Vallis). The first Adhyaya is considered to be of older origin than the second. The Upanishad is the legendary story of a little boy, **Nachiketa** – the son of Sage Vajasravasa, who meets Yama (the deity of death). Their conversation evolves to a discussion of the nature of man, knowledge, Atman (Self) and moksha (liberation). In the Katha Upanishad Brahman is said to be the "intelligence of the intelligent,".

Katha Upanishad says:

एतद्ध्येवाक्षरं ब्रह्म एतद्ध्येवाक्षरं परम् ।
एतद्ध्येवाक्षरं ज्ञात्वा यो यदिच्छति तस्य तत् (1.2.16)

etaddhyevākṣaraṃ brahma etaddhyevākṣaraṃ param .
etaddhyevākṣaraṃ jñātvā yo yadicchati tasya tat. (1.2.16)

Meaning: This syllable (Om) indeed is the (lower) Brahman; this syllable indeed is the higher **Brahman**; whosoever knows this syllable, indeed, attains whatsoever he desires.

ऋतं पिबन्तौ सुकृतस्य लोके
गुहां प्रविष्टौ परमे परार्धे ।
छायातपौ ब्रह्मविदो वदन्ति
पञ्चाग्नयो ये च त्रिणाचिकेताः (1.3.1)

ṛtaṃ pibantau sukṛtasya loke
guhāṃ praviṣṭau parame parārdhe .
chāyātapau brahmavido vadanti
pañcāgnayo ye ca triṇāciketāḥ (1.3.1)

Meaning: The knowers of Brahman and those who kindle the five fires and propitiate the Nachiketa Fire thrice, speak of as light and shade, the two that enjoy the results of righteous deeds, entering within the body, into the innermost cavity (of the heart), the supreme abode (of **Brahman**).

यः सेतुरीजानानामक्षरं ब्रह्म यत् परम् ।
अभयं तितीर्षतां पारं नाचिकेतँ शकेमहि (1.3.2)

yaḥ seturījānānāmakṣaraṃ brahma yat param .
abhayaṃ titīrṣatāṃ pāraṃ nāciketam̐ śakemahi (1.3.2)

Meaning: May we be able to know the Nachiketa Fire which is the bridge for the sacrificers, as also the imperishable **Brahman**, fearless, as well as the other shore for those who are desirous of crossing (the ocean of samsara).

नाचिकेतमुपाख्यानं मृत्युप्रोक्तँ सनातनम् ।
उक्त्वा श्रुत्वा च मेधावी ब्रह्मलोके महीयते (1.3.16)

nāciketamupākhyānaṃ mṛtyuproktam̐ sanātanam .
uktvā śrutvā ca medhāvī brahmaloke mahīyate. (1.3.16)

Meaning: Narrating and hearing this eternal story of Nachiketas told by Death, the intelligent man attains glory in the world of **Brahman**.

हन्त त इदं प्रवक्ष्यामि गुह्यं ब्रह्म सनातनम् ।
यथा च मरणं प्राप्य आत्मा भवति गौतम (2.2.6)

hanta ta idaṃ pravakṣyāmi guhyaṃ brahma sanātanam .
yathā ca maraṇaṃ prāpya ātmā bhavati gautama (2.2.6)

Meaning: I will describe to thee, O Gautama, this secret ancient **Brahman** and also what becomes of the Self after death.

य एष सुप्तेषु जागर्ति कामं पुरुषो निर्मिमाणः ।
तदेव शुक्रं तद्ब्रह्म तदेवामृतमुच्यते ।
तस्मिँल्लोकाः श्रिताः सर्वे तदु नात्येति कश्चन । एतद्वै तत् (2.2.8)

ya eṣa supteṣu jāgarti kāmaṃ puruṣo nirmimāṇaḥ .
tadeva śukraṃ tadbrahma tadevāmṛtamucyate .
tasmim̐llokāḥ śritāḥ sarve tadu nātyeti kaścana . etadvai tat
(2.2.8)

Meaning: This Purusha who is awake when all are asleep, creating all things cherished, is certainly pure; that is **Brahman**; that is called the Immortal. All worlds are strung on that; none passes beyond that. This verily is that (thou seekest).

ऊर्ध्वमूलोऽवाक्शाख एषोऽश्वत्थः सनातनः ।
तदेव शुक्रं तद्ब्रह्म तदेवामृतमुच्यते ।
तस्मिँल्लोकाः श्रिताः सर्वे तदु नात्येति कश्चन । एतद्वै तत् (2.3.1)

ūrdhvamūlo'vākśākha eṣo'śvatthaḥ sanātanaḥ .
tadeva śukraṃ tadbrahma tadevāmṛtamucyate .
tasmim̐llokāḥ śritāḥ sarve tadu nātyeti kaścana . (2.3.1)

Meaning: This peepul tree with root above and branches down is eternal. That (which is its source) is certainly pure; that is Brahman and that is called immortal. On that are strung all the worlds; none passes beyond that. This verily is that (thou seekest).

यदा सर्वे प्रमुच्यन्ते कामा येऽस्य हृदि श्रिताः ।
अथ मर्त्योऽमृतो भवत्यत्र ब्रह्म समश्नुते ॥ 2.3.14 ॥

yadā sarve pramucyante kāmā ye'sya hṛdi śritāḥ .
atha martyo'mṛto bhavatyatra brahma samaśnute. (2.3.14)

Meaning: When all longings that are in the heart vanish, then a mortal becomes immortal and attains **Brahman** here.

मृत्युप्रोक्तां नचिकेतोऽथ लब्ध्वा
विद्यामेतां योगविधिं च कृत्स्नम् ।
ब्रह्मप्राप्तो विरजोऽभूद्विमृत्यु-
रन्योऽप्येवं यो विदध्यात्ममेव ॥ 2.3.18 ॥

mṛtyuproktāṃ naciketo'tha labdhvā
vidyāmetāṃ yogavidhiṃ ca kṛtsnam .
brahmaprāpto virajo'bhūdvimṛtyu-
ranyo'pyevaṃ yo vidadhyātmameva. (2.3.18)

Meaning: Nachiketas then, having acquired this knowledge imparted by Death, as also the instructions on Yoga in entirety, attained **Brahman** having become dispassionate and deathless. So does become anyone else also who knows the inner Self thus.

9.4 Brahman in Kena Upanishad

The Kena Upanishad is a Vedic Sanskrit text classified as one of the primary or Mukhya Upanishads that is embedded inside the last section of the Talavakara Brahmanam of the Samaveda. It is listed as number 2 in the Muktikā, the canon of the 108 Upanishads of Hinduism.

The Kena Upanishad was probably composed sometime around the middle of the 1st millennium BCE. It has an unusual structure where the first 13 are verses composed as a metric poem, followed by 15 prose paragraphs of main text plus 6 prose paragraphs of epilogue. The latter prose section of the main text is far more ancient than the poetic first section, and this Upanishad bridged the more ancient prose Upanishad era with the metric poetic era of Upanishads that followed.

Kena Upanishad is notable in its discussion of **Brahman** with attributes and without attributes, and for being a treatise on "purely conceptual knowledge". It asserts that the efficient cause of all the gods, symbolically envisioned as forces of nature, is Brahman. This has made it a foundational scripture to Vedanta school of Hinduism, both the theistic and monistic sub-schools after varying interpretations. The Kena Upanishad is also significant in asserting the idea of "Spiritual Man", "Self is a wonderful being that even gods worship", "Atman (Self) exists", and "knowledge and spirituality are the goals and intense longing of all creatures".

Kena Upanishad says:

यद्वाचाऽनभ्युदितं येन वागभ्युद्यते ।
तदेव ब्रह्म त्वं विद्धि नेदं यदिदमुपासते (1.5)

yadvācā'nabhyuditaṃ yena vāgabhyudyate .
tadeva brahma tvaṃ viddhi nedaṃ yadidamupāsate (1.5)

Meaning: That which is not uttered by speech, that by which the word is expressed, know That alone to be **Brahman**, and not this (non-Brahman) which is being worshiped.

यन्मनसा न मनुते येनाहुर्मनो मतम् ।
तदेव ब्रह्म त्वं विद्धि नेदं यदिदमुपासते (1.6)

yanmanasā na manute yenāhurmano matam .
tadeva brahma tvaṃ viddhi nedaṃ yadidamupāsate (1.6)

Meaning: That which one does not think with the mind, that by which, they say, the mind is thought, know That alone to be Brahman, and not this (non-Brahman) which is being worshiped.

यच्चक्षुषा न पश्यति येन चक्षूँषि पश्यति ।
तदेव ब्रह्म त्वं विद्धि नेदं यदिदमुपासते (1.7)

yaccakṣuṣā na paśyati yena cakṣūm̐ṣi paśyati .
tadeva brahma tvaṃ viddhi nedaṃ yadidamupāsate (1.7)

Meaning: That which man does not see with the eye, that by which man sees the activities of the eye, know That alone to be Brahman, and not this (non-Brahman) which is being worshiped.

यच्छ्रोत्रेण न शृणोति येन श्रोत्रमिदं श्रुतम् ।
तदेव ब्रह्म त्वं विद्धि नेदं यदिदमुपासते (1.8)

yacchrotreṇa na śṛṇoti yena śrotramidaṃ śrutam .
tadeva brahma tvaṃ viddhi nedaṃ yadidamupāsate (1.8)

Meaning: That which man does not hear with the ear, that by which man hears the ear's hearing, know That alone to be Brahman, and not this (non-Brahman) which is being worshiped.

यत्प्राणेन न प्राणिति येन प्राणः प्रणीयते ।
तदेव ब्रह्म त्वं विद्धि नेदं यदिदमुपासते (1.9)

yatprāṇena na prāṇiti yena prāṇaḥ praṇīyate .
tadeva brahma tvaṃ viddhi nedaṃ yadidamupāsate (1.9)

Meaning: That which man does not smell with the organ of smell, that by which the organ of smell is attracted towards its objects, know That alone to be Brahman, and not this (non-Brahman) which is being worshiped.

यदि मन्यसे सुवेदेति दहरमेवापि वर दभ्रमेवापि
नूनं त्वं वेत्थ ब्रह्मणो रूपम् ।
यदस्य त्वं यदस्य देवेष्वथ नु
मीमाँस्यमेव ते मन्ये विदितम् (2.1)

yadi manyase suvedeti daharamevāpi var dabhramevāpi
nūnaṃ tvaṃ vettha brahmaṇo rūpam .

yadasya tvaṃ yadasya deveṣvatha nu
mīmāṁsyameva te manye viditam (2.1)

Meaning: If you think, 'I know Brahman rightly', you have known but little of Brahman's (true) nature. What you know of His form and what form you know among the gods (that too is but little). Therefore Brahman is still to be inquired into by you. I think Brahman is known to me.

नाहं मन्ये सुवेदेति नो न वेदेति वेद च ।
यो नस्तद्वेद तद्वेद नो न वेदेति वेद च (2.2)

nāhaṃ manye suvedeti no na vedeti veda ca .
yo nastadveda tadveda no na vedeti veda ca (2.2)

Meaning: I think not I know Brahman rightly, nor do I think It is unknown. I know (and I do not know also). He among us who knows that knows It (Brahman); not that It is not known nor that it is known.

ब्रह्म ह देवेभ्यो विजिग्ये तस्य ह ब्रह्मणो
विजये देवा अमहीयन्त (3.1)

brahma ha devebhyo vijigye tasya ha brahmaṇo
vijaye devā amahīyanta (3.1)

Meaning: It is well-known that Brahman indeed achieved victory for the gods. But in that victory which was Brahman's the gods reveled in joy.

सा ब्रह्मेति होवाच ब्रह्मणो वा एतद्विजये महीयध्वमिति
ततो हैव विदाञ्चकार ब्रह्मेति (4.1)

sā brahmeti hovāca brahmaṇo vā etadvijaye
mahīyadhvamiti

tato haiva vidāñcakāra brahmeti (4.1)

Meaning: It was Brahman. In the victory that was Brahman's you were reveling in joy. Then alone did Indra know for certain that It was Brahman.

तस्माद्वा एते देवा अतितरामिवान्यान्देवान्यदग्निर्वायुरिन्द्रस्ते ह्येनन्नेदिष्ठं पस्पर्शुस्ते ह्येनत्प्रथमो विदाञ्चकार ब्रह्मेति (4.2)

tasmādvā ete devā atitarāmivānyāndevānyadagnirvāyurindraste hyenannediṣṭhaṃ pasparśuste hyenatprathamo vidāñcakāra brahmeti (4.2)

Meaning: Therefore, these gods viz. Agni, Vayu and Indra excelled other gods, for they touched Brahman who stood very close and indeed knew first that It was Brahman.

तस्माद्वा इन्द्रोऽतितरामिवान्यान्देवान्स ह्येनन्नेदिष्ठं पस्पर्श स ह्येनत्प्रथमो विदाञ्चकार ब्रह्मेति (4.3)

tasmādvā indro'titarāmivānyāndevānsa hyenannediṣṭhaṃ pasparśa sa hyenatprathamo vidāñcakāra brahmeti (4.3)

Meaning: Therefore is Indra more excellent than the other gods, for he touched Brahman who stood very close and indeed knew first that It was Brahman.

उपनिषदं भो ब्रूहीत्युक्ता त उपनिषद्ब्राह्मीं वाव त उपनिषदमब्रूमेति (4.7)

upaniṣadaṃ bho brūhītyuktā ta upaniṣadbrāhmīṃ vāva ta upaniṣadamabrūmeti (4.7)

Meaning: (Disciple:) "Revered sir, speak Upanishad to me." (Teacher:) "I have spoken Upanishad to thee. Of Brahman verily is the Upanishad that I have spoken."

The Self is ear of the ear, mind of the mind, speech of speech. He is also breath of the breath, and eye of the eye. Having given up the false identification of the Self with the senses and the mind, and knowing the Self to be Brahman, the wise, on departing this life, become immortal.

CHAPTER 10

THE BRAHMAN IN BRAHMA SUTRAS

10.1 The enquiry into Brahman and its pre-requisites (BS 1.1.1)

अथातो ब्रह्मजिज्ञासा (1.1.1)

athāto brahmajijñāsā (1.1.1)

Meaning: Now, therefore, the enquiry into **Brahman**.

10.2 Definition of Brahman (BS 1.1.2)

जन्माद्यस्य यतः (1.1.2)

janmādyasya yataḥ oṃ (1.1.2)

Meaning: Brahman is that from which the origin etc., (i.e. the origin, sustenance and dissolution) of this (world proceed).

10.3 BS 1.1.10:

गतिसामान्यात् (1.1.10)

Gatisāmānyāt (1.1.10)

Meaning: On account of the uniformity of view (of the Vedanta texts, **Brahman** is to be taken as that cause).

10.4 BS 1.1.11:

श्रुतत्वाच्च (1.1.11)

Śrutatvācca (1.1.11)

Meaning: And because it is directly stated in the Sruti (therefore the all-knowing **Brahman** alone is the cause of the Universe).

10.5 Anandamaya is Para Brahman (BS 1.1.12)

आनन्दमयोऽभ्यासात् (1.1.12)

ānandamayo'bhyāsāt (1.1.12)

Meaning: Anandamaya means Para Brahman on account of the repetition (of the word 'bliss' as denoting the Highest Self).

10.6 BS 1.1.15:

मान्त्रवर्णिकमेव च गीयते (1.1.15)

māntravarṇikameva ca gīyate (1.1.15)

Meaning: Moreover that very **Brahman** which has been re-referred to in the Mantra portion is sung (i.e. proclaimed in the Brahmana passage as the Anandamaya).

10.7 The being or person in the Sun and the eye is Brahman (BS 1.1.20)

अन्तस्तद्धर्मोपदेशात् (1.1.20)

Antastaddharmopadeśāt (1.1.20)

Meaning: The being within (the Sun and the eye) is **Brahman**, because His attributes are taught therein.

10.8 The word Akasa must be understood as Brahman (BS 1.1.22)

आकाशस्तल्लिङ्गात् *(1.1.22)*

ākāśastalliṅgāt (1.1.22)

Meaning: The word Akasa, i.e., ether here is **Brahman** on account of characteristic marks (of that, i.e., Brahman being mentioned).

10.9 The word 'Prana' must be understood as Brahman (BS 1.1.23)

अत एव प्राणः *(1.1.23)*

ata eva prāṇaḥ (1.1.23)

Meaning: For the same reason the breath also refers to **Brahman**.

10.10 The light is Brahman (BS 1.1.24)

ज्योतिश्चरणाभिधानात् *(1.1.24)*

jyotiścaraṇābhidhānāt (1.1.24)

Meaning: The 'light' is **Brahman**, on account of the mention of feet in a passage which is connected with the passage about the light.

10.11 BS 1.1.28:

प्राणस्तथानुगमात् *(1.1.28)*

prāṇastathānugamāt (1.1.28)

Meaning: Prana is **Brahman**, that being so understood from a connected consideration (of the passage referring to Prana).

10.12 BS 1.1.30:

शास्त्रदृष्ट्या तूपदेशो वामदेववत् *(1.1.30)*

śāstradṛṣṭyā tūpadeśo vāmadevavat (1.1.30)

Meaning: The declaration (made by Indra about himself, viz., that he is and with **Brahman**) is possible through intuition as attested by Sruti, as in the case of Vamadeva.

10.13 The Manomaya is Brahman (BS 1.2.1)

सर्वत्र प्रसिद्धोपदेशात् *(1.2.1)*

sarvatra prasiddhopadeśāt (1.2.1)

Meaning: (That which consists of the mind 'Manomaya' is Brahman) because there is taught (in this text) (that

Brahman which is) well-known (as the cause of the world) in the Upanishads.

10.14 BS 1.2.2:

विवक्षितगुणोपपत्तेश्च (1.2.2)

vivakṣitaguṇopapatteśca (1.2.2)

Meaning: Moreover the qualities desired to be expressed are possible (in Brahman; therefore the passage refers to **Brahman**).

10.15 BS 1.2.7:

अर्भकौकस्त्वात् तद्व्यपदेशाच्च नेति चेन्न निचाय्यत्वादेवं
व्योमवच्च (1.2.7)

arbhakaukastvāt tadvyapadeśācca neti cenna
nicāyyatvādevaṃ
vyomavacca (1.2.7)

Meaning: If it be said that (the passage does) not (refer to **Brahman**) on account of the smallness of the abode (mentioned i.e. the heart) and also on account of the denotation of that (i.e., of minuteness) we say, no; because (**Brahman**) has thus to be meditated and because the case is similar to that of ether.

10.16 The Eater is Brahman (BS 1.2.9)

अत्ता चराचरग्रहणात् (1.2.9)

attā carācaragrahaṇāt (1.2.9)

Meaning: The Eater (is Brahman), because both the movable and immovable (i.e. the whole world) is taken (as His food).

10.17 BS 1.2.10:

प्रकरणाच्च (1.2.10)

prakaraṇācca (1.2.10)

Meaning: And on account of the context also the (eater is Brahman).

10.18 The dwellers in the cave of the heart are the individual soul and Brahman(1.2.11)

गुहां प्रविष्टावात्मानौ हि तद्दर्शनात् (1.2.11)

guhāṃ praviṣṭāvātmānau hi taddarśanāt (1.2.11)

Meaning: The two who have entered into the cavity (of the heart) are indeed the individual soul and the Supreme Soul, because it is so seen.

10.19 The person within the eye is Brahman (1.2.13)

अन्तर उपपत्तेः (1.2.13)

antara upapatteḥ (1.2.13)

Meaning: The person within (the eye) (is **Brahman**) on account of (the attributes mentioned therein) being appropriate (only to **Brahman**).

10.20 The internal ruler is Brahman (BS 1.2.18)

अन्तर्याम्यधिदैवादिषु तद्धर्मव्यपदेशात् *(1.2.18)*

antaryāmyadhidaivādiṣu taddharmavyapadeśāt (1.2.18)

Meaning: The internal ruler over the gods and so on (is **Brahman**) because the attributes of that (**Brahman**) are mentioned.

10.21 That which cannot be seen is Brahman (BS 1.2.21)

अदृश्यत्वादिगुणको धर्मोक्तेः *(1.2.21)*

adṛśyatvādiguṇako dharmokteḥ (1.2.21)

Meaning: The possessor of qualities like indivisibility etc., (is **Brahman**) on account of the declaration of Its attributes.

10.22 Vaisvanara is Brahman (BS 1.2.24)

वैश्वानरः साधारणशब्दविशेषात् *(1.2.24)*

vaiśvānaraḥ sādhāraṇaśabdaviśeṣāt (1.2.24)

Meaning: Vaisvanara (is **Brahman**) on account of the distinction qualifying the common terms ("Vaisvanara" and "Self").

10.23 BS 1.2.28:

साक्षादप्यविरोधं जैमिनिः *(1.2.28)*

sākṣādapyavirodhaṃ jaiminiḥ (1.2.28)

Meaning: Jaimini (declares that there is) no contradiction even (if by Vaisvanara) (**Brahman** is) directly (taken as the object of worship).

10.24 The abode of heaven, earth etc. is Brahman (BS 1.3.1)

द्युभ्वाद्यायतनं *(1.3.1)*

dyubhvādyāyatanaṃ svaśabdāt (1.3.1)

Meaning: The abode of heaven, earth, etc., (is **Brahman**) on account of the term, 'own' i.e., 'Self'.

10.25 Bhuma is Brahman (BS 1.3.8)

भूमा सम्प्रसादादध्युपदेशात् *(1.3.8)*

bhūmā samprasādādadhyupadeśāt (1.3.8)

Meaning: Bhuma (is **Brahman**) because it is taught after the state of deep sleep (i.e. after Prana or the vital air which remains awake even in that state).

10.26 Akshara is Brahman (BS 1.3.10)

अक्षरमम्बरान्तधृतेः *(1.3.10)*

akṣaramambarāntadhṛteḥ (1.3.10)

Meaning: The Imperishable (is **Brahman)** on account of (its) supporting everything up to Akasa (ether).

10.27 The Highest person to be meditated upon is the Highest Brahman (BS 1.3.13)

ईक्षतिकर्मव्यपदेशात् सः *(1.3.13)*

īkṣatikarmavyapadeśāt saḥ (1.3.13)

Meaning: Because of His being mentioned as the object of sight, He (who is to be meditated upon is **Brahman**).

10.28 BS 2.3.5:

स्याच्चैकस्य ब्रह्मशब्दवत् *(2.3.5)*

syāccaikasya brahmaśabdavat (2.3.5)

Meaning: It is possible that the one word ('sprang'—Sambhutah) may be used in a secondary and primary sense like the word **Brahman**.

10.29 When meditating on a symbol, the symbol should be considered as Brahman and not Brahman as the symbol (BS 4.1.5)

ब्रह्मदृष्टिरुत्कर्षात् *(4.1.5)*

brahmadṛṣṭirutkarṣāt (4.1.5)

Meaning: (The symbol) is to be viewed as **Brahman** (and not in the reverse way), on account of the exaltation (of the symbol thereby).

CHAPTER 11

THE BRAHMAN IN SRIMAD BHAGAVAD GITA

11.1 The Brahman in Srimad Bhagavad Gita

श्रीभगवानुवाच ।

कुतस्त्वा कश्मलमिदं विषमे समुपस्थितम् ।
अनार्यजुष्टमस्वर्ग्यमकीर्तिकरमर्जुन ॥ 2.2 ॥

śrībhagavānuvāca .

kutastvā kaśmalamidaṃ viṣame samupasthitam .
anāryajuṣṭamasvargyamakīrtikaramarjuna (2.2)

Translation: Shri Bhagavan (Lord Krishna) said: My dear Arjuna, how have these impurities come upon you? They are not at all befitting a man who knows the value of life. They lead not to higher planets but to infamy.

Explanation: Lord Krishna is referred to as Bhagavan throughout the Gita. Bhagavan is the ultimate in the Absolute Truth. Absolute Truth is realized in three phases of understanding, namely **Brahman**, or the impersonal all-pervasive spirit; Paramatma, or the localized aspect of the Supreme within the heart of all living entities; and Bhagavan, or the Supreme Personality of Godhead, Lord Krishna.

न त्वेवाहं जातु नासं न त्वं नेमे जनाधिपाः ।

न चैव न भविष्यामः सर्वे वयमतः परम् ॥ 2.12 ॥

na tvevāhaṃ jātu nāsaṃ na tvaṃ neme janādhipāḥ .
na caiva na bhaviṣyāmaḥ sarve vayamataḥ param (2.12)

Translation: Never was there a time when I did not exist, nor you, nor all these kings; nor in the future shall any of us cease to be.

Explanation: The Māyāvadi theory, that after liberation, the individual soul, separated by the covering of Māyā, or illusion, will merge into the impersonal **Brahman** and lose its individual existence is not supported herein by Lord Krishna the supreme authority. Nor is the theory that we only think of individuality in the conditioned state supported herein. Krishna clearly says herein that in the future also the individuality of the Lord and others, as it is confirmed in the Upanishads, will continue eternally. This statement of Krishna is authoritative because Krishna cannot be subject to illusion. If individuality were not a fact, then Krishna would not have stressed it so much—even for the future. The Māyāvadi may argue that the individuality spoken of by Krishna is not spiritual, but material. Even accepting the argument that the individuality is material, then how can one distinguish Krishna's individuality? Krishna affirms His individuality in the past and confirms His individuality in the future also. He has confirmed His individuality in many ways, and impersonal **Brahman** has been declared to be subordinate to Him. Krishna has maintained spiritual individuality all along; if He is accepted as an ordinary conditioned soul in individual consciousness, then His Bhagavad-Gita has no value as authoritative scripture. A common man with all the four defects of human frailty is unable to teach that which is worth hearing. The Gita is above such literature.

श्रुतिविप्रतिपन्ना ते यदा स्थास्यति निश्चला ।
समाधावचला बुद्धिस्तदा योगमवाप्स्यसि ॥ 2.53 ॥

śrutivipratipannā te yadā sthāsyati niścalā .
samādhāvacalā buddhistadā yogamavāpsyasi (2.53)

Translation: When your intellect ceases to be allured by the fruitive sections of the Vedas and remains steadfast in divine consciousness, you will then attain the state of perfect Yoga.

Explanation: To say that one is in samadhi is to say that one has fully realized Krishna consciousness; that is, one in full samadhi has realized **Brahman**, Paramatma and Bhagavan. The highest perfection of self-realization is to understand that one is eternally the servitor of Krishna and that one's only business is to discharge one's duties in Krishna consciousness. A Krishna conscious person, or unflinching devotee of the Lord, should not be disturbed by the flowery language of the Vedas nor be engaged in fruitive activities for promotion to the heavenly kingdom. In Krishna consciousness, one comes directly into communion with Krishna, and thus all directions from Krishna may be understood in that transcendental state. One is sure to achieve results by such activities and attain conclusive knowledge. One has only to carry out the orders of Krishna or His representative, the spiritual master.

एषा ब्राह्मी स्थितिः पार्थ नैनां प्राप्य विमुह्यति ।
स्थित्वास्यामन्तकालेऽपि ब्रह्मनिर्वाणमृच्छति ॥ 2.72 ॥

eṣā brāhmī sthitiḥ pārtha naināṃ prāpya vimuhyati .
sthitvāsyāmantakāle'pi brahmanirvāṇamṛcchati (2.72)

Translation: That is the way of the spiritual and godly life, after attaining which a man is not bewildered. If one is thus situated even at the hour of death, one can enter into the kingdom of God.

Explanation: One can attain Krishna consciousness or divine life at once, within a second—or one may not attain such a state of life even after millions of births. It is only a matter of understanding and accepting the fact. Actual life begins after the completion of this material life. For the gross materialist it is sufficient to know that one has to end this materialistic way of life, but for persons who are spiritually advanced, there is another life after this materialistic life. Before ending this life, if one fortunately becomes Krishna conscious, he at once attains the stage of brahma-nirvana. There is no difference between the kingdom of God and the devotional service of the Lord. Since both of them are on the absolute plane, to be engaged in the transcendental loving service of the Lord is to have attained the spiritual kingdom. In the material world there are activities of sense gratification, whereas in the spiritual world there are activities of Krishna consciousness. Attainment of Krishna consciousness even during this life is immediate attainment of **Brahman**, and one who is situated in Krishna consciousness has certainly already entered into the kingdom of God. **Brahman** is just the opposite of matter.

कर्म ब्रह्मोद्भवं विद्धि ब्रह्माक्षरसमुद्भवम् ।
तस्मात्सर्वगतं ब्रह्म नित्यं यज्ञे प्रतिष्ठितम् ॥ 3.15 ॥

karma brahmodbhavaṃ viddhi brahmākṣarasamudbhavam

.

tasmātsarvagataṃ brahma nityaṃ yajñe pratiṣṭhitam (3.15)

Translation: Regulated activities are prescribed in the Vedas, and the Vedas are directly manifested from the Supreme Personality of Godhead. Consequently the all-pervading Transcendence is eternally situated in acts of sacrifice.

Explanation: Yajnartha-karma, or the necessity of work for the satisfaction of Krishna only, is more expressly stated in this verse. If we have to work for the satisfaction of the yajnaa-purusha, Vishnu, then we must find out the direction of work in **Brahman**, or the transcendental Vedas. The Vedas are therefore codes of working directions. Anything performed without the direction of the Vedas is called vikarma, or unauthorized or sinful work. Therefore, one should always take direction from the Vedas to be saved from the reaction of work. As one has to work in ordinary life by the direction of the state, one similarly has to work under direction of the supreme state of the Lord. Such directions in the Vedas are directly manifested from the breathing of the Supreme Personality of Godhead. The Lord, being omnipotent, can speak by breathing air, for as it is confirmed in the Brahma-samhita, the Lord has the omnipotence to perform through each of His senses the actions of all other senses. In other words, the Lord can speak through His breathing, and He can impregnate by His eyes. In fact, it is said that He glanced over material nature and thus fathered all living entities. After creating or impregnating the conditioned souls into the womb of material nature, He gave His directions in the Vedic wisdom as to how such conditioned souls can return home, back to Godhead. We should always remember that the conditioned souls in material nature are all eager for material enjoyment. But the Vedic directions are so made that one can satisfy one's perverted desires, then return to Godhead, having finished his so-called enjoyment. It is a chance for the conditioned souls to attain liberation; therefore the conditioned souls must try to follow the process of yajna by becoming Krishna conscious. Even those who have not followed the Vedic injunctions may adopt the principles of

Krishna consciousness, and that will take the place of performance of Vedic yajnas, or karmas.

तत्त्ववित्तु महाबाहो गुणकर्मविभागयोः ।
गुणा गुणेषु वर्तन्त इति मत्वा न सज्जते ॥ 3.28॥

tattvavittu mahābāho guṇakarmavibhāgayoḥ .
guṇā guṇeṣu vartanta iti matvā na sajjate (3.28)

Translation: One who is in knowledge of the Absolute Truth, O mighty-armed, does not engage himself in the senses and sense gratification, knowing well the differences between work in devotion and work for fruitive results.

Explanation: The knower of the Absolute Truth is convinced of his awkward position in material association. He knows that he is part and parcel of the Supreme Personality of Godhead, Krishna, and that his position should not be in the material creation. He knows his real identity as part and parcel of the Supreme, who is eternal bliss and knowledge, and he realizes that somehow or other he is entrapped in the material conception of life. In his pure state of existence he is meant to dovetail his activities in devotional service to the Supreme Personality of Godhead, Krishna. He therefore engages himself in the activities of Krishna consciousness and becomes naturally unattached to the activities of the material senses, which are all circumstantial and temporary. He knows that his material condition of life is under the supreme control of the Lord; consequently he is not disturbed by all kinds of material reactions, which he considers to be the mercy of the Lord. One who knows the Absolute Truth in three different features—namely **Brahman**, Paramatma, and the Supreme Personality of Godhead—is called tattva-vit, for he knows also his own factual position in relationship with the Supreme.

ये त्वेतदभ्यसूयन्तो नानुतिष्ठन्ति मे मतम् ।
सर्वज्ञानविमूढांस्तान्विद्धि नष्टानचेतसः ॥ 3.32 ॥

ye tvetadabhyasūyanto nānutiṣṭhanti me matam .
sarvajñānavimūḍhāṃstānviddhi naṣṭānacetasaḥ (3.32)

Translation: But those who, out of envy, disregard these teachings and do not follow them, are to be considered bereft of all knowledge, befooled, and ruined in their endeavors for perfection.

Explanation: The flaw of not being Krishna conscious is clearly stated herein. As there is punishment for disobedience to the order of the supreme executive head, so there is certainly punishment for disobedience to the order of the Supreme Personality of Godhead. A disobedient person, however great he may be, is ignorant of his own self, and of the Supreme **Brahman**, Paramatma and the Personality of Godhead, due to a vacant heart. Therefore there is no hope of perfection of life for him.

जन्म कर्म च मे दिव्यमेवं यो वेत्ति तत्त्वतः ।
त्यक्त्वा देहं पुनर्जन्म नैति मामेति सोऽर्जुन ॥ 4.9 ॥

janma karma ca me divyamevaṃ yo vetti tattvataḥ .
tyaktvā dehaṃ punarjanma naiti māmeti so'rjuna (4.9)

Translation: One who knows the transcendental nature of My appearance and activities does not, upon leaving the body, take his birth again in this material world, but attains My eternal abode, O Arjuna.

Explanation: One who can understand the truth of the appearance of the Personality of Godhead is already liberated from material bondage, and therefore he returns to the kingdom of God immediately after quitting this present material body. Such liberation of the living entity from material bondage is not at all easy. The Vedic version *tat tvam asi* is actually applied in this case. Anyone who understands Lord Krishna to be the Supreme, or who says unto the Lord "You are the same Supreme **Brahman**, the Personality of Godhead," is certainly liberated instantly, and consequently his entrance into the transcendental association of the Lord is guaranteed.

ब्रह्मार्पणं ब्रह्म हविर्ब्रह्माग्नौ ब्रह्मणा हुतम् ।
ब्रह्मैव तेन गन्तव्यं ब्रह्मकर्मसमाधिना ॥ 4.24॥

brahmārpaṇaṁ brahma havir brahmāgnau brahmaṇā hutam
brahmaiva tena gantavyaṁ brahma-karma-samādhinā (4.24)

Translation: For those who are completely absorbed in God-consciousness, the oblation is **Brahman**, the ladle with which it is offered is **Brahman**, the act of offering is **Brahman**, and the sacrificial fire is also **Brahman**. Such persons, who view everything as God, easily attain Him.

Explanation: How activities in Krishna consciousness can lead one ultimately to the spiritual goal is described here. There are various activities in Krishna consciousness, and all of them will be described in the following verses. But, for the present, just the principle of Krishna consciousness is described. A conditioned soul, entangled in material contamination, is sure to act in the material atmosphere, and yet he has to get out of such an environment. The process by which the conditioned soul can get out of the material atmosphere is Krishna consciousness. The word brahma (**Brahman**) means "spiritual." The Lord is spiritual, and the rays of His transcendental body are called brahmajyoti, His spiritual effulgence. Everything that exists is situated in that brahmajyoti, but when the jyoti is covered by illusion (mäyä) or sense gratification, it is called material. This material veil can be removed at once by Krishna consciousness; thus the offering for the sake of Krishna consciousness, the consuming agent of such an offering or contribution, the process of consumption, the contributor, and the result are—all combined together—**Brahman**, or the Absolute Truth. The Absolute Truth covered by mäyä is called matter. Matter dovetailed for the cause of the Absolute Truth regains its spiritual quality. Krishna consciousness is the process of converting the illusory consciousness into **Brahman**, or the Supreme. When the mind is fully absorbed in Krishna consciousness, it is said to be in samädhi, or trance. Anything done in such transcendental consciousness is called yajna, or sacrifice for the Absolute. In that condition of spiritual consciousness, the contributor, the contribution, the consumption, the performer or leader of the performance, and the result or ultimate gain—everything—becomes one in the Absolute, the Supreme **Brahman**. That is the method of Krishna consciousness.

दैवमेवापरे यज्ञं योगिनः पर्युपासते ।
ब्रह्माग्नावपरे यज्ञं यज्ञेनैवोपजुह्वति ॥ 4.25 ॥

daivamevāpare yajñaṃ yoginaḥ paryupāsate .
brahmāgnāvapare yajñaṃ yajñenaivopajuhvati (4.25)

Translation: Some yogis perfectly worship the demigods by offering different sacrifices to them, and some of them offer sacrifices in the fire of the Supreme **Brahman**.

Explanation: A person engaged in discharging duties in Krishna consciousness is also called a perfect yogi or a first-class mystic. But there are others also, who perform similar sacrifices in the worship of demigods, and still others who sacrifice to the Supreme **Brahman**, or the impersonal feature of the Supreme Lord. So, there are different kinds of sacrifices in terms of different categories. Such different categories of sacrifice by different types of performers only superficially demark varieties of sacrifice. Factually sacrifice means to satisfy the Supreme Lord, Vishnu, who is also known as Yajna. All the different varieties of sacrifice can be placed within two primary divisions: namely, sacrifice of worldly possessions and sacrifice in pursuit of transcendental knowledge. Those who are in Krishna consciousness sacrifice all material possessions for the satisfaction of the Supreme Lord, while others, who want some temporary material happiness, sacrifice their material possessions to satisfy demigods such as Indra, the sun-God, etc. And others, who are impersonalists, sacrifice their identity by merging into the existence of impersonal **Brahman**. The fruitive workers sacrifice their material possessions for material enjoyment, whereas the impersonalist sacrifices his material designations with a view to merging into the existence of the Supreme. For the impersonalist, the fire altar of sacrifice is the Supreme **Brahman**, and the offering is the self being consumed by the fire of **Brahman**. The Krishna conscious person, like Arjuna, however, sacrifices everything for the satisfaction of Krishna, and thus all his material possessions as well as his own self—everything—is sacrificed for Krishna. Thus, he is the first-class yogi; but he does not lose his individual existence.

ब्रह्मण्याधाय कर्माणि सङ्गं त्यक्त्वा करोति यः ।
लिप्यते न स पापेन पद्मपत्रमिवाम्भसा ॥ 5.10॥

brahmaṇyādhāya karmāṇi saṅgaṃ tyaktvā karoti yaḥ .
lipyate na sa pāpena padmapatramivāmbhasā (5.10)

Translation: One who performs his duty without attachment, surrendering the results unto the Supreme Lord, is unaffected by sinful action, as the lotus leaf is untouched by water.

Explanation: Here brahmani means in Krishna consciousness. The material world is a sum total manifestation of the three modes of material nature, technically called the pradhana. Brahma indicate that everything in the material world is a manifestation of **Brahman**; and although the effects are differently manifested, they are nondifferent from the cause. Everything is related to the Supreme **Brahman**, or Krishna, and thus everything belongs to Him only. One who knows perfectly well that everything belongs to Krishna, that He is the proprietor of everything and that, therefore, everything is engaged in the service of the Lord, naturally has nothing to do with the results of his activities, whether virtuous or sinful. Even one's material body, being a gift of the Lord for carrying out a particular type of action, can be engaged in Krishna consciousness. It is then beyond contamination by sinful reactions, exactly as the lotus leaf, though remaining in the water, is not wet.

इहैव तैर्जितः सर्गो येषां साम्ये स्थितं मनः ।
निर्दोषं हि समं ब्रह्म तस्माद् ब्रह्मणि ते स्थिताः ॥ 5.19॥

ihaiva tairjitaḥ sargo yeṣāṃ sāmye sthitaṃ manaḥ .
nirdoṣaṃ hi samaṃ brahma tasmād brahmaṇi te sthitāḥ (5.19)

Translation: Those whose minds are established in sameness and equanimity have already conquered the conditions of birth and death. They are flawless like **Brahman**, and thus they are already situated in **Brahman**.

न प्रहृष्येत्प्रियं प्राप्य नोद्विजेत्प्राप्य चाप्रियम्।
स्थिरबुद्धिरसम्मूढो ब्रह्मविद् ब्रह्मणि स्थितः ।। 5.20।।

na prahṛiṣhyet priyaṁ prāpya nodvijet prāpya chāpriyam
sthira-buddhir asammūḍho brahma-vid brahmaṇi sthitaḥ
(5.20)

Translation: Established in God, having a firm understanding of divine knowledge (Brahman) and not hampered by delusion, they neither rejoice in getting something pleasant nor grieve on experiencing the unpleasant.

बाह्यस्पर्शेष्वसक्तात्मा विन्दत्यात्मनि यत्सुखम् ।
स ब्रह्मयोगयुक्तात्मा सुखमक्षयमश्नुते ॥ 5.21 ॥

bāhyasparśeṣvasaktātmā vindatyātmani yatsukham .
sa brahmayogayuktātmā sukhamakṣayamaśnute (5.21)

Translation: Such a liberated person is not attracted to material sense pleasure but is always in trance, enjoying the pleasure within. In this way the self-realized person enjoys unlimited happiness, for he concentrates on the Supreme **Brahman**.

योगी युञ्जीत सततमात्मानं रहसि स्थितः ।
एकाकी यतचित्तात्मा निराशीरपरिग्रहः ॥ 6.10 ॥

yogī yuñjīta satatamātmānaṃ rahasi sthitaḥ .
ekākī yatacittātmā nirāśīraparigrahaḥ (6.10)

Translation: A transcendentalist should always engage his body, mind and self in relationship with the Supreme **Brahman**; he should live alone in a secluded place and should always carefully control his mind. He should be free from desires and feelings of possessiveness.

Explanation: Krishna is realized in different degrees as **Brahman**, Paramatma and the Supreme Personality of Godhead. Krishna consciousness means, concisely, to be always engaged in the transcendental loving service of the Lord. But those who are attached to the impersonal **Brahman** or the localized Super-soul are also partially Krishna conscious, because impersonal **Brahman** is the spiritual ray of Krishna and Super-soul is the all-pervading partial expansion of Krishna. Thus the impersonalist and the meditator are also indirectly Krishna conscious. A directly Krishna conscious person is the topmost transcendentalist because such a devotee knows what is meant by **Brahman** and Paramatma. His knowledge of the Absolute Truth is perfect, whereas the impersonalist and the meditative yogi are imperfectly Krishna conscious. Nevertheless, all of these are instructed herewith to be constantly engaged in their particular pursuits so that they may come to the highest perfection sooner or later. The first business of a transcendentalist is to keep the mind always on Krishna. One should always think of Krishna and not forget Him even for a moment. Concentration of the mind on the Supreme is called samädhi, or trance. In order to concentrate the mind, one should always remain in seclusion and avoid disturbance by external objects. He should be very careful to accept favorable and reject unfavorable conditions that affect his realization. And, in perfect determination, he should not hanker after unnecessary material things that entangle him by feelings of possessiveness.

कच्चिन्नोभयविभ्रष्टश्छिन्नाभ्रमिव नश्यति ।
अप्रतिष्ठो महाबाहो विमूढो ब्रह्मणः पथि ॥ 6.38 ॥

kaccinnobhayavibhraṣṭaśchinnābhramiva naśyati .
apratiṣṭho mahābāho vimūḍho brahmaṇaḥ pathi (6.38)

Translation: O mighty-armed Krishna, does not such a man, who is bewildered from the path of transcendence, fall away from both spiritual and material success and perish like a riven cloud, with no position in any sphere?

Explanation: There are two ways to progress. Those who are materialists have no interest in transcendence; therefore they are more interested in material advancement by economic development, or in promotion to the higher planets by appropriate work. When one takes to the path of transcendence, one has to cease all material activities and sacrifice all forms of so-called material happiness. If the aspiring transcendentalist fails, then he apparently loses both ways; in other words, he can enjoy neither material happiness nor spiritual success. He has no position; he is like a riven cloud. A cloud in the sky sometimes deviates from a small cloud and joins a big one. But if it cannot join a big one, then it is blown away by the wind and becomes a nonentity in the vast sky. The brahmana pathi is the path of transcendental realization through knowing oneself to be spiritual in essence, part and parcel of the Supreme Lord, who is manifested as **Brahman**, Paramatma and Bhagavan. Lord Krishna is the fullest manifestation of the Supreme Absolute Truth, and therefore one who is surrendered to the Supreme Person is a successful transcendentalist. To reach this goal of life through **Brahman** and Paramatma realization takes many, many births. Therefore the supermost path of transcendental realization is bhakti-yoga, or Krishna consciousness, the direct method.

यदक्षरं वेदविदो वदन्ति
विशन्ति यद्यतयो वीतरागाः ।
यदिच्छन्तो ब्रह्मचर्यं चरन्ति
तत्ते पदं सङ्ग्रहेण प्रवक्ष्ये ॥ 8.11 ॥

yadakṣaraṃ vedavido vadanti
viśanti yadyatayo vītarāgāḥ .
yadicchanto brahmacaryaṃ caranti
tatte padaṃ saṅgraheṇa pravakṣye (8.11)

Translation: Persons who are learned in the Vedas, who utter onkara and who are great sages in the renounced order enter into **Brahman**. Desiring such perfection, one practices celibacy. I shall now briefly explain to you this process by which one may attain salvation.

Explanation: Lord Krishna has recommended to Arjuna the practice of sat-cakra-yoga, in which one places the air of life between the eyebrows. Taking it for granted that Arjuna might not know how to practice sat-cakra-yoga, the Lord explains the process in the following verses. The Lord says that **Brahman**, although one without a second, has various manifestations and features. Especially for the impersonalists, the akhara, or omkara—the syllable OM—is identical with **Brahman**. Krishna here explains the impersonal **Brahman**, in which the renounced order of sages enter. In the Vedic system of knowledge, students, from the very beginning, are taught to vibrate OM and learn of the ultimate impersonal **Brahman** by living with the spiritual master in complete celibacy. In this way they realize two of **Brahman**'s features. This practice is very essential for the student's advancement in spiritual life, but at the moment such brahmachari (unmarried celibate) life is not at all possible.

किं पुनर्ब्राह्मणाः पुण्या भक्ता राजर्षयस्तथा।
अनित्यमसुखं लोकमिमं प्राप्य भजस्व माम्॥ 9.33॥

kiṁ punar brāhmaṇāḥ puṇyā bhaktā rājarṣhayas tathā
anityam asukhaṁ lokam imaṁ prāpya bhajasva mām(9.33)

Translation: What then to speak about kings and sages with meritorious deeds? Therefore, having come to this transient and joyless world, engage in devotion unto Me.

Explanation: When even the most abominable sinners are assured of success on the path of bhakti, then why should more qualified souls have any doubt? Kings and sages should be even more reassured of attaining the supreme destination by engaging in ananya bhakti (exclusive devotion). Shree Krishna thus beckons Arjun, "A saintly king like you should become situated in the knowledge that the world is temporary (maya) and a place of misery. Engage yourself in steadfast devotion to Me (**Brahman**), the possessor of unlimited eternal happiness. Else the blessing of birth in a kingly and saintly family, good education, and favorable material circumstances will all be wasted, if they are not utilized in the pursuit of the supreme goal.

अर्जुन उवाच।
पश्यामि देवांस्तव देव देहे
सर्वांस्तथा भूतविशेषसङ्घान्।
ब्रह्माणमीशं कमलासनस्थ-
मृषींश्च सर्वानुरगांश्च दिव्यान्॥ 11.15॥

arjuna uvācha
paśhyāmi devāns tava deva dehe
sarvāns tathā bhūta-viśheṣha-saṅghān
brahmāṇam īśhaṁ kamalāsana-stham

ṛiṣhīnśh cha sarvān uragānśh cha divyān (11.15)

Translation: Arjun said: O Shree Krishna, I behold within Your body all the gods and hosts of different beings. I see **Brahma** seated on the lotus flower; I see Shiva, all the sages, and the celestial serpents.

कस्माच्च ते न नमेरन्महात्मन्
गरीयसे ब्रह्मणोऽप्यादिकर्त्रे।
अनन्त देवेश जगन्निवास
त्वमक्षरं सदसतत्परं यत्।। 11.37।।

kasmāch cha te na nameran mahātman
garīyase brahmaṇo 'py ādi-kartre
ananta deveśha jagan-nivāsa
tvam akṣharaṁ sad-asat tat paraṁ yat (11.37)

Translation: O Great One, who are even greater than **Brahma**, the original creator, why should they not bow to you? O Limitless One, O Lord of the devatās, O Refuge of the universe, You are the imperishable reality beyond both the manifest and the non-manifest.

ब्रह्मणो हि प्रतिष्ठाहममृतस्याव्ययस्य च।
शाश्वतस्य च धर्मस्य सुखस्यैकान्तिकस्य च।। 14.27।।

brahmaṇo hi pratiṣhṭhāham amṛitasyāvyayasya cha
śhāśhvatasya cha dharmasya sukhasyaikāntikasya cha
(14.27)

Translation: I am the basis of the formless **Brahman**, the immortal and imperishable, of eternal dharma, and of unending divine bliss.

ॐ तत्सदिति निर्देशो ब्रह्मणस्त्रिविधः स्मृतः।

ब्राह्मणास्तेन वेदाश्च यज्ञाश्च विहिताः पुरा || 17.23||

oṁ tat sad iti nirdeśho brahmaṇas tri-vidhaḥ smṛitaḥ
brāhmaṇās tena vedāśh cha yajñāśh cha vihitāḥ purā
(17.23)

Translation: The words "Om Tat Sat" have been declared as symbolic representations of the Supreme Absolute Truth, (**Brahman**) from the beginning of creation. From them came the priests, scriptures, and sacrifice.

CHAPTER 12

QUANTUM SCIENCE INTERPRETATION OF MĀYĀ AND THE BRAHMAN

12.1 Classical Physics vs. Quantum Physics

Science tells us that the laws which operate in the classical world do not work in the quantum world and laws which operate in the quantum world do not work in the classical world. From this statement, it would seem that both of them are functioning in different worlds. Why does this happen? What is the difference between these two worlds? According to Vedanta, there is a fully functioning subtle universe and a fully functioning gross universe. The subtle universe is made up of 'vrittis' or waveforms operating with the individual mind and the cosmic mind. The gross universe is the universe which is made of 'memory' objects. In the gross or physical universe, you only find 'memory' objects, you will not find any 'now' objects.

As explained earlier in this book that the world is Māyā, a projection of Brahman in the material form.

12.2 Brief (non-mathematical) Introduction of Quantum Physics

Quantum Physics brings science face-to-face with metaphysics, and that is unpleasant to some of the scientists, considering the manner in which they conduct the twenty-first-century science. However, as we shall see shortly that the Māyā, and the Brahman can be explained satisfactorily by the quantum physics, and not by the classical physics. So, let us begin introducing quantum mechanics from the point of a layman.

Picture the nucleus of an atom in the centric position of our sun. According to Bohr's model of the atom, the nucleus is positively charged and composed of neutral "particles" called neutrons and positively-charged protons. The neutrons and protons are made up of subatomic "particles" known as quarks, leptons and bosons; however, these subclasses are not immediately pertinent to our discussions here. The positive charge of the protons in the nucleus is balanced to neutrality by an equal number of electrons spinning around the nucleus, much the way the planets in our solar system revolve about our sun.

12.2.1 What is Quantum?

A quantum is a discrete packet of energy, proposed for the first time by Max Planck, in 1900. It denotes that the energy exchange between the two bodies can take place in terms discrete quanta (plural of quantum) of light: one quantum, two quanta, three quanta, but never half quantum and never continuous exchange of energy. One quantum of radiation of energy is one photon. The energy carried by a photon is directly proportional to the frequency associated with it.

The electrons revolving about the nucleus of the atom can increase or decrease their energy levels (orbits) by interaction with a variety of forces, including photons of appropriate energy. For example, a low energy electron encircling the nucleus can be excited or stimulated by a number of methods with an appropriately energetic photon to "jump" to a higher energy orbit, or the reverse can occur, an electron can "jump" from the higher orbit down to the lower energy orbit with a consequent emission of energy, usually in the form of a photon. Using this model, often called the "Old Quantum Mechanics," we can derive and describe a number of useful conclusions based on the laws of quantum mechanics

But to dig deeply into the metaphysics of quantum theory, we must make the transition to the New Quantum Mechanics, as developed in the mid-1920s by Werner Heisenberg, Erwin Schrödinger, and other astute theoreticians. However, a word of caution and clarity–despite the practical effectiveness of quantum mechanical models, most physicists believe that atoms, electrons, neutrons and protons are not solid particles, as these models might imply. They are more precisely, packets of information and energy. That being said, quantum mechanics can explain numerous properties of what we, with our five senses, perceive to be the stuff of our universe. More important, and perhaps quite surprising, it can provide you with a more accurate perspective of your true reality, and thereby give you specific tools that can significantly enhance your quality of life and well-being.

In all that follows, almost no mathematics and only elementary concepts in physics will be used. We will touch on the following *profound phenomena.* They are derived directly from quantum theory.

12.2.2 Quantum Jumps

One of these revolutionaries was Einstein. He was working as a clerk at the patent office in Zurich at the time he published his first research paper on the quantum theory (1905). Challenging the then-popular belief that light is a wave phenomenon, Einstein suggested that light exists as a quantum—a discrete bundle of energy—that we now call a photon. The higher the frequency of the light, the more energy in each bundle.

Even more revolutionary was Danish physicist Niels Bohr, who in 1913 applied the idea of light quanta to suggest that the whole world of the atom is full of quantum jumps. We all have been taught that the atom resembles a tiny solar system, that electrons rotate around a nucleus much as the planets rotate around the sun. It may come as a surprise to learn that this model, originated by the British physicist Ernest Rutherford in 1911, has a crucial flaw that Bohr's work resolved. In an atom, negatively-charged electrons can be considered to be whirling about the atom's positively-charged nucleus, occupying different energy levels or orbits. There are many ways to stimulate an electron to jump from one energy level or orbit to another, either to a higher or lower level. This movement is called a "quantum jump." In the process, the electron is initially present at say lower energy level 1, and then jumps to higher energy level 2. Before and after the jump, it can be observed at each of these respective energy levels. However, during the quantum jump process, it exists nowhere in between. Quantum mechanics forbids its existence between the levels.

12.2.3 Uncertainty Principle

According to Nobel laureate Werner Heisenberg, small or microscopic objects such as electrons and atoms are not "real" in our everyday sense. They exist as "potentialities," and hence what we call the domain of "potentia," where there exist infinite possibilities and one of them is created by the **collapse of the wave function** to a specific state or set of conditions, as a consequence of our observation. Heisenberg proved mathematically that any observation disturbs things enough to prevent disproval of quantum mechanic's assertion that observation creates the property observed. Stated another way, the more accurately you know the exact position of a moving particle, say an electron, the less accurately you know its velocity, and conversely. This same principle applies to large objects, but the calculated uncertainties are so small as to be immeasurable. Because of this, we need only use Newton's laws or Newtonian mechanics as opposed to quantum mechanics to track spaceships, satellites and planets. Newtonian mechanics is an approximation or simplified form of quantum mechanics.

12.2.4 Wave-Particle Duality

The focus of quantum physics is on understanding the wave/particle duality. This would mean that the focus of quantum physics is on the subtle universe (Brahman), while the focus of classical physics is on the gross world (Māyā). In the classical (Newtonian) worldview, you are a determined machine, with no uncertainty. We know that the gross world is made up of 'memory' objects only, while the subtle universe is made up of 'now' objects. Therefore, the focus of quantum physics is on 'now' objects while the focus of classical physics is 'memory' objects.

It is for this reason that the laws of quantum physics do not apply to the gross/physical world, only the classical laws will work in the physical world. The same reasoning will apply to the subtle universe; the classical laws will not be suitable, only the quantum laws will work in the subtle universe.

De Broglie had posited that any physical object has the wave/particle duality. It is both a wave and also a particle. This is exactly the same as the subtle/gross duality referred to in Vedanta. The subtle state, which is the Brahman is nothing but a pool of waves (a field of infinite possibilities), while the gross body ((Māyā) is the physical universe. Even Schrodinger's wave equation is really talking about 'vrittis' or waves of the Brahman. The only place you can have waves is in the Brahman, there are no waves in the physical universe. The observed system (the world or Māyā), which collapses the Schrodinger probability wave function is nothing but the World, which is the underlying reality of everyone. All the waves in the Brahman collapse and result into Māyā.

The Quantum Physics observes that that the world we see is not reality itself but a projection onto our Brahman. In the ancient Indian texts known as the Upanishads, they found echoes of their theories, and a philosophical foundation to ensure they would no longer be cast adrift by the implications of quantum mechanics.

The Austrian-Irish physicist Erwin Schrödinger proposed at it in 1926, called the Schrödinger's equation.

12.2.5 Copenhagen interpretation of Quantum Science

According to the Copenhagen interpretation of quantum mechanics, observing an object causes it to lose its quantum nature and collapse into the classical form we're used to. This collapse of the wave function implies that the reality we see exists only when we are there to observe it. And an observer does not merely observe reality; she creates it.

When does something stop behaving like a wave and start behaving like a piece of matter, an object composed strictly of particles? This happens when we observe it.

If left to themselves, things would remain as waves until somebody observed them. Einstein, who could not reconcile himself with this, summed up the strangeness of quantum physics when he asked a friend, "Do you believe the Moon exists only when I look at it?"

12.2.6 Contribution of Schrodinger's Quantum Theory to the Upanishads, Brahman and Māyā

The Upanishads are transmitted orally from teacher to student over thousands of years (Shruti). While the Vedas prescribe rituals to appease deities, the Upanishads are concerned with the nature of reality (the Brahman), mind and the self.

Schrödinger was first exposed to Indian philosophy around 1918, through the writings of the German philosopher Arthur Schopenhauer. An ardent student of the Upanishads, Schopenhauer had declared, "In the whole world there is no study so beneficial and so elevating as that of the Upanishads. It has been the solace of my life. It will be the solace of my death."

The Upanishads describe the relationship between the Brahman, the Atman and the Māyā. Brahman is the universal self or the ultimate singular reality. The Atman is the individual's inner self, the soul. A central tenet of the Upanishads is *tat tvam asi*, which means the Brahman and the Atman are identical. There is only one universal self, and we are all one with it.

The Isha Upanishad states, "the Brahman forms everything that is living or non-living … the wise man knows that all beings are identical with his self, and his self is the self of all beings."

Quantum physics eliminates the gap between the observer and the observed. The Upanishads say that the observer and the observed are the same things. In his 1944 book 'What is Life?', Schrödinger took on a peculiar line of thought. If the world is indeed created by our act of observation, there should be billions of such worlds, one for each of us. How come your world and my world are the same? If something happens in my world, does it happen in your world, too? What causes all these worlds to synchronize with each other?

He found his answer, again, in the Upanishads. "There is obviously only one alternative," he wrote, "namely the unification of minds or consciousnesses. Their multiplicity is only apparent, in truth there is only one mind. This is the doctrine of the Upanishads."

According to the Upanishads, Brahman alone exists. Everything we see around us is Māyā, a distortion of the Brahman caused due to our ignorance and imperfect senses. The Chandogya Upanishad says, "All this is Brahman. Everything comes from Brahman, everything goes back to Brahman, and everything is sustained by Brahman."

On this, Schrödinger wrote, "… there is only one thing and that what seems to be a plurality is merely a series of different aspects of this one thing, produced by a deception (the Indian Māyā); the same illusion is produced in a gallery of mirrors, and in the same way Gaurishankar and Mt Everest turned out to be the same peak seen from different valleys."

It is easy to see why such a concept would have appealed to Schrödinger. Quantum physics insists that reality exists as waves, and wave-particle duality arises due to our observation. Because we cannot perceive the true wave nature of reality, our observation reduces it to the incomplete reality we see. This reduction is what we know as the collapse of the wave function. The emergence of Māyā thus explains the collapse.

Schrödinger was not making passing references to the Upanishads; instead, he had wholly internalized their core message. "Myriads of suns, surrounded by possibly inhabited planets, multiplicity of galaxies, each one with its myriads of suns... According to me, all these things are Māyā."

The Upanishads uphold an idealist view – that the Brahman exists by itself, and that the physical world (Māyā) depends on it. There is no objective reality that exists independently of the observer. Schrödinger supported this view and lamented the aversion for it: "it must be said that to Western thought this doctrine has little appeal, it is unpalatable, it is dubbed fantastic, unscientific. Well, so it is because our science – Greek science – is based on objectivation, whereby it has cut itself off from an adequate understanding of the subject of cognizance, of the mind."

Schrödinger was moved by the Upanishads. He discussed it with everyone he met and made determined efforts to incorporate it in his life. The epitaph on his tombstone reads, "... So all Being is alone and only Being; And that it continues to be when someone dies; [this] tells you, that he did not cease to be."

The Upanishads provided solace – a conception of reality and the universe based on observation and reasoning. In the precepts of these texts, the physicists found moral comfort, intellectual courage and spiritual guidance.

Nothing attests to the importance of these philosophical edifices less than absurd claims that Schrödinger and other scientists merely baked the lessons of the Upanishads into quantum theory. Such statements are misleading through and through. Schrödinger was, foremost, a physicist deeply entrenched in the methods of science. Indian philosophy soothed his soul but it is unlikely that it helped him frame mathematical equations.

Indeed, Schrödinger was often critical of many Indian ideas and pointed out that they were prone to superstition. Modern science, according to him, represented the zenith of human thought. He sought Indian philosophy not to replace the methods of science but to be inspired. He was aware that mixing two systems of thought separated by thousands of years was not easy.

12.3 Opening Remarks on Māyā and Quantum Physics

Māyā is invisible and beyond sense-perception. No human can see beyond the quantum screen. Dvaita Hinduism tells us about the duality of nature and existence. These dual poles of Tamas and Rajas are connected via consciousness. It is about the quantum possibility wave vibration between two poles.

What is the difference between a quantum physicist and an ancient Indian rishis? The quantum scientist with his DNA (97% junk) with pre-conceived notions of mathematical concepts with a past baggage from Isaac Newton is without any self-realization (Atma-Bodh). The rishis knew how to get from ordinary to a realized state. They got to see beyond the apparition of Māyā. The distinction between the self and the Universe is a false dichotomy.

When you see beyond the quantum screen of Māyā, everything become crystal clear.

The greatest thing that quantum physics did for the spiritually minded person was to show that the world as the senses tell us and as the Newtonian scientists had been telling us, is not a solid thing. These physicists went to the heart of matter and were astounded by what they saw. Matter was not solid at all as our senses tell us but merely energy in motion. In fact matter is composed of subatomic particles that have no design or shape and do not follow any standard order. Sometimes they behave like waves and sometimes like particles and sometimes they are both as well as many things at same time. Hence these physicists actually proved the Māyā theory in a scientific way. Our Puranas have been telling us this truth for centuries but we, with our dependence and total belief in the theories of western science were most scornful of them. But now when the western scientists themselves say the same thing, but of course not in the same words, we are forced to believe them even though our senses believe this truth.

The second shock came with Einstein's theory of relativity. Time and space had always been accepted as absolute and unchangeable facts of life but Einstein and many of the scientists who came after him proved that time and space are relative. This was a shocking idea which even now we who are bound to our clocks and time schedules find hard to accept. The Gita as well as our Puranas have always declared that what binds us to wheel of samsara are the three mental bonds known as *desa, kaala and nimitta*, - space, time and causality and that these are purely mental bonds which we have created ourselves.

We have created this world of concrete objects and superimposed a false reality on them. Again and again our scriptures tell us that Absolute reality is beyond these three upadhis -desha, kaala and nimitta or space time and causality. This world which we think we see is Māyā or an appearance. It has no permanent reality. It is only a passing show and has no permanence. Our bodies which are made of the same material - the five elements are also perishable. BUT we are not solely these bodies. Our reality is something far greater since we are actually the atman - which is imperishable and eternal and untouched by the changes of the body which take place in the world of space /Time. The moment we demarcate ourselves as belonging to a specified place and time, that moment we separate ourselves from our roots and thus bring suffering on ourselves. We are the creators of time and space. When we bring energy to conscious awareness, through the act of perception we create separate objects that exist in space through a measured continuum called time. By creating time and space we create our own separateness.

Another important thing that the physicist saw was that these subatomic particles had no meaning by themselves in isolation but only in relationship with everything else. At its elemental level, which is the quantum level, matter could not be chopped up into intelligible units but was completely indivisible. If we want to understand the universe we will have to see it as a dynamic web of interconnectedness. Human beings are a coalescence of energy in a field of energy which is connected to every other thing in this universe. This energy field is the central engine of our being. We can never be estranged from the other aspects of this universe since we are all bound fundamentally to this field!.

The zero-point field is the most fundamental state of matter and this is a heaving sea of energy - one vast quantum field. On the quantum level all living beings including human beings are packets of quantum energy constantly exchanging information with this inexhaustible field of energy., which is known as the "*chitta*' in Hindu terminology. Information about all aspects of life, is relayed through the interchange of information on the quantum level. Have you watched a flight of birds winging their way across the sky and how suddenly all of them veer to a different course as if at some hidden signal? The same phenomenon can be noticed in schools of fish. Till now it was assumed that these birds and fish had a novel method of communicating with each other by some radar or some noise signal which we cannot hear but now experiments on the quantum field proved that they are all in touch with this field and receive their orders simultaneously from it. The functions of our minds -like thinking, feeling etc. draw information from the quantum field which is pulsing simultaneously through our body and brain. In fact we resonate with the universe. Every breath we take is part of the universal breath and every breath we give out is our contribution to universal life. This prana, this life force is the same in everything and everyone and is spread everywhere simultaneously. Our lives can only become perfect if we participate in this great interchange with the universe. As the Gita tells us in chapter 3, " *Sahayajna praja sristwa purovacha prajapati.*" - The creator created all of us and instilled the idea of yajna or selfless action in us. No man is an island and no one can live without any sort of dependence on others and on nature. There is no me and mine as we think but all things are connected in an amazing way to the energy field. "*Mamta and ahamta*" (me and mine) have always been considered to be the two knots which alienate us from God. In this unified field there is no place for me and mine.

Pure energy as it exists on the quantum level is not bound by time or space but exists as a vast continuum of fluctuating change which exists here and now. This moment, this tiny bit of time and space we are existing now is the only truth and reality. Whereas Newtonian science had totally divorced man from the universe, quantum science has demonstrated that there is a purpose and unity in life and we are an important part of it. What we do and think is critical in creating our world. We are not isolated beings living our desperate lives on a lonely planet in an indifferent universe. We are always in the centre of everything. We have the power both individually and collectively to heal ourselves and improve our own lives and the lives of others around us.

This raises another interesting subject which again the scientists have proved for us. Are we capable of controlling our future. When our mind connects to the universal mind which we call *Chitta* in Hinduism, we are actually capable of controlling our future. This is because this *chitta* or zero-point field provides a holographic blueprint of the world for all time, past and future. So one who can tap this field can well predict the future. Thus we can conclude as our scriptures tell us that everything in the future already exists at some bottom rung level in the realm of pure potential and when we look into the future or the past we help to shape it and bring it into being just as we do with a quantum entity in the present, by the simple act of observation. Information transferred through subatomic waves do not exist in time or space but somewhere in the ever present. The past and present blur into one vast here and now and our brain picks up these signals and forms our own future. Our future exists in some nebulous state that we may begin to actualize in this very present. Again we must remember that this field (the Brahman) is the field of all possibilities and what actually happens, happens because we will it either consciously or subconsciously.

Another great thing the quantum scientists did for ancient spirituality is that they found out that individual consciousness does not die with the death of the body which is what Hinduism has been saying all the time. Krishna says, "Like a man changing his clothes so also the spirit changes one body for another." But the spirit lives on so why grieve when someone dies. It is only his body, which was unreal in any case, which has passed on to the elements from which it came into existence. His reality is the atman which was never born and thus can never die.

Living consciousness is not an isolated entity. It is not the personal property of one individual. This much has been discovered in the quantum field. We think that each of us has a separate atman even though our scriptures tell us that when this apparently separate atman is covered with the body, it is called the *jivatma* but this *jivatma* is the same as the Paramatma - meaning to say it is not an isolated entity. This lives on even after the body dies since it has never been isolated from the whole so there is no question of going back. It simply slips into what it ever was. Like the water in the bottle returning to the water of the pool when the bottle is broken. This consciousness of people has incredible powers. It can increase order in the world and make it as we wish it to be. If a number of individuals concentrate and wish for the same thing it has even greater force. That is why we say that communal prayer has more power. The all-absorbing topic of the day is how to control the climatic changes which are being increasingly felt all over the world. If enough people had a burning desire to change the situation, they would do far better if they got together and meditated on this topic, willing the minds of people to change and thus stop the terrible effects we have brought upon ourselves.

Thus we see that even though quantum physics has gone a long way in supporting the Advaitic view of Hindu spirituality of a shadow world of Māyā, as well as of a human consciousness which is universal and eternal, it still has not been able to postulate or prove an ultimate reality which has ever existed and which will ever exist and which alone is - Sat-chit and Ananda. Not only that it EXISTS but that it is pure CONSCIOUSNESS and that it is filled with BLISS. This can only be experienced by the sage, the seer and the mystic who connects himself with that source and thus draws his inspiration from it. As the Gita says such a man can no longer be labeled as a human being but has to be given the title of God. The future of the world lies in the production of such god men and not in the production of more nuclear weapons.

Vedanta is the apex of the knowledge of the Vedic tradition, exactly as Quantum Mechanics and allied fields are the most advanced subjects in Western science. None of the quantum scientists (except Erwin Schrodinger, to some extent) have categorized Vedanta as a religious and authentic work. It is amazing that the timeless Vedic tradition remains relevant even today and easily expressible in terms of contemporary scientific concepts.

Hinduism believes that God has given us 5 senses of narrow bandwidth, so that we do NOT have an information overload breakdown. The quantum world cannot be observed by our 5 senses, and they do NOT follow the cause-and-effect laws of classical physics.

One of the laws of the quantum realm – an event is a particle (matter) and a wave (energy) simultaneously. Body is a collection of particles. Brahman is a collection of waves (a field of infinite possibilities); and Māyā (the matter) displays the particle picture, subsequent to a collapse of the wavefunction. Quantum Physics in Vedanta tell us that particles and waves are the same thing. Your intention determines whether you see a particle or a wave.

The timeless principles of Vedanta is expressed in the technical language of Quantum Science and the philosophy of science, even today, with little or no attenuation of meaning.

12.4 Further on Quantum Physics Interpretation of Māyā and The Brahman

Advaita Vedanta is considered the culmination point among all the Indian philosophical systems. Referring to the Upanishadic statements, the founder of this Vedantic school Adi Sankaracharya and his followers like Swami Vivekananda, Sarvopally Radhakrishnan and others have lucidly elucidated on the concepts of Consciousness and Self. According to Shankaracharya, Atman (soul) or **Brahman** (transcendental self) has the nature of undifferentiated consciousness. Atman is eternal, self-luminous, universal consciousness which shines by its own light and reveals Jiva (the empirical self). It is devoid of externally enjoying nature and activity, yet appears to be an enjoying and active agent owing to its limiting adjuncts. Ever liberated Atman is beyond space, time and causality.

The Brihadaranyaka Upanishad states that consciousness is the ultimate reality. It is cosmic consciousness which, according to Vedanta is the basis of cosmic energy. Where does motion or mass or energy come from? It is nothing but very subtle energy in the form of spirit, the will of **Brahman** mixing with consciousness that is the spiritual spark, which by way of physical analogy might be thought of as spiritual particles.

According to Advaita Vedanta, these different categories of consciousness are classified as absolute consciousness (brahma-chaitanya), cosmic consciousness (Ishvara-chaitanya), individual consciousness (jīva-chaitanya), and indwelling consciousness (sākshi-chaitanya) (Brahmaprana, "Consciousness in Advaita Vedanta").

The natural question that arises is: How did absolute consciousness— undivided, unmoved, and unchanging— become this world of multiplicity and change? The Great seer and philosopher Shankaracharya resolved this paradox with his theory of superimposition, vivartavāda (involution). Advaita Vedanta states that this world is and is not. By is not, it is not suggested that the world is an illusion without a basis, a shadow without substance, or a void. Shankaracharya's interpretation means that the world as it appears to us is unreal because this world-appearance has no absolute existence. But for a rishi or seer whose vision is clear, the world is ever real because it is, essentially, nothing less than Brahman mistaken as a world of matter. This cosmic superimposition of the unreal on the real is due to Māyā (illusion), which literally means "that which measures the immeasurable." To show its twin faculty of concealing the reality and projecting the apparent, Māyā is often compared to a veil. Advaita Vedanta is not mere philosophical speculation or theory; it has direct experience as its basis as well as ultimate proof.

To lift the veil of Māyā, Advaita Vedanta exhorts the spiritual seeker to take the testimony of the Vedas (scriptures) and illumined souls, use reason, reflection, and meditation, and attain direct experience. These capacities are the compasses, maps, and sails needed to steer successfully to the highest union with Brahman. One must transcend the effects of Māyā in order to know the nature of its cause.

Quantum Physics emerged as a part of physics that studied sub-atomic particles. The major discovery of Quantum physics is that at a microscopic level, the universe is not continuous. Thus, a modified notion of the universe as a continuum was called for. Space-time existed not as a sheet but as a chunk of units called quanta. Subatomic particles or quantum particles did not follow any deterministic laws.

They exhibited a dual nature and behaved both as particle and wave, which in essence derives from the classical energy-matter equivalence. Quantum consciousness is a new concept that is emerging from the field of quantum physics. The acts of making conscious choices and observations are nothing but attributes of consciousness. This understanding came to be of paramount importance in the field of quantum physics. Thus, consciousness became a primary subject of physics with the advent of quantum physics. Max Planck said: "Consciousness I regard as fundamental. I regard Matter (Māyā) as derivative of Consciousness. We cannot get behind consciousness. Everything that we talk about, everything that we regard as existing postulates consciousness." 2) Nobel physicist Eugene Wigner stated: "There are two kinds of reality or existence—the existence of my consciousness and the reality of existence of everything else (Māyā). This latter is not absolute, but only relative. Excepting immediate sensations, the content of my consciousness, everything else is a con struct." He also stated that that it is the Consciousness of the observing scientist which is itself the hidden variable. He asserted that it is impossible to give an accurate and certain description of quantum processes "without explicit reference to consciousness." 3) Quantum physicist Werner Heisenberg stated that while observing quantum particles, uncertainty or indeterminacy would always remain and cannot be eliminated. Einstein, who did not believe in this uncertainty principle, said that there must be a "hidden variable" somewhere which is responsible for the uncertainty. 4) Famous contemporary scientist Fritjof Capra has asserted that Consciousness is an essential feature of David Bohm's Holon Theory, according to which the movement of one single particle is connected with the movement of the entire universe.

Ancient Vedic and Vedantic thought and quantum mechanics are very close today. The ancient seers realized that there is an invisible and formless force which controls the universe and the individual's life trajectory as well. It is everywhere in the living and in the nonliving. It cannot be seen or touched. It is **Brahman**, but masquerades as the package of energy of quarks and electrons in quantum mechanics. According to quantum physicist Dr. Mani Lal Bhaumik, through "both the Vedic concepts and quantum physics that entity having created this universe is also present everywhere, thereby supporting and governing everything in this universe" (Code Name God). Everything changes, but the unified field, just like **Brahman**, is eternal. **Brahman** is the spiritual package of energy just as the Higgs boson containing particles and **waves may be compared to Purusha and Prakrit (particle and wave)** within the quantum mechanical domain. When waves are active, particles are dormant and when particles are active, waves are dormant. Both phenomena exist within the same state, yielding a deeper, more synthesizing understanding of ultimate reality. According to Advaita Vedanta, **Brahman** is the ultimate character or structure of the universe. In fact, the universe is **Brahman** in disguise when it is reduced to its starkest nakedness. It is Brahman intelligence reflected in mind. Therefore, "I am Brahmn" (*aham brahmasmi*), "you are Brahmn" (*tat tvam asi*), "all are Brahman"' (*Sarvam khalu idam brahma*).

Ancient Hindu Rishis wanted to define what they intuitively knew as Brahman, the unchanging, permanent, highest reality. But how were they to explain something as vast and all-encompassing as that? The Upanishads thus described Brahman as neti, neti, neti. Neither this, not this, nor this. These seers also spoke of two fundamental characteristics of the world: Shunyata (or nothingness) and Māyā (or illusion). Amazingly, researchers in quantum physics are now finding that our world is characterized by empty space. At the atomic and subatomic levels there is no rigidity. What we call 'matter' consists of fuzzy waves that can manifest as particles and switch back just as quickly. Energy and matter are interchangeable. The solidity of our world is illusory. The world is indeed characterized by Shunyata and Māyā.

In the quantum world, everything seems to be an ocean of interconnected possibilities. Every particle is just a wave function and could be anywhere at any time; it could even be at several places simultaneously. This hazy view of the world fits almost perfectly with what our sages said about Brahman: 'It moves; it moves not; it is far; it is near; it is within this; it is outside this.' In fact, many early quantum researchers such as Schrodinger, Heisenberg and Bohr had been exposed to Vedic and Vedantic philosophy. Māyā (or illusion) can be interpreted as the collapse of wavefunction of the Brahman or the projection of Brahman in the matter (or world), which, according to Vedantic philosophy is transitory and not permanent.

To conclude, Only the Brahman is the Reality, Permanent, Attribute-less, and Absolute. Everything else is transitory, impermanent, illusory, Māyā and Mithyā.

Om Shanti: Shanti: Shanti:

BIBLIOGRAPHY

Ayyar, D. Krishna. "Advaita Vedanta: A Bird's Eye View". Year of Publication (?)

Barnett, L.D. " Brahma-Knowledge: An Outline of the Philosophy of the Vedānta" , John Murray, London, 1911.

Chakraborty, Nirod Baran. "The Advaita Concept of Falsity- A Critical Study" Published by The Principal, Sanskrit College, Calcutta. 1967.

Das, Sreepati. "A study on Brahma and the External life enlightened in the Shankara's Advaita Vedanta", Ph.D. Thesis, University of Chittagong, 2022.

Devanandan, P.D. "The Concept of Maya", Y.M.C.A. Publishing House, Calcutta, 1954.

Dudeja, Jai Paul. "Quantum Physics of Consciousness and Non-Duality in Eastern Philosophy", Blue Rose Publishers, 2021.

Joshi, K.L.; O.N. Bimali; and Bindiya Trivedi. "112 Upanishads (Sanskrit Text, English Translation, An Exclusive Introduction, and Index of Verses)", Vol. 1, Parimal Publications, Delhi, 2016.

Krishnananda, Swami. " The Realisation of the Absolute", Divine Life Society, Year (?)

Panda, N.C. "Māyā in Physics", Motilal Banarsidass Publishers, Delhi, 1991.

Pandya, Dr. Pranav and Dr. Abhay Saxena. "Virtual Reality and the Concept of Maya (illusion)", https:/www.researchgate.net, Sep 2015.

Pattanaik, Devdutt. "Myth = Mithya: A Handbook of Hindu Mythology", Penguin 2008.

Prabhupada, Swami. "Bhagavad-gita As It Is", Bhaktivedanta Book Trust International, California, 2004.

Radhakrishnan, S. "The Vedanta Philosophy and the Doctrine of Maya", International J. of Ethics, Vol. 24. No. 4. pp. 431-451, 2014.
Shastri, Prof. Prabhu Dutt. "The Doctrine of Māyā" Luzag and Co. London, 1911.
Sivananda. Swami. "The Moksha Gita", (Commentary by Swami Krishnananda, The Divine Life Society, 1949.
Sivananda. Swami. "Vedanta for Beginners", Divine Life Society, 1996.
Sivananda. Swami. "Brahma Sutras: Text, Word-to-Word Meaning, Translation and Commentary", Divine Life Society, 2008.

INDEX

Abhedavedanta, 22
Achintya-Bheda-Abheda, 21, 28-29
Adhikarana, 15, 108
Adhyāropa, 42
Adhyasa, 64-65
Adhyāsa, 38, 41-42
Advitīyatva, 26
Adyasa, 141
Ajnana, 174
Ajñāna, 36, 52
Anādi, 42
Anandamaya Kosha, 96, 172, 174
Anirvacanīya-khyāti, 33
Annamaya, 96, 171, 173-177, 179
Anukramani, 82
Anumanam, 108
Apavāda, 42
Ātma-jñāna, 40
Aupādhika Bhedābheda, 22
Avarana, 38, 51-52
Āvaraṇashakti, 36
Bādarāyana, 107-108
Bhāskara, 22

Bhāvarūpa, 36-37, 45
Bhedābheda, 21-22
Brihadaranyaka, 12, 27, 44, 124, 169, 236
Chāndogya Upanishad, 25, 33, 132, 147, 161, 227
Chatushtaya, 42, 149
Chulika Upanishad, 90
Gaudapada, 22
Jīvanmukti, 43
Jīvātman, 21
Kabirdas, 71
Lokacharya, 24
Madhusudana, 141, 143-144
Madhvacharya, 25, 28, 146
Mahā vākya, 160-161
Mahavakyas, 42, 144
Māndūkya Upanishad, 87
Manomaya, 96, 171-172, 174-178, 180
Māyin, 75, 86, 110
Mrigtrishna, 37, 69
Nammalvar, 25
Nididhyasana, 59
Nirakara, 41, 162
Nirguṇa, 41, 162
Nirguna, 8, 31, 84
Nirviśeṣādvaita, 27
Nivritti, 144
Palayana, 151
Panchtatva, 38
Paramarthika, 39, 118

Prajnanam brahma, 168
Pranamaya, 96, 171-172, 174-177, 180
Prārabdha-karma, 43
Prātibhāsika-satya, 40
Pratyaksham, 108
Rajas, 49, 61, 68-69, 71, 124, 133, 179-180, 229
Ramanuja, 16, 24-25, 28, 54, 62
Sadasad-vilasaṇa, 34
Sagulna, 80
Satcitananda, 27
Sattva, 49, 68-69, 71, 179-180
Shadasad vilakshana, 152
Shravaṇa, 42
Shuddadvaita, 27
Srishti, 53-54
Sutrakara, 107
Svābhābika Dvaitādvaita, 22
Svadhyaya, 149
Svetasvatara Upanishad, 11-12
Swaminarayan Sampraday, 25
Swarūpa-lakshaṇa, 166
Tādātmya, 42
Taittiriya, 12, 44, 81
Tamas, 45, 49, 61, 68-69, 71, 124, 133, 169, 179-180, 229
Tanmatras, 130
Tattvavada, 25
Tenkalai, 24
Totapuri, 154-156
Uparati, 149

Vadakalai, 24
Vallabhā sampradaya, 27
Vārttika, 44
Vedānta sūtra, 107
Vedartha samgraha, 25
Vicara, 53
Videhamukti, 43
Vikshepa, 38, 51-52, 124
Vikshepa-Shakti, 51, 124
Vikshepashakti, 36
Vishishtadvaita, 8, 15, 21, 24-25, 28, 144
Vivarana, 143
Vivarta, 30, 36, 41, 54, 64, 163
Vivartavāda, 36, 237
Vivekachudamani, 33
Vritti, 25
Vrittis, 176, 220, 224
Vyavaharika, 118
Vyāvahārika-satya, 40
Yamunacharya, 25

Milton Keynes UK
Ingram Content Group UK Ltd.
UKHW020213191223
434575UK00010B/125

9 798891 333239